The Islamic Republic of Dewsbury

Danny Lockwood

The Press News Ltd

This edition first published November 2011 by
The Press News Ltd
Edward Latham House
1 Oates Street,
Dewsbury
West Yorkshire WF13 1BB

Tel: +44 01924 439498
Fax: +44 01924 457994

email: news@thepressnews.co.uk
web: thepressnews.co.uk

ISBN: 978-0-9570964-0-0

Body text set in 11pt Century Schoolbook

Printed in Gt Britain by
EuroPrint Ltd
14 Hanover Square,
London W1S 1YH

CONTENTS

INTRODUCTION

'Flying The White Flag'

DEWSBURY TOWN HALL, its magnificent 19th century edifice a forlorn testament to the former glories of this once-proud Yorkshire mill town, spent most of 2010 under a massive shroud.

The town was (and is) on its knees in so many ways – economically, socially, politically and criminally – but the local authority decided that a couple of million quid's-worth of sandblasting and pointing was the best restorative for the place. Or was that all they were up to?

That all-encompassing shroud – a familiar look round these parts, although admittedly not in the jet black cloth that's de rigeur on the streets of the town centre.

Would the council just cut a narrow slit across the front of the garb from which the town hall could peer out suspiciously upon the world? Was this an attempt to set a world record for the biggest niqab (Muslim face veil) ever made? Was that to be Dewsbury's regenerative path back to fame and fortune? To entice even more Islamic pilgrims – they travel here from all over the planet – to come witness this curiosity?

Or was it simply the final slap in the face for an indigenous population already beaten to its knees by the failed mantra of multi-culturalism?

In my weekly newspaper column, I wondered whether perhaps when the great unveiling came, the town hall clock tower might have been replaced by a minaret. It wasn't, and indeed the grand old façade looked as good as new (although those ventilation units on the roof look decidedly eastern in architectural influence; probably my paranoia).

Not that it was going to make a blind bit of difference to Dewsbury's wider fortunes, however reinvigorated the building appeared. No meaningful decisions affecting the town's precarious prospects are made inside those walls. The town hall was and remains little more than a handsome, Victorian folly. A reminder of what once was.

Most surprisingly, to me at least, was the ragged presence of the Union flag, still hanging limply there on its stanchion. Hope springs eternal, eh? Because in Dewsbury, we've been flying the white flag for years now.

DURING the final editing of this book I was visited by an esteemed journalist and author, Matthew Engel, the much-admired long-time writer for The Guardian, now occasional columnist for the Financial Times, former editor of the cricket bible Wisden and the News International Visiting Professor of Media at Oxford University for 2010/11. He was passing through while researching a book on the various counties of England and was curious to see our little town.

We spent a late afternoon driving round and talking. I showed him the house of Karen Matthews, the disgrace of a 'mother' who supposedly kidnapped her own daughter and we visited the flat of Mick Donovan where little Shannon Matthews was found safe and reasonably well.

The writer witnessed the derelict buildings and empty shops, the tattooed, tracksuit wearing single mothers, beer-bellied or baseball capped blokes, the veil-clad Muslim sisterhood, and we fantastically ended up inside the largest teaching mosque in western Europe, thanks to the refreshing friendliness of a young Muslim security guard, wearing his faith like a beacon. I'm not sure his elders would have approved. Not if they'd known who one of the visitors was – the troublesome owner of the local paper.

Towards the end of our time together Matthew asked a simple enough question. "Why Dewsbury?" he said. "Other towns have large scale immigration, economic and social deprivation. So why should Dewsbury have to suffer more than other places?"

It was a timely question given where I was in completing this book. I'd thought about exactly that over a long period of time. This wasn't my exact reply, but it would have worked: "A perfect storm. Our civic pride and governance has been systematically stripped away. Our industrial bedrock has gone. Mass immigration has brought all kinds of challenges that we haven't come close to understanding, let alone dealing with. Throw in three decades of promoting single-motherhood and life on benefits, judicial dereliction of duty and this is what you get. The perfect storm. Oh, and some bad luck too. Lots of that."

There would have been plenty in that for Matthew Engel to chew on as he deliberated over his planned book.

'THE ISLAMIC Republic of Dewsbury? Are you sure?' I'm sure. People's reaction to that title says so much about the stigma – the institutionalised fear – of the mere possibility of misusing a simple single word, of putting it in a context that might inflame community relations, ethnic tensions.

But why should it? 'Islam' is a word, no more. I am a journalist and this is a factual story. Why should words terrify? Why should one particular word so inhibit us? The fact that it does, in itself justifies the title of this book.

Would I hesitate to describe a social chronicle as The Roman Catholic Republic of Dewsbury? It wouldn't make much of a book, but then it didn't happen. My ancestors came to this industrial and industrious town in the old West Riding of Yorkshire from their homes in Ireland for the very same reasons as the 20th and 21st century influx of south Asian migrants, but the impacts and outcomes have been radically different.

This is that story, that history, of the fundamental, mostly silent but occasionally violent social revolution within our town. And nothing defines that change more than that single word – Islam.

I'm prepared for the rancour and vitriol both the title and the subject matter will garner from the same old tired quarters. I could name many of this work's detractors now, but you'll be introduced to some of them soon enough.

Having endured so many years of being vilified every time I've written or published an opinion or even a factual news story in the slightest way critical of anything relating to the Muslim or Asian community, it's long been the proverbial water off a duck's back.

So why bother writing a chronicle which will predictably be portrayed as a provocation, as an undermining of supposedly worthy efforts towards 'community cohesion'? Why construct a narrative which appears to blatantly poke a finger of blame at one group of people, for the ills bedevilling so many others?

Firstly, 'community cohesion' in its tired, race industry dogma, is a myth; it's a political and bureaucratic construction whose only effective purpose is the self-perpetuation of the lucrative race industry.

Paradoxically, and intentionally or not – probably not – the selectively deaf, goose-stepping march of the 'community cohesion' zealots creates the exact division and resentment they pretend to address. Without tension and division there is no need for their fools' mission. Thus, mission accomplished, the lucrative wheels of the race industry turn.

Secondly, any finger-pointing in this story is definitively not aimed where those race and diversity and equality self-interests will misleadingly pretend.

This is not about Islam. It is about individuals and organisations who manipulate religion, ethnicity and colour for personal, political and criminal gain. Such as a finger points anywhere, it is inwards at the white, liberal British establishment whose attempts at social engineering have so fundamentally failed all of our citizens, of all faiths and nationalities.

Such as mixed ethnic communities rub along just fine in Dewsbury, it is in spite of, and not because of, meddling quangos and public-funded interest groups.

In essence this is a small story of a small town that has seen far better days. It is a chronicle of its recent history, in an attempt to explain where Dewsbury came from and where it has ended up.

That is not about an ethnic conspiracy or a religious masterplan, despite the clear wishes for a global caliphate that are harboured behind so many walls in this town. This is a story about far smaller matters, of ambition, greed and opportunism. Race and creed are just distractions when considering those very human foibles.

This story is about Politically Correct madness creating the perfect conditions for social division, criminal behaviour and economic disintegration. That it has also inadvertently empowered an alien culture to create a de facto state within a state might be completely farcical, but makes it no less real. Just a by-product of fools' errands.

Some Dewsbury people will not recognise parts of this story. Others will choose not to. By nature of creating this portrait, the humdrum everyday of so many lives is necessarily overlooked. In a town so geographically small, people of such radically different cultures cannot help but share so many areas of their lives. It would be unfair to pretend that for the greatest part people don't manage to cut along in a mostly civil fashion.

We do business with each other where mutual interests coincide and we share common courtesies, though less than you'd imagine. There are pockets of neighbourliness, of cross-cultural acquaintance and friendship.

People are people, at heart. Most of us want to bring our families up peacefully, for our children to have a good education and decent opportunities in life. It is how we set about achieving those goals that causes the fractures to appear and ultimately widens the chasm.

Culture is the biggest barrier between Dewsbury's two main communities, far more than religion.

But while our differences aren't so extreme as to prevent ordinary people going about their daily business, the tensions between two frankly incompatible cultures are undeniable; the frustration and resentment is visible mostly in small ways, but occasionally it explodes. And through it all the separatism increases, not diminishes.

You don't have to point the finger of blame to acknowledge that in a town like Dewsbury.

The race industry trumpets small, manufactured, photo-opportunity victories but only because it serves to justify its own existence. It tries to ignore and at other times buries its violent failings – often by diverting attention to people like outspoken local newspaper editors.

During the editing of this manuscript 'community cohesion' turned its blind eyes away from yet another unfortunate victim. Nazakat Alam and Nisar Shah have been charged with the murder of Jack Carter, an innocent victim caught up in a violent row between Asian and white neighbours. Mr Carter, 39, was allegedly beaten to death in the street while visiting friends.

Not long afterwards the district had three nights of drive-by shootings involving Pakistani drug gangs. You probably didn't read, see or hear of any of that, not even on regional tv news programmes, let alone News at Ten. So much of what happens here flies beneath the public radar – the police and authorities do their best to ensure that.

There was a time when Dewsbury, and its neighbouring town along the valley, Batley, were defined by an industry and by the proud, if occasionally rough-hewn character of the men and women who belonged here. No more.

In 2011 there is not an area of life in Dewsbury, from health to education, from politics to crime, from economic stagnation to social deprivation, that has not been massively impacted upon by our significant and rapidly burgeoning Islamic community, its needs, its demands and its cultural differences.

That relationship defines most significantly what the town has become. There is barely a civic or corporate decision made without reference to, or predominantly influenced by, its impact on the Muslim community. Their social, economic and religious appetites and ambitions increasingly shape the future of this town, on every level.

This book does not pretend to possess an answer to, or a solution for, Dewsbury's multitude of challenges, let alone other places like it. It serves only to describe what has happened to us and what your town or community can expect if the same circumstances prevail.

That's all.

Danny Lockwood, November 11th, 2011

1 – SETTING THE SCENE

Dewsbury, West Yorkshire.

IT IS THURSDAY, July 7th, 2011. Typical English 'summer' weather. It can't make its mind up whether to scorch us or drown us. The gusty breeze is coming from the prevailing west, over the Pennines a dozen miles up the Calder valley, bringing with it a real ration of 'Woolworth's weather' – pick'n mix. I'm standing in a small children's play area created out of a corner of overgrown spare land, on a rise above Dewsbury railway station and the town centre beyond, and I'm overlooking a battlefield.

From here I can see the escarpment two-and-a-half miles away, from atop which Lord Fairfax's Parliamentarian army pounded the Royalist forces of Lord Savile into submission during the one-sided Battle of Thornhill Hall. That was 1648, in the fledgling days of English democracy.

In the foreground I can see the eponymous Savile Road, snaking its way south out of Dewsbury, through the brooding Muslim enclave of Savile Town and past the former public house that now houses 'our' Sharia court. It was up Savile Road that a rampaging Muslim mob charged in June 1989, besieging and ransacking another pub in a battle whose repercussions resonate in this district to this day.

Not that war has ever been declared. We submitted

before hostilities were ever formally acknowledged. Democracy has come full circle in these parts. And some. At least the civil war between Cromwell and the Stuarts was 'in the family' between Englishmen who considered themselves thus, whatever their divergent politics.

In the railway station car park a few yards down below me, a hoped-for battleground of new English democrats didn't quite work out as anticipated when they descended on the town a few Saturdays ago. The English Democratic League chose Dewsbury to stage their latest rally in protest at the Islamification of the country and sure enough they rolled into town like so many 1970s football hooligans, all guttural, monosyllabic chants and pulsating veins, hoping/expecting things to kick off.

Their bait had been predictably taken by the Kirklees Unite Against Fascism rabble, a collection of various Socialist Workers Party, loony left and race industry professionals, who can always be guaranteed to rise to the occasion. I've no time for either motley crew.

It was a battlefield without a battle on this occasion. This week is also the 10th anniversary of the bloody Bradford riots, eight miles north up the Spen valley, and the police have learned their lessons. The EDL were 'kettled' like so many cheese and onion crisps, and the anti-fascists herded into another car park further down the ring road.

If the traffic stopped long enough they'd probably just about be able to hear each other's chanted insults. The EDL say they'll be back, but don't sound inclined to give the police as much notice next time, probably because they never got to provoke the confrontation they desired. We shall see.

My mother, now in her mid-70s, lives just a couple of hundred yards behind where I'm standing, in a small estate of local authority houses and flats, not more than a half mile from where she grew up in the town's Irish immigrant community, and only half that distance from the Moorlands Maternity Home where I was born just before Christmas in 1958.

I'm facing directly south, where 12 miles away stands the beacon that is Emley Moor television mast, at 1,068 feet the tallest structure in the UK, pointing like a giant finger to the heavens. There's an ironic symbolism there. The mast has carried far and wide the word of Dewsbury's disgraces over recent years from being the home of the leader of the July 7th 2005 suicide bombers, Mohammed Siddique Khan, to dissolute mother Karen Matthews, who faked the kidnapping of her daughter Shannon. I'm not aware of any local disputes claiming Emley Moor's spiritual significance for one particular set of gods or other, but the cynic in me supposes it can only be a matter of time.

In the foreground, on the opposite side of the town's small ring road from where I'm standing, is Dewsbury's handsome Minster Church, founded in 627AD by the Roman missionary Paulinus. It is still an imposing, beloved and well used house of worship; every Christmas Eve the 'Devil's Knell' is rung out on its bells, one toll for every year since Christ's birth, just as it has been the past 600 years – since Sir Thomas de Soothill murdered a servant boy by throwing him into a mill pond, and by way of penance donated a bell, Black Tom, to the church.

Temper and violence. Nothing new in Dewsbury then. We just don't see much repentance these days.

There certainly wasn't much repentance in the eyes of Peter William Sutcliffe, the Yorkshire Ripper, when he climbed the steps into the dock of the old magistrates court housed in our magnificent town hall one momentous evening in January 1981.

Sutcliffe's eyes looked dead as he glanced at we journalists ranked and packed in the public gallery behind him. He studiously avoided the desperate gaze of his wife Sonia, blankly staring at a spot above the head of the magistrate as the world witnessed the first public accountability of his crimes.

When caught with a prostitute in Sheffield who may have been his next intended victim, Sutcliffe's car was sporting license plates stolen from a motor spares yard in the Dewsbury division, hence him being brought here. It wasn't his only link to the town though. One of the girls he murdered, Helen Ritka, had been living under the care of my aunt until shortly before her pimp came and took her away – again – to work the streets of Huddersfield, where she met her grisly fate.

The town hall, like the Minster, is an imposing reminder of what Dewsbury once was, but the walls of the fabulous civic building echo mostly with memories these days. Virtually all of our local governance is based up the valley in Huddersfield, the seat of a woeful bureaucratic confection, Kirklees Council.

Kirklees has systematically dismantled – or tried to – every element of the old Dewsbury County Borough that represented local pride and self-determination, up to and including trying to flog the civic silverware. They even managed to 'misplace' the bandstand from our handsome public park. How do you lose something as big as a flaming bandstand? Those little things still rankle hereabouts.

The beautiful period courtroom where Sutcliffe stood was replaced in the 1980s by a purpose built courthouse in the town centre, but we can't even take pride in dealing with our own criminals for much longer. If such a high profile arrest happened again on our patch we would be spared much of the media spotlight because the police have decamped their command team to Huddersfield. Meanwhile our 'new' courts are set to close and be crammed into a far less suitable building, also in Huddersfield.

If you detect a sense of grievance, you'd be right. It's widely shared by Dewsbury people. Huddersfield gets everything, we don't even seem to get the crumbs from their table, just another increased Council Tax or business rates bill.

As the town hall is much diminished in civic stature, so the Minster is far from being Dewsbury's dominant religious establishment any longer, not locally and certainly not in terms of global influence. That honour belongs to the far bigger, brooding and secretive mass of the Markazi mosque complex, less than a mile beyond the Minster as I look southwards. I'm regarding its prominent minaret – one of very many in these parts. As another church rings its final bell, another two mosques begin their calls to prayer.

But while the doors of one house of worship, the Minster, are open to any man, woman or child of any faith who passes by and seeks spiritual solace, the other is high walled, ringed by security cameras and forbidding warnings not to try photographing it.

Outside Saudi Arabia, the Markazi mosque is the worldwide headquarters of Tablighi Jamaat, a secretive, fundamentalist sect which preaches a global caliphate – an Islamic world. To use a more familiar Christian analogy they're a bit 'old testament' in their teachings; back-to-basics religion. Tablighis profess a peaceful path to their goal although clearly not all of their adherents follow that teaching to the letter of the law. Neither theirs nor ours.

You may have heard of some of Tablighi Jamaat's followers, people like Richard Reid the failed and infamous shoe-bomber who tried to bring a plane down over America, or maybe Shehzad Tanweer, one of London's July 7th bombers. Tanweer attended prayers at the Markazi, which was built and paid for by Saudi money here in Dewsbury, starting construction in 1978, being completed in 1982, and whose creeping, radical tentacles reach far beyond our town's Sharia court, corrupt politics, criminal gangs and simmering racial tensions.

Less clear is how devoted to Tablighi Jamaat's goals and means was the leader of the July 7th plot, Mohammed Siddique Khan. Just last night I read on a Muslim internet forum that he despised the cult; others say that he attended prayers there with Tanweer. We'll probably never know.

Certainly Khan, who died along with five innocent bystanders on the Edgware Road train that morning, won't be enlightening us. From where I stand I can't quite see the street where Khan lived, just across the valley in the adjacent settlement to Savile Town of Thornhill Lees, on the flood plain of the river Calder.

When Khan bade farewell to his pregnant wife on that fateful morning of July 7 to lead his fellow martyrs off to claim 52 innocent lives, it was from a tidy council house in a quiet cul de sac, Lees Holm. I used to live in Lees Holm, though some years before Khan and his family arrived. Another of my aunts and her family lived there too, just across the road from him. Small world. Small town.

I'VE JUST finished putting The Press 'to bed' – it's a weekly newspaper covering the goings-on in this crowded valley, an extended neighbourhood of small former mill towns of which Dewsbury is the largest, followed by Batley, Mirfield, Heckmondwike, Cleckheaton and Birstall; it is 'North' Kirklees as defined by the language of the 1972 Local Government Act.

One of our main news stories this week regards a pronouncement by the extremist Islamic group Muslims Against Crusades (MAC) calling for the founding of three Islamic emirates in the UK – in the London borough of Tower Hamlets, Bradford and here in Dewsbury.

MAC are the gang who burned poppies during last year's

Remembrance Day parades. Their war cry this week is for those three nominated districts to seal themselves off against the outside secular world, to school their children separate from our infecting influences, to establish Sharia law in their protectorate and to cease from trading with us.

I can't speak for Tower Hamlets and Bradford, but as I look across at Savile Town I can safely say that the taxi drivers, corner shop and curry house owners apart – oh and the drug dealers of course – the rest is pretty much in place already.

You'd think such an inflammatory appeal from Muslims Against Crusades would be front page news in a town like this. Well, it got a brief mention on page 1 but that's all. It's hardly earth-shattering stuff given what we see and live with, week in week out.

Our front page tomorrow will be the story of Darren Thornton, a troubled young man who was born with severe hearing impairments and became alcoholic, but who was found dead in a seedy drug den, about 100 yards from where I'm standing.

Darren almost certainly wasn't a heroin addict unlike the men who's company he was in. The inquest hasn't concluded yet, but his family believe it may have been his first injection that killed him, administered by a third party. He was left handed, and the needle mark was in his left arm.

Even that isn't news in Dewsbury these days. The Kirklees death rate from accidents and suicides is almost double the national average and much of that will be explained by the regularity of the heroin deaths here in Dewsbury and our neighbouring towns.

The reason it's on our front page is because Darren's family were devastated not just by their troubled son's death but by my rival newspaper, the Dewsbury Reporter, printing that he was the tyrannical, drug raddled neighbour whose flat was well known as an addict's haven. They even cocked up the apology, so the family rang and asked me to write something to honour Darren's tragic memory. I grew up across the road from his mum, many years ago.

It was the least I could do for the latest in the long, long roll call of young people in this town whose lives have been lost, mostly silently, to this plague. Young Pakistani men control Dewsbury's prolific heroin industry. They deal brazenly on the road just behind me, according to local residents who have tired of reporting it to police and seeing no action taken. They deal with impunity on pretty much every road, come to that.

FROM MY vantage point I'm regarding a broad landscape of distant hills where the district breathes and expands. Beyond the crowded terraced homes buffering the Markazi mosque in Savile Town lie the neighbouring settlements of Thornhill Lees and beyond that Thornhill, atop the escarpment beyond the Calder flood plain. From there the countryside opens up, until it hits the urban sprawl of Wakefield to the south-east, but all the way west and south to the Pennines and Peak District, dotted with picturesque villages amidst which sits the Emley Moor tv mast. This part of West Yorkshire is a mass of contradictions – from violent social and religious strife, to an idyllic pub lunch on the village green, in just 10 or 15 minutes.

In the foreground too many disused mills and empty factories characterise the working face of the district. Dewsbury town centre is hidden in the bowl below me, littered with its empty shops and mistrustful people, soundtracked by flash cars with young drivers, barking out hip-hop, rap and gangsta noises that assault the sensibilities of passers by. Cast a disapproving glance at their racket however and receive back what one local politician described as “a thousand yard stare”.

I’ve often thought about driving my modest family saloon slowly round Savile Town with the windows open, wearing my smartest business suit and tie, with some Matt Monro or Val Doonican playing at full volume. Not a good idea really. Three or four judiciously parked cars would turn Savile Town into a fortress, sealing off the outside world. It’s not a place to try to be funny. It’s not even a place to try walking past on a dark night.

At night in the town centre you will no longer find homeward bound cinema or theatre-goers, nor even couples returning from restaurants or late-night revellers spilling out of crowded nightclubs; just empty streets and trouble for the most part.

As mixed as the summer weather of 2011 has been it’s remained clear so far today, but there aren’t any children in the playground I’m standing in, early in the afternoon. I don’t think I have ever seen any children playing in it, come to that. It was probably some well-meaning local councillor or council officer’s bad idea of a good idea. Some Leisure Services budget money left over? Let’s turn this overgrown pervert’s hideaway into a kiddies’ playground, shall we?

The district is littered with such recreational follies, like the broken down shells of burnt out tanks marking some desperate military combat, all passion and zeal in its moment but now absently forgotten. Wary mums and dads don’t let their kids come out and play unsupervised in places like this. Not in a town like this has become. Not any longer. Not if they’ve any sense.

And where kids do roam the streets and the playgrounds at will – well, in Dewsbury today, those families and ‘communities’ are synonymous with characters like Karen Matthews, who became the face of Dewsbury for several months in 2008 when she was convicted of orchestrating the kidnap of her own daughter Shannon.

I'm still not sure that was the full story by the way – a farcical 'kidnap' plot with the intention of claiming a reward for her own child's discovery. You wouldn't get that plot past a tv producer, but the police somehow managed to get it past a judge and jury – probably for the lack of a more plausible explanation. Maybe we'll discover one day.

As a brief aside, I came as close as I ever will to getting a 'million pound' photograph when they found little Shannon in Mick Donovan's council flat, barely 100 yards from the Woodman Inn where the CID officers hunting for the child used to go for an occasional beer after work.

I got a tip that the child had been found alive and well, and as I ran up the cul de sac with my camera in hand and a work experience student galloping behind, Shannon was bundled into a police car and Donovan dragged bodily out of his flat and whisked away. I was seconds too late for a photograph that would have been on every tv screen and every newspaper front page around the world in minutes! Bugger.

Instead the student and I sat on a wall, talking to a couple of bemused housewives, and waited for the world's media to arrive. Dewsbury would be back in the headlines again, but there was a happy-ish ending to this tale. No one, least of all the police, thought there was a prayer of finding little Shannon alive.

The Matthews 'family' lived a mile or so from where I'm standing today, and Shannon was found a little closer than that.

IT IS A shame about these children's play areas. This one I'm standing in sports a health-and-safety-proof rubber compound surface, and some attractively functional playground slides and see-saws and roundabouts which, surprisingly, haven't been vandalised.

If I had a golf club and ball I could whack it onto the police station roof from here – that's how close at hand the forces of law and order are. A crowd of 200-300 angry left-wing activists and Muslims gathered outside that police station one Sunday afternoon last summer, calling for my blood because I'd used the 'P' word. We'll come back to that.

Despite the law's proximity no one uses the playground. Policemen are rarely seen except for the occasional Police Community Support Officers – hobby bobbies – walking round in scaredy-cat pairs in mid-morning, ironically when the kids are at school and the druggies are still in bed.

In one of the flats directly behind me I remember reporting a story of a man who killed his partner by choking her to death in what he claimed was a consensual sex act. No ligatures were involved. Use your imagination.

I also recall that more recently a girl was raped on this very spot – incredible, when you think that it is overlooked by those dozen or more local authority flats just a few yards away, and is closer still to the entrance to the railway station. The culprit was disturbed in the act and chased by a local teenager and despite escaping by train, was tracked down by the police and successfully convicted. A result for the good guys. Dewsbury doesn't seem to have many of them these days – good results.

But it isn't just because of the marginal threat of sexual predators that kids don't play in areas like these in 21st century Dewsbury. It's just as likely to be the worry and danger of the commonplace race attacks that seem to go increasingly unpoliced and unpunished.

I read a report about Dewsbury on the Times website the other day where it stated that incidents of racial violence are rare because the white and Muslim communities simply don't encounter each other in daily life.

I don't know where the author got that information from, on either count. No doubt some 'authority' with a vested interest in pretending otherwise. It would have been instructive for the journalist to have his car experience a bump with one driven by an Asian man down there in Savile Town, over the hill in Batley Carr, or just along the valley in Scout Hill or Ravensthorpe. He might even be impressed at first, then scared stiff, by how fast so many 'independent' witnesses could appear on he scene, surrounding him and his vehicle, to 'help' establish the cause of the accident. Or rather the accident that he caused. So many witnesses. That's a daily occurrence round here.

Still, I suppose that's not 'violence' per se. But to assert there's very little race crime? Sorry. Not true.

I'm reminded of the case of a schoolboy, set on fire by a pair of Asian youths in the town centre in broad daylight. It was on Saturday, near the market, at a time and in a place where the town's at its busiest. Proper shopping tourists still come to Dewsbury from all over the county, on coach trips even, to visit our renowned outdoor market.

As emblems of this town's once-proud heritage go, Dewsbury market is like the flag that General Custer's men stuck in the ground during their last stand. It was named the country's best outdoor market in 2007. It didn't prevent this lad being sprayed with a flammable substance and being set light to, in front of dozens of witnesses. His attackers were never caught. So much for the CCTV cameras seemingly on every other lamppost.

THE RACE attacks aren't exclusive to one ethnic group upon another. From the playground I can look down through the windows of the West Riding Refreshment Rooms, formerly the train station's waiting room and now a real ale pub.

It's an excellent one too, the town centre's best pub, if ever you fancy breaking your train journey from York or

Leeds, on the way to Manchester or Liverpool. Or vice versa of course.

Just along the platform from the door to the pub a young Asian student, waiting for the Huddersfield train with his pals on a Christmas shopping trip, was inexplicably knifed to death by two white teenage drug-addicts.

Ahmed Hassan was a model pupil, a quiet boy, who went to the same school as my son at the time he was killed. Most of the victims of race violence in our town tend to be minding their own business. Unlike Ahmed however, most also tend to be white. The colour doesn't make the difference. Crime is crime and never victimless, racially motivated or not. It's authority's tacit submission to it as an acceptable part of the town's social fabric that angers and frightens conscientious parents most. They're not sure anyone is on their side any longer, not the police, not the politicians, not anyone in authority.

The crime isn't ignored by police because of the ethnic involvement, rather because of the crime itself. But by trying to create that illusion of public safety, they only serve to fuel suspicion and misplaced motive. As in most things the police do for well-meaning reasons round here, it backfires regularly.

Just beyond the West Riding pub, on the inside of the small ring-road which encircles the town, stands the prow-shaped Yorkshire-stone building through whose doors I nervously took my first steps as a trainee journalist in the late summer of 1978, the Dewsbury Reporter, at the very time they were laying the foundation stones of the Markazi.

By the time I returned as editor-in-chief of the newspaper and its sister titles in 1993 it had a bustling, thriving staff of around 95 people and was hugely profitable, part of the Yorkshire Post stable of newspapers. Today there are probably only a dozen or so downtrodden employees rattling around inside the big, handsome

Victorian building. The company profits have headed due south in step with the 'efficiencies' and 'downsizing' of rapacious modern publishing companies.

Not that I care about the dwindling fortunes of their owners Johnston Press overmuch. I'm persona non grata at the Dewsbury Reporter these days, despite all my years of honourable service, the business success stories we shared, the awards we won – the millions we made.

In 2002 I launched my own independent newspaper, The Press, whose offices can't quite be seen from here, a further couple of hundred yards down the hill in the bowl of the town centre. The Press has suffered in recent years too, partly because of the economic downturn that's hit everyone so hard, but also as a result of the damage suffered during a long and painful legal battle with Dewsbury's former Labour MP, Shahid Malik.

Malik sued The Press, a local Tory councillor Jonathan Scott, and me personally, for libel based on a letter Scott wrote in our pages. Malik didn't sue the Dewsbury Reporter, our competitor, which also published the letter. That's a story in itself.

However, and highly unusually these days, the case staggered all the way to a hugely expensive two-week trial at the Royal Courts of Justice in London. It shouldn't have come to that – it wasn't much of a grievance that prompted the lawsuit in the first place – but Malik and I are equally proud, equally stubborn characters, and we went down together kicking and scratching and fighting like a couple of alley cats. The jury couldn't separate us, failing to reach a verdict, and we talked sense into each other before stepping into the ring for a re-match that would have left all and sundry bankrupt.

Pride, an expensive commodity.

There was a good news ending to that bloody episode in a couple of senses. Firstly the lawyers got their backsides bitten for a fortune, as Malik was on a no-win no-fee agreement throughout and our lawyers did the trial part of the battle on a similar footing. At least we weren't the only ones left out of pocket. And secondly, at the General Election in June 2010 Malik was booted out of office and, temporarily at least, out of Dewsbury.

Down below me a trans-Pennine service train pulls to a halt, on the near platform – eastbound. I can't see if any young Muslim men have disembarked having caught the train from Manchester, the fervour of their faith shining brightly, suitcases or holdalls at hand, heading outside onto the station forecourt looking for a taxi to take them to the Markazi mosque.

They travel here week in, week out, not just from around Britain but from all over the world, to take residence at the religious seminary housed within the sprawling, secure compound of the mosque. The quest for a global Islamic caliphate has many encampments in the territories of the Kuffar – the infidel, the unclean, the non-believers. Us. But none of those havens are quite so embedded, secure, influential and completely unaccountable as the Markazi, here in the heart of Dewsbury. In the heart of what I used to think was my town.

Now it's the town of Baroness Warsi of Dewsbury. Small, sweet, smiling, witty Sayeeda, who just a few years ago was sitting in a hairdresser's chair unwittingly alongside one of my former members of staff. She was wondering aloud whether to accept the political courting of Labour or Conservative, both astutely aware of the value of an educated, articulate and politically ambitious Muslim woman. She certainly backed the right horse.

At times I've fondly imagined I played some meaningful role in putting Sayeeda there, and then I think I can still detect the dainty, metaphorical footprints on my back and shoulders where my 'friend' manipulated my media usefulness on her cynical climb to fame – and power.

This is now the town of Sheikh Yakub Munshi, a senior cleric at the Markazi who has run Dewsbury's Sharia court for years, and his teenage grandson Hammaad Munshi, arrested at the gates of his school while still in uniform (it was my school once, too) and hauled off to be convicted and jailed as Britain's youngest terrorist bomb plotter, aged 16, in 2008.

It's the town of Aishah Azmi, not coincidentally a young lady with close family ties to the Munshis. She became another Islamic cause celebre as the fundamentalist school teaching assistant, who sued over her 'human right' to wear the full face niqab veil in front of young children. She lost her case – a rare setback for the brotherhood's incessant march to dominance in every corner, every crevice, of Dewsbury life.

From commerce to crime, politics to property, this isn't the town it was any longer. How did we get into this sorry state? Dewsbury has been changing for a long time, since the death of the textile industry when we were the beating heart of Yorkshire's 'Heavy Woollen District'. The wealth has seeped away, to be replaced by a new economic dynamic.

As the immigrants came from south Asia to take low-paid mill and public transport jobs in the 50s and 60s, so the world turned again. But our new neighbours were and are nothing if not innovative and industrious. Many of the mills have found a new use. Dewsbury and Batley are the bed-manufacturing capitals of the UK now, an industry dominated by the Asian business community.

As public transport gave way to the social phenomenon of a motor car outside almost every home so they capitalised on the private hire revolution. There are taxis for man and dog round these parts and it is an industry dominated almost totally by that ethnic representation. Meanwhile it sometimes seems there are more curry takeaways than there are customers in the valley, but there's rarely a week or month goes by that another doesn't open. Cash businesses are always popular, even when it's sometimes difficult to envisage where the cash is coming from.

Oh and of course there's the drugs industry, as I've mentioned. Nowhere does heroin quite as cheaply and plentifully as Dewsbury – all the other recreational drugs too, because profit is profit, and customer demand is king – but heroin's the killer, quite literally.

This is a different town in every way you can describe it, from the one I was born and grew up in. No aspect of life remains untouched by Islam, not our schools, not our health service. There are more mosques than pubs, let alone churches. Indeed many of our old pubs and working men's clubs are mosques.

The criminal landscape revolves around the drug industry rooted by supply in their communities, but touching, too often fatally, every street in ours. It's a troubling blight on young Asian people's parents and mullahs and imams every bit as much as it is on the parents of our addicts and orphans. It just isn't publicly acknowledged by either.

The streets in many parts of town are not safe to walk, be that the threat of sexual harassment for young women (increasingly from the 'new' migrants of eastern Europe and the middle east) or random, casual violence on mostly young men by other young men. That's a fact, no matter the police pretence otherwise. Neither does our political landscape bear much resemblance to a democratic system that people outside this ethnic morass would recognise. Electoral fraud and voter intimidation are an annual accomplice of polling day in these parts.

Meanwhile in everyday, workaday Dewsbury, the 'nice' shops have gone. When Marks & Spencer called it a day, you could almost have hung up the 'Closed For Business' sign. Now it's a 'poundtown' of discount and charity shops, of shabby takeaways and boarded up frontages, of those drunken east European immigrants slumped against town centre walls, or care-in-the-community foul-mouths screaming at each other across car parks and out of state-funded apartment windows.

A few good people, a few organisations continue to fight the good fight, to hang on to some of the traditions which once punctuated Dewsbury life. People like The Collegians am-dram group, putting on their annual panto, despite the Council banning local groups from displaying banners on the town hall to advertise their efforts, or selling their own bags of sweets to kiddies – health and safety, don't you know. The market traders persist with their 'Dewsbury on Sea' summer festival and Santa's grotto, despite the PC brigade's ongoing efforts to remove the 'Christ' from Christmas for fear of giving offence.

I CAN SEE dark clouds starting to roll down the valley and even the sheets of rain hitting the hills to the west of Thornhill. The first drops are starting to fall. It looks like this burst will be heavy. What a lousy summer it is.

I'd better get back to the office – I need to collect the photograph of Darren Thornton we borrowed for tomorrow's front page and return it to his folks. It's a lovely picture taken when he was in an alcoholics' hostel run by the Betel Christian organisation over the Pennines in Wigan. Darren was doing so well until this past April when he had an alcoholic lapse and had to leave the hostel.

He'd been back with his mum and dad and doing all right, but went to stay with a pal for a few days and the heroin got him. I hope tomorrow's story gives Allan and Sue some comfort at least.

2 – THE BATTLE OF DEWSBURY

IF HISTORICAL references to the Battle of Thornhill Hall in 1648 are scant, there is still plenty of documentary and eyewitness evidence of the Battle of Dewsbury, of Saturday June 24th 1989. Editions of the Dewsbury Reporter, Huddersfield Examiner and Yorkshire Post describe the day's events in words and images and witnesses – victims even – are still abundant.

For the purposes of this study of Dewsbury's waning fortunes and its social and economic disintegration, and despite portraits in future chapters of the town's 1,400 year journey as a seat of Christianity, I've chosen this date to effectively begin my chronicle. That Saturday afternoon marked the sea-change in everything about the relationship between Islam and the rest of the world as witnessed through Dewsbury people's eyes.

Geoff McGill, former pit electrician and subsequent landlord of the Scarborough Hotel on the corner of Savile Road and Orchard Street, at the effective 'entrance' to the already predominantly Muslim enclave of Savile Town, was enjoying a Saturday afternoon game of cards with pals and pub regulars when the protests over the Salman Rushdie novel Satanic Verses exploded upon Dewsbury's town centre streets, a little over half a mile away.

Rushdie's book sparked global protests but nowhere was the effigy-burning more vitriolic than in West Yorkshire where the increasingly militant young generation of Muslims for the first time really made their voices and anger heard.

The tv cameras caught the fiery protests in Bradford and other increasingly confident Asian communities, while 10 miles down the road in Dewsbury, more trouble fomented.

The police had made a complete hash of managing a planned rally that Saturday in Dewsbury town centre by the right-wing British National Party, which was in 1989 a quite recent derivation from the more radically voiced National Front. In itself it was an opportunistic protest nominally at the book burning scenes in Bradford and other heavily-Muslim areas mostly across the industrial north of England.

The rally was also justified by the BNP at the time as being in support of an episode two years before when a group of white Dewsbury parents had fought a very public – and successful – battle against Kirklees Council, who were trying to force them to send their children to an overwhelmingly Muslim primary school.

The parents in Thornhill Lees, next door to Savile Town, insisted on having a say in their children's schooling and fought a long and bloody battle with Kirklees Council and its arch-socialist meddler, former Labour Councillor Denis Ripley. Even in the 1980s, Ripley was ahead of his time in the multi-cultural science of white subjugation.

In the parents of Thornhill Lees he met his match. They kept their children at home, set up their own ad hoc school and fought him all the way to the high court in London, where Ripley's and Kirklees's manipulative agenda was eventually revealed. The children were sent to school up on the crest in Thornhill, which was then and still remains a predominantly white bastion on its perch above Savile Town.

But in essence the BNP's 1989 rally was nothing more

than an act of blatant provocation in a town with a large and growing Muslim population. The first, not the last.

In response, and to throw petrol onto the potential for an explosive outcome, a left-wing outfit self-titled the Black Workers' Group was allowed to quickly rally the angry young Muslims of Savile Town (and further afield) to their cause and stage a tit-far-tat public display.

They held their gathering a few hundred yards away from the BNP, outside the town's main public library.

About 750 people attended that Black Workers' Group gathering – mostly Asians from across the north of England – and they were addressed by a number of speakers including another of Labour's main architect of the Politically Correct agenda in Kirklees, Councillor John Harman. Harman would later be knighted by Tony Blair and made a highly-paid quango chief, generally accepted as bring in exchange for giving up a promised Parliamentary seat in favour of one of Blair's lackeys.

Their rally broke up at 1.30pm – the BNP's was due to start across town at 2pm – and despite loudhailer requests for the crowd to disperse (surely naïve given the malignantly coincidental timing of the rally's conclusion) gangs of young Asians, many wearing headbands daubed with the slogan 'Islam' broke away and stormed through the busy town centre.

Many of the rampaging Asian youths contented themselves with terrorising shoppers and damaging cars and shop windows, although a policeman was injured when a gang hurled stones at officers, before one group confronted young white drinkers outside the Black Bull public house in the town's Market Place.

As police moved to break-up that skirmish more Asian youths, joined by a separate mob that had moved in from the direction of Savile Town, converged on the site of the BNP rally behind the town hall, only to find themselves being held at bay by a line of police.

An uneasy stand-off followed, whereby the estimated 200 BNP supporters were urged not to become confrontational and after listening to several speeches, were bussed rapidly out of town. Ironically it was local white youths, and not attendees of the BNP rally, who then got caught up in abusive confrontations with the Black Workers Group and their allies.

At that point the police started trying to herd the Muslim protesters away from the town centre and back towards Savile Town. Missiles were hurled at the police and at about 3pm duty commanding officer Supt Neil Reece gave the order for arrests to be made if necessary.

As the police herded the angry Muslim mob back across the river over the main Savile Bridge, one very traditional symbol of white Britain stood before them a few hundred yards up Savile Road – the Scarborough pub, with Geoff McGill and his pals inside.

I need to make a declaration of interest at this point. Geoff McGill was a good friend of 30 years standing until his premature death in 2007. Most of the people with him that day in the Scarborough were and continue to be similarly close acquaintances of mine.

The Scarborough had a reputation of being a 'top' Tetley's pub – no mean accolade in this beer drinking part of Yorkshire – and Geoff one of its most popular landlords. He used to watch the rugby league team I played for, though he was never a player himself unlike some of his acquaintances that day, Colin Webber and Phil Andruchow, former teammates of mine at Dewsbury Celtic, the town's premier amateur rugby league club.

Phil takes up the story.

"We were in the Scarborough and it was lunchtime – there were probably about a dozen of us, having a drink and playing cards, mostly blokes but a couple of women. This was usually where we went on a Saturday lunch.

"We knew there was something going on in town, and around 1-ish we noticed this bloke – a white bloke, in casual clothes – just sitting on the bench across Savile Road from the pub. He was just sitting there and it seemed a bit funny so I went over and had a word with him. He said he was a police officer and I asked him to give us a shout in the pub if there was anything to worry about.

"Later on I popped out to see if he was still there and he wasn't. He'd simply disappeared. I turned and looked down Savile Road towards town and I'd never seen anything like it. There was a mass of people pouring up the road, packing it, literally hundreds of them charging up the hill.

"I could see the police had stopped at the junction with Mill Street, by the Savile Arms, and all these Asian people were heading our way and getting closer.

"I looked around and the grocer's shop just along the road had taken in all its fruit and veg that was normally stocked outside. Local residents, Asian folk, used to use Geoff's car park at the pub, but all the cars had been moved out of it – there was only David Hirst's left there. Dave was in the pub with us. His car ended up a write-off.

"I slammed the door shut and locked it, and no sooner had I done that than they set about the building, trying to smash the door down. I don't know what they used on the door but it must have been a sledgehammer to knock it down. Geoff's pub had these shatterproof windows that the brewery had put in, so they didn't actually manage to break the glass – instead the entire windows were banged completely out of the frame.

"We'd phoned the police straight away and told them what was happening, then we retreated up the stairs into the living quarters and gathered there. The mob just set about everything in the pub, throwing furniture about, smashing the optics, glasses, everything, just wrecking the place. I don't know how long it went on. Twenty minutes, maybe half an hour, but it seemed like an eternity. We must have called the police four or five times.

"We were starting to panic because we thought they were going to burn the pub down and we were stuck and there was no sign of the police.

"We'd placed ourselves in the hallway at the top of the stairs because that was the easiest place to defend if they came after us, the narrowest area – we'd looked around for anything we could use as weapons. Scared? Of course we were scared. You'd be a liar if you said you weren't."

Eventually the police arrived, and as quickly as they'd arrived the mob fled. Geoff McGill and Phil Andruchow, Colin Webber, David Hirst, Nigel and Sarah Clayton and their friends descended to be met by riot police.

"The place was a shambles," said Phil. "They'd just gone mad. But the funny thing was on the table by the back window, the cards were still sitting there, undisturbed. All this mayhem and wreckage and the cards were the only things that hadn't moved.

"We'd been playing a game called 'shit cart' and the call went out, 'gentlemen, the cards!' We opened a bottle, sort of in symbolic defiance, and sat down and finished the hand.

"Then we started sweeping up and clearing the mess. Fair play to Geoff, he opened up the next day, with his windows boarded up – business as usual!"

THE OUTPOURING of militant Islamic feeling regarding the publishing of Rushdie's provocative Satanic Verses signalled a marked thrust forward in the assertiveness of the generally south Asian but specifically Muslim migrants who had taken root in industrial towns across the north like Dewsbury, Batley, Keighley and Bradford, and across the Pennines in Burnley, Oldham and Blackburn. Larger metropolitan centres like Leicester and Birmingham had their booming Muslim populations too – indeed as did most sizeable population centres.

The socio-political dynamics within those towns and cities are for others to observe and comment upon. I can only remark upon what happened in the town of my birth and chronicle the events as they unfolded here.

Dewsbury changed visibly that day.

Whether Satanic Verses was the trigger that fired Islamic zeal, or simply a totemic excuse to hang around the neck of a movement whose time had inexorably come, is moot. Lots of social sands were shifting as BBC and ITV news cameras televised images of young men burning books and effigies of the acclaimed 'British' writer Rushdie.

If angry young Muslims are the visible face of the so-called Anti-Fascists who came into their own at that time, then my experience has been of very white, middle-class individuals pulling their strings in the background.

Whatever other repercussions Britain experienced in the times of the fatwa issued by the Ayatollahs on Rushdie, but before global Islamic terrorism was on the vaguest of horizons, those events of the summer of 1989 signalled a marked change in the political dynamic within our district.

In widening the growing schism between Muslim and indigenous communities, despite the hurried onset of multi-cultural appeasement, they were seismic. Just, I suspect, as the mullahs of Savile Town's Markazi mosque silently prayed for. The 'community' had publicly flexed its muscles for the first time, but by far from the last. How our political and governmental authorities responded would be critical.

What filled the vacuum in the first place was a socialist (as opposed to socially) motivated piece of opportunism. Britain's race industry found its wings, a cause, and ultimately a ceaseless supply of funding.

What spewed forth from that confrontation on June 24th

1989 in Dewsbury set a tone that was to dominate the nature of political, police and community relations – certainly in this district – to this day. The path has been exclusively downhill if anyone's intention was ever to bring Muslim and white communities closer together in a framework of respect and understanding.

Paradoxically and as I have opined, peaceful co-existence is the last thing the race industry needs. Without tension and division, it has no raison d'etre; it relies on grievances – real or imagined, contrived or otherwise, in order to justify its existence and its budgets.

In the kind of tragic irony that we have become used to, that Saturday was supposed to be the launch of Festival Dewsbury, one of many initiatives our hard-working and undyingly enthusiastic commercial stalwarts have implemented to try to stimulate trade in the town and the involvement of local people who might otherwise drift towards the far bigger nearby commercial centres of Leeds, Wakefield, Huddersfield and Bradford.

My good friend Mark Ashley, then Managing Director of the Dewsbury Reporter and now a publisher across 'the hill' in Wigan, was at that time chairman of Enterprise Dewsbury, a local voluntary group that chose the day to launch its activities less than a mile away in the town's Crow Nest Park.

As the festival got underway, the crowds in attendance couldn't help but be distracted by the police helicopter over the town centre. Afterwards Mark Ashley decried the unfortunate distraction and its timing, while presciently remarking on the malign motives of both left and right wing extremism. The riots had well and truly peed on the festival's parade.

Councillor Jack Brooke was an Irish Catholic Labour stalwart and chairman of the Kirklees Equal Opportunities Committee at the time, an organisation soon to be superseded by the Kirklees Racial Equality Committee and a succession of far more zealously political chairmen.

Jack Brooke wasn't interested in Salman Rushdie's book or whoever had or hadn't been on the end of a good kicking – the rallies had been staged on the town's busiest shopping day, thus impacting negatively on already hard-pressed traders. Which fool had allowed that?

No one was seriously hurt during the riot, although Geoff McGill's days at the Scarborough were numbered, despite his persevering British Bulldog spirit. Geoff soon left and the pub limped along like a festering sore literally on the side of the Muslim enclave, until Tetley's eventually succumbed to the inevitable and sold it for a song to a wealthy local businessman who converted it into a dwelling.

In the fall-out over the riot, police eventually made over 70 arrests of both white and Muslim agitators, although in what was to be a sign of things to come, the response from one community became a signal beacon for what the future held.

A group backed by the largely white left-wing membership of the Kirklees Black Workers Group, styling itself 'The Dewsbury 59 Defence Campaign', organised a public rally at the town hall to protest at the arrest of the Muslim men on the day and subsequently at the quite novel use of CCTV pictures in an attempt to bring them to book. Of the men arrested, 59 were Muslim.

The meeting itself was roundly criticised by politicians and police alike and only one local councillor, a diehard Labour leftie Sue Powell, attended in her formal capacity.

What was clear was that the Muslim community, quietly assisted by white Marxist third parties, was becoming militant and lobbying for special treatment in trying to influence the exercising of both policing and, when the cases came to court, judgements.

The admirable Supt Neil Reece insisted that arrests

would continue to be made and that the police would not be intimidated by the calling of the public meeting. I suspect that may have been Supt Reece's career swansong.

Certainly no senior police officer with responsibility for the division since that day has displayed such chutzpah, and I've known pretty much every one of them. He didn't last long after that.

Dewsbury had actually had a Conservative MP between 1983 and 1987, triggered by the former Labour MP David Ginsberg jumping ship to the newly formed Social Democrats, splitting the vote and allowing local Tory solicitor John Whitfield to briefly turn the solidly red town, into a surprised Conservative blue.

Whitfield was the prospective candidate again for the Tories in 92, and attended the Black Workers Group meeting in an unofficial capacity, observing afterwards that the crowd was a mix of professional anti-racists plus impressionable local Muslim youths.

The overall message to emerge from it, he reported, was that the Muslims had been defending themselves against BNP aggression (though the far right party had no involvement in the day's actual dramas), that the police were an unofficial extension of the racist BNP and that the protestors now insisted that the Labour Party was duty bound to support the arrested men, who were all martyrs and heroes. No mention whatsoever was made of their casual violence or the attack on the Scarborough pub.

The meeting went nowhere in itself, certainly at that point in terms of influencing the police or local magistrates, but combined with public left-wing broadsides against anyone who failed to support it – the new Labour MP Ann Taylor and her subsequent successors particularly – its influences resonated in a manner that still prevails.

In what might have been one of her last stances of principled and neutral reason, at least that I can recall,

Ann Taylor stood by her decision not to support the meeting. In return she was accused of appeasing the racist voters of Dewsbury. That label would not stick for long as Taylor, swiftly detecting which way the wind was blowing, became the champion of all things Muslim.

The message from the activist left, visibly Muslim for public purposes but intellectually white left-wing, was loud and clear: if you do not agree with us, you are a racist. Broad brush strokes were applied to politician, policeman, journalist and public alike. They still are and it still works.

At the time that Supt Reece was pressing ahead with his arrests, Geoff McGill commented to the Dewsbury Reporter: "It doesn't matter what colour the rioters are. If people go about causing trouble and wrecking places they should be punished. They shouldn't think they are above the law. I'm 100 per cent behind the police on this matter."

He went on: "These people are using racism as a shield. They think they can get away with breaking the law and escape justice by claiming they are being victimised and threatening people with the Race Relations Act."

And in case anyone thinks landlord McGill might have been biased, it should be noted that his own son was one of the white youths arrested in the fighting, and duly charged and sentenced by the local bench. Geoff never defended his actions either.

3 – THE 'P' WORD

FROM THAT first violent example of a community finding its public voice and muscle, I want to flash forward 21 years almost exactly – I don't know what it is about June in Dewsbury – to another, far more sophisticated example of how the militant Muslim community is ready, willing and able to carry on its aggressive march of influence.

I'm also about to cause a few raised eyebrows. The BBC may have come to terms with the 'C' word and quite a few other adult expressions after the 9pm watershed, but 21st century Britain has a far bigger taboo. The 'P' word. Well gird your loins, because here it comes.

All I can promise in advance is that this is a phrase, an expression, which lays much of the groundwork for what is to come in the pages ahead and – I should stress – its etymology is entirely someone else's. Not mine. I refer to something I've spoken about many times in the pages of my newspaper – 'Paki Politics'.

I am full aware that the 'P' word, like its culturally unacceptable forerunner the 'N' word, is entirely in the domain of the people it purports to describe. Once it was little more than a simple abbreviation, now it is the lowest form of insult.

People of Pakistani origin can still use it however, casually, in ironic humour, or aggressively to thrust in the white mainstream face of whoever their grievance-of-the-day is with. But any attempt by someone like you or I at using or even explaining the 'P' word hits a barrier, a Berlin Wall of an obstacle within the English language.

My defence in using it here lies in the quotation marks. You see it honestly isn't my expression. It isn't any white or Christian man or woman's expression. It certainly isn't intended as an insult – it describes more of a philosophy if you must know. Let me explain.

On the afternoon of Sunday June 7th 2010, I drove from my home 40 miles away in York into my company's offices in Dewsbury. I publish a Rugby League newspaper, League Weekly, which comes out on a Monday morning so it's a pretty hectic day for the staff.

I occasionally work from home on a Sunday, but on this particular day I was aware that a public demonstration had been organised outside Dewsbury Police Station for 4pm.

The subject of the demonstration, and of a concerted campaign to have West Yorkshire Police instigate race-hate charges, was me and the newspaper, The Press, and specifically my weekly 'Ed Lines' column, which I've written on and off for nearly 18 years.

I had used the expression 'Paki Politics' in my column on the previous Friday and a lot of people had taken exception. Some of them were even Pakistani and Muslim. But by no means all, and certainly not the key individuals trying to prompt legal and public redress against me and the business.

The roots of that expression will become clear, but what took me by surprise was the inflamed level of antagonism towards it; you see I'd used the phrase 'Paki Politics' and explained it a number of times previously, to absolutely no comment at all.

Not only had I *not* used the term 'Paki' in a derogatory manner, I had explained its roots, at least in the context of its Dewsbury usage in conjunction with the 'politics' suffix.

But on this occasion, in association with offence taken against something else I'd written (by no means unusual) the people who pull the strings of the Savile Town rent-a-crowd were kicking off.

The internet and Facebook were ablaze with protests against the 'racist' Danny Lockwood and Dewsbury Press. Text messages zipped around the district encouraging the white left-wing and Muslim brotherhood to register their objections, to join the public protests.

I was actually due to depart out of Doncaster's Robin Hood Airport on the Sunday evening to Mallorca on literally a flying 48-hour visit, but took a detour to the office in Dewsbury to make sure everyone and everything was ok.

Our building is in a relatively quiet side street (okay, derelict if you insist) only 50 yards from the town centre's main thoroughfare, but even so police are not often in evidence, despite the divisional HQ being about 200 yards away. That proximity doesn't appear to count for much, whether it's protecting property or people.

A few years ago we were burgled but the wailing alarm was neither use nor ornament. When I arrived to switch it off in the early hours and clear up the smashed window I found a cigarette end on the office floor, so put a drinking glass over it as evidence. Believe it or not, DNA tests exposed the culprit who pleaded guilty to nicking one of our computers! He's currently paying us back at a rate which should yield a new Apple Mac in 30 years or so.

Still, it was something of a result, more than I can say about the Sunday morning when I watched four blokes steal the Yorkshire stone roof off the derelict building opposite ours.

The property was a nightmare. Addicts used to go shoot up in a roofless former outside toilet – at times we've had to call ambulances for them overdosing. A tramp slept rough on the stone toilet floor for a while, but the addicts made his life hell, gave him a hard time if he got in their way. He was sleeping on discarded needles and used condoms from young teenage girls earning themselves a fix. It's not a pretty picture. The police and authorities knew about it. They did nothing. And we're not talking about a time too long ago.

So you can understand that I was delighted when the roof thieves said they were demolishing the building, because I'd threatened the owners that I'd turn up for work one day with a sledgehammer and start myself if they didn't deal with it.

On that occasion I spoke to the gang and even photographed them in the act from our office windows – I had even known the bloke who drove the lorry which took the stone slates away for 35 years. He and I had brought the town centre to a standstill in our teens, physically slugging it out over long-forgotten youthful disputes, mostly centred around inter-school rivalries.

When it turned out it was brazen theft my first reaction was that it would at least hasten the demolition, but I did my public duty and gave the cops my photos, and testified. However it still took them 18 months to bring charges against just one of the thieves – not the bloke I knew – and the accused walked free from the court inside about 10 minutes, such was the shoddy case preparation. Meanwhile every villain in town knew that Lockwood was a grass.

Hey-ho. That's hardly news.

On the Sunday afternoon of the public protest against me however all was quiet at the office. I drove past the police station at 3.40pm but no protestors were yet in evidence. I couldn't wait until 4pm and the scheduled protest because I was late for Doncaster and the airport.

I didn't know how late. I got there in plenty of time for the 6pm flight. Unfortunately I was exceedingly late for the 6am flight, which it had been. I know, I know. How could you? Well, I'm a busy bloke. Lots on my mind, especially that Sunday.

I managed to get on a 7am Monday morning flight out of Leeds/Bradford airport and was cruising along the A64 York-Leeds road at about 5.20am when my mobile phone went. It was an 'Unknown' caller and I ignored it. It went every 10 minutes.

Once I'd parked up I listened to an answer phone message from the Duty Inspector at Kirklees Police saying they wished to speak to me urgently. I took the call expecting to be asked to report to the station to be questioned about the complaints of inciting racial hatred, plus the public protest of the previous afternoon.

'Are you on your way to work Mr Lockwood?' asked the Inspector. He was obviously a duty Plod as opposed to a detective, because who in an office job is on their way to work at 5.45am?

'No officer,' I replied. 'I'm on my way to Mallorca.'

It transpired the police did not want to caution me or otherwise; they had been made aware of text messages doing the rounds between characters they described as 'persons of interest' who were trying to track down my exact home address.

I had moved my family out of Dewsbury 18 months previously though not for reasons of personal security as a reporter from the Daily Telegraph once asked, inquiring if I was living in a police safe house. I nearly wet myself laughing at that.

We moved because we could afford to and we wanted to put distance between many of the issues that can be expected to beguile a newspaper editor, but which were not necessarily conducive to a quiet family life. But my large extended network of family and friends and my businesses were still in the town, as was I more often than not.

The Inspector explained that no overt threats had been

made, but as a matter of protocol they were contacting me to see if I was concerned – I wasn't – and to open a line of dialogue. They said they would inform North Yorkshire Police just to make them aware. I asked them not, under any circumstances, to tell my wife. That would cause me far more problems than any imaginary crowd scene from Zulu.

I later learned that some 200-300 protestors had assembled outside Dewsbury Police Station on the Sunday afternoon, having been herded up like so many obedient sheep in Savile Town and marched down to the rallying point, whereupon they milled around without much idea of what the hell was going on.

I'm sure that most of them could read and write, but I doubt that many had actually seen the words being complained about – they were just extras in the crowd scene of this pseudo-political production.

My business colleague and then-editor of The Press, Martin Shaw, went along to observe as did a photographer, recording the rather pointless rabble of a gathering which milled around muttering to one another before dispersing, probably wondering what the hell all that had been about.

TV cameras didn't turn up. No other media showed interest. A couple of bright-lemon uniformed PCSOs stood and watched it all pass without incident. There was barely a raised voice.

Few among the overwhelmingly young Asian crowd were anyone we recognised at The Press. However it was impossible to miss the trusted lieutenants, staff members and hangers-on of our former MP Shahid Malik, who had been ousted from the Parliamentary seat just five weeks before and who, in his agonised farewell speech, blamed the malevolent press. Which should have actually read Press with a capital 'P'. As in Lockwood and his troublesome crew.

The protest over my use of the expression 'Paki Politics'

was orchestrated by Malik's white sidekicks using a few young Muslim stooges for a front. As a payback aimed at me for his public decline and fall, the public protest really wasn't effective or damaging, but it was typical of the way the malleable Muslim community is ever available, at a moment's notice, to militarise, to shove an angry hand in the chest of authority and try to force it from its already defensive position, making it retreat one more small step.

On that particular Sunday afternoon it was a peaceful demonstration motivated by personal grudges towards me, but the crowd's heart wasn't in it much.

Previously these mass gatherings out front of Dewsbury Police Station have been for a variety of reasons – from something as trivial as a taxi driver arrested after protesting about a parking ticket he was issued, to a rather more robust protest over the arrest of several men for affray, howling their demands for their friends' release and creating violent mayhem in the process.

These events never create the slightest ripple among the wider media. Meanwhile the tiresome, predictable outcome remains the same. Senior police officers call on 'community leaders' to mediate with the angry young men, they pull on their ultra-sensitive kid gloves and everything is quietly swept under the carpet until next time.

Cue the police and politicians to take one more backward step in the face of waving arms and raised voices, cue ordinary white people's resentment at perceived favouritism and appeasement of one ethnic community to be ratcheted up another level.

Confronting authority is a tried and tested tactic rolled out by the Muslim community time and again, certainly in Dewsbury and Batley, although as a cultural observation it's worth looking outside our local and even national boundaries and realising that this is actually a very common form of social expression in the Arab world.

It's not something we're used to seeing in our 'ever-so-polite' English democracy – at least not on such a micro level – but it's a fact of life elsewhere.

We can rally 100,000 people and more to march through London and decry the Poll Tax, the hunting of foxes and the introduction of university tuition fees, but those are on a grand scale, mass-political demonstrations.

What we witness in Dewsbury is a far more tempestuous and reactionary willingness to flex the community muscle in the face of authority. No cause is too trivial. Why wait for empty promises made over a ballot box when we can mobilise and make the point today? It has its plus points results wise, I'll say that much.

The difference between the protests before a few hobby bobbies outside Dewsbury police station and a city square in the dictatorial Middle East is that soldiers with stony faces and guns will provide a rather different reception as we've witnessed in the bloody Arab Spring of 2011. One crowd is banging its fists against a steel wall, the other is pushing against an open door.

My view will necessarily conflict with that of senior local police officers and politicians – what I consider their collective policy of any price worth paying for a quiet life – but in terms of community relations in Dewsbury and Batley their appeasement and constant retreat ultimately adds to the problem.

Why wouldn't an ethnic community keep repeating the strategy if it gets a positive result nine times out of 10? Even if the outcome isn't immediate, the wearing effect on officialdom has its own erosive benefits – albeit at the cost of a corrosive deterioration of relationships with the wider public.

It is thankfully a tactic that has lost some of its weight since Kirklees police pulled their command team out of Dewsbury and tucked them behind distant desks in the

Huddersfield HQ nine miles away. The Dewsbury station is a major divisional HQ, or it was until the West Yorkshire force merged it with Huddersfield to create the county's largest force, based in the seat of the 'Kirklees' local authority.

Where we recently had our own Chief Superintendent, Detective Supt of CID and three Chief Inspectors, now we have just one Community Inspector for each town.

That was one big backward step, in more ways than one, although I suspect that from policing perspectives it was as much for show as for dough. The senior force management flies under the public radar far more easily now.

The Sunday afternoon protest over my newspaper column passed swiftly and quietly and, suffice to say, Shahid Malik didn't actually show up himself.

That was a shame, given that 'Paki Politics' was Malik's own catchphrase. He first used it in my company when he was trying to win my editorial friendship and favours in his bid to become the town's MP back in 2004.

'PAKI POLITICS'. It doesn't become any more comfortable with the repeating of it. There happens to be a very popular website, paki.com, which is a social networking site with over 650,000 members. The word itself, like the unspoken 'n' word of Afro-American heritage, is now the private literal domain of the people whose ethnicity it describes.

Despite being condemned forever and a day to being a 'Pommie bastard' to every Aussie and sundry, or a 'Limey' to Americans, I haven't a problem with that ownership of the 'P' word. Language changes. It's long been unacceptable to refer to people with physical or mental disabilities as spastics or retards and that's all for the good.

I loathe Political Correctness from a very deep place in me, but common courtesies, civilities and basic manners are quite something else. 'Queer' used to be a common descriptive term of homosexual; it has become an insulting, disparaging word in modern parlance. But if words pass from casually accepted usage into spiteful and derogatory weapons, then reasonably intelligent and articulate people ought to be respectful of that.

Remember when Prince Harry was 'outed' as having referred to a fellow army officer as 'Paki'? However innocently it was meant, however socially acceptable within their private relationships, you could sense that even television newsreaders weren't happy having to repeat it.

The BBC's Huw Edwards already has a top lip that appears to be on a string when he makes certain facial expressions. On the occasion of having to say the 'P' word it nearly took his left eye out. Huw and crew all seemed to wear that lemon-grimaced look of sour distaste as the two syllables tainted their educated lips.

But they were just doing their job. The word had to be uttered to maintain the context, the integrity of the story. However if anyone working for the BBC was caught using that expression anywhere but in the privacy of their own home – and possibly even there, as the Big Brother society intrudes ever closer – their balls would be hanging off the front of a Cultural Diversity Oberleutnant's desk as fast as the fact could be tweeted.

My only chance of escaping the wrath of the 21st century Language Nazis on that occasion of protest lay in the quotation marks around those supposedly deeply offensive words – 'Paki Politics'. It was and is an expression that speaks of a syndrome that I had been aware of long before the first British-born Muslim MP and eventual Minister for Justice Shahid Malik MP walked into my office.

The occasion was Malik whirlwinding his way over the Pennines from Burnley in 2004, as he fancifully put it in his best Lancashire brogue, seeking and successfully winning the Labour nomination to stand for MP for Dewsbury.

Actually, far from being a good 'ol Burnley lad, Malik had long been a metropolitan Londoner as he pushed his career ambitions this way and that, carrying his firebrand reputation before him.

If trouble didn't quite follow young Mr Malik around, it had a worrying habit of turning up before very long, whether it be the street riots that plagued his hometown and the policeman's cosh that laid him out on one occasion, or the political wars of words that seemed to blight his every attempt to win elected office around the country. All of those were before he turned up on our doorstep.

Dewsbury, as a hotbed of the British National Party, needed Malik like it needed Salman Rushdie to publish a follow-up to Satanic Verses and stage a book signing on our town hall steps. But not for any small reason was our local Labour party renowned for having a collective IQ slightly below room temperature.

With the odd intellectual exception, the Dewsbury Labour Party was a Working Men's Club committee – without the ability to run the proverbial piss-up in a brewery, let alone display expertise at darts and dominoes.

They gave Malik the nod (though it is notable, in the subsequent political debate over the Alternative Vote system, that he was by no means the unanimous choice and only succeeded by the vagaries of AV).

Still, comrades all, they fell in behind their new totem, hoping they would get a better and more committed local representative than their previous MP Ann Taylor, who worked incredibly hard and won the just rewards of those endeavours – for herself though, not the town.

If Burnley-born Malik's reputation ran before him, his first venture into Dewsbury brought him colliding face-first into my own. He stepped off the train, put his tee-total foot inside the West Riding pub (which he henceforth always described as his 'local') and immediately his left-wing firebrand foot soldiers warned him off about Lockwood and The Press newspaper. Indeed that was absolutely the first thing he revealed to me at our meeting.

"They told me I shouldn't deal with you Danny," was his opening gambit without specifying who 'they' were. Not that I needed to ask. "But I believe in giving everyone a chance. I'm a what-you-see-is-what-you-get type of guy" (or words to that effect. I still have the transcribed note somewhere).

It was an encouraging opening gambit even if not completely convincing. I already knew, and was disheartened by, the company Malik was keeping. His main aide-de-camp Terry McKay was a far-left troublemaker who had communicated dire warnings that The Press could suffer the same fate as the Oldham Chronicle – firebombed in the 2001 riots – if we continued carrying news that he and his colleagues disapproved of.

Another of Malik's cosy new coterie, Tahir 'Terry' Zaman was an interesting character, one minute driving a taxi to make a living and flirting with the law, the next minute cruising round in a Ferrari and bragging that he had £15 million to invest in property development in Dewsbury.

In and out of trouble with authority generally, before you knew it Terry was being declared bankrupt ... and then he was bouncing back with his property deals again, before being fined for being a slum landlord and managing to land his tenant (Malik) deep in the dirt over confused accounts about the MP's rent expenses.

My previous run-ins with both these characters informed me that any friendly overtures from the new Labour Parliamentary candidate in 2004 might be short-lived.

Both McKay and Zaman had vastly different interests in aligning themselves to Shahid Malik's cause; neither involved being cosy with an inquisitive newspaper which didn't subscribe to their questionable agendas.

Zaman had known not to bother with us following one occasion, when after reporting upon his latest brush with the law, Martin Shaw came back from interviewing him and said he'd offered us a new bed each.

All other things apart, this area is now known as 'Sleepy Valley' for its proliferation of bed-manufacturing companies, one of which Terry Zaman had ended up being Managing Director of for a spell. God knows how. It didn't last. We politely declined his 'offer' and reported the story. He didn't like that, but then again he never did, and Terry had an unhelpful (for him) habit of creating news and controversy wherever he went.

But back to mine and Malik's first meeting.

"I like to make my own mind up about people – I thought I'd give you a chance," he graciously effused.

This was a sparring session, the first round of what looked like being a long boxing match. Neither of us had any idea how bloody it would turn out.

I don't mind admitting that Shahid Malik can be quite the charmer in a down-to-earth, homespun way. He is always at great pains to convince people how plain-spoken, trusting, and implicitly honest he is. And he absolutely believes it too. I know that much from experience, even in the contradictory face of his own prior words and actions.

However and as I had also long come to recognise, what Malik displayed on the witness stand is a cultural trait (and that's probably a racist remark in itself).

I can only speak from my own experience and it isn't easy to say – but within the Pakistani community so often the 'truth' of yesterday doesn't necessarily mean it's the 'truth' today. It's as if the turning of the clock has immutably changed everything.

"This is what I'm saying now and that's all that counts. How dare you question it? That's racist! It's just because of my colour/religion, isn't it? Racist!"

Of course it is. Prefer to just be called a liar do you? In my days as a reporter, covering cases in the Magistrates court, I used to sit in wonder as men pleaded not guilty to crimes that they had no possible defence for, other than that they were not British, thus, presumably, incapable of breaking British law.

Quite often they would feign ignorance of the language, when it was clear they had at the very least passable grasps of it. You only had to watch them following the court conversations to know that. Some had backgrounds and jobs which clearly illustrated they had a working knowledge of English, but I never saw them challenged over it.

I once asked an English-born Pakistani friend what the idea was behind this. I can't offer any validity other than his account, but he said, basically, that if they pleaded innocent within their understanding of the offence, they could return to their communities with head held high; they had been effectively 'stitched up' by the English legal system.

I don't know how true that generalisation was or is, but it's as good an explanation as anything I could ever come up with for some of the things I've seen and heard.

It was thus in our first discussion, as Malik sought to reassure me of his one-town, one-society credentials as a political moderniser, that he offered up the following sentiment, and one of the central themes in this attempt to chronicle our town's sad decline in Britain's brave new multicultural world:

"I don't do Paki politics," he said. I knew what he meant.

I'd been a journalist for more than 25 years at that time, and an editor in Dewsbury for 11 years and understood that 'Paki Politics' referred to something far more than corrupting or manipulating the electoral process.

It was and remains an attitude, a bi-focal value system pertaining to every facet of public life. I welcomed Malik's refreshing commitment.

'Paki Politics' wasn't just about people of a certain ethnic community playing fast and loose with British democracy; of Muslim councillors and MPs' actions being dictated by the mosque; of widescale fraudulent voting, intimidation at the polling booth, physical attacks on elected members even; 'Paki Politics' in my understanding was about an entire culture and I'm not sure that Shahid Malik even understood that himself.

I accepted his commitment at face value. He was coming to Dewsbury to play a straight bat, to be a unifying, modernising Muslim politician. "Time will be the judge of that," I replied, or words to that effect.

His problem was a simple one and it would end up haunting him time and again. Basically his attraction to the local Labour party was his influence over the growing Muslim vote. Obvious. But that was a path fraught with inherent dangers.

The electoral support of the Muslim community was malleable, not based on any political ideology, and winning that support had a cost which quite often flew at direct odds with some of the positions any politician of reasonable virtue might have to take on occasion. Simply, Malik – any Muslim politician – had to sell himself to that community of voters quite differently from the political values he espoused to the wider, traditional voting public.

Some years later when community-based post offices were being closed down with gay abandon, Savile Town's was one of those earmarked for closure. Given the massive dependency on benefits within the district and the 'cash' ethos of their community it was a ridiculous intent anyway.

Malik was ever the campaigning MP and he crowed his celebration loudly when he 'saved' Savile Town post office by virtue of an exhaustive report into the reasons it had to survive. However that blew up in his face when the Post

Office declared that instead it would shut the Thornhill Edge office, in a completely white part of the constituency.

You can imagine the public indignation.

In fairness Malik argued on Thornhill Edge's behalf too, but a major source of embarrassment stemmed from his refusal to divulge exactly how he had 'saved' Savile Town. It emerged that he'd played the race card about as blatantly as possible with all kinds of outlandish claims about the negative impact and indeed social dangers of shutting it.

Even when Freedom of Information requests were submitted to have his report made public, the powers-that-be threw themselves four-square behind Malik and assisted in disguising his discomfort.

Ultimately Thornhill Edge post office was saved too, but the case served to highlight the inherent dangers of trying to serve two disparate communities in distinctly different ways – however altruistic the politician's intent.

But neither was his case helped by his own propensity for putting his foot in his mouth, and showboating for Britain's Muslims. In October 2008 he appeared at something termed a Global Peace and Unity Conference, which was actually an Islamic event.

His audience was a world away from the doorsteps of the Dewsbury hustings, but it is difficult to imagine any reasonably streetwise individual – and especially a junior minister – not foreseeing the outcome of a performance like the one he gave.

This is an excerpt of his speech as seen around the world thanks to the wonders of the internet sharing site Youtube.

"ALTHOUGH I am now Minister for Justice working alongside the Lord Chancellor Jack Straw, who sends his good wishes, I was until three weeks ago Minister for International Development *(NB: the role was newly created, the most junior in the department, and unpaid).*

"It has also been a privilege working with Islamic Relief, Muslim Aid, Muslim Hands and many others ... come on, a round of applause for the Muslim NGOs *(Non-Governmental Organisations – a smattering of applause can be heard from the cavernous conference centre).*

"My work as International Development Minister has resulted, over the next three years, with the UK assisting Bangladesh to the tune of 370 million pounds, Pakistan Insh'allah 480 million pounds, Palestine Insh'allah 243 million pounds, Yemen in excess of 100 million pounds, not to mention Sudan and Somalia.

"I'm proud of the achievements of the Muslims of this country from 97. In 1997 we got our first Muslim MP. In 2001 we had two Muslim MPs. In 2005 we had four Muslim MPs, Insh'allah in 2009/10 we shall have eight Muslim MPs, in 2014 we shall have 16 Muslim MPs. At this rate the whole Parliament will be Muslim!

"But just to say – in case there are journalists here today – that is not my objective.

"But you know we've got four Muslim MPs, there should be 20 Muslim MPs in Parliament and Insh'allah very shortly we'll see that.

"And I'm confident as Britain's first Muslim minister that Insh'allah in the next 30 years or so we'll see a Prime Minister of this country who happens to share my faith."

IGNORE the fact that as the (unpaid) most junior of all members of the International Development department, Malik was trying to take personal and specific credit for securing over a billion pounds of aid for Muslim countries, clearly a gross exaggeration and overstatement of his actual standing.

Whatever he was trying to achieve with his Muslim audience, there was only ever going to be one predictable reaction from the disenfranchised white voters of Dewsbury. It beggars belief that he couldn't see it coming.

In the wake of the video going viral on the internet – because the BNP and their associates were always going to have a field day with comments like that – his spokesman lamely tried to explain that Mr Malik had been "joking".

What was funny? Not the very real statistics about the hundreds of millions of pounds worth of funding for what a great many people considered terrorist states, at a time in late 2008 when the global economy was falling apart. Northern Rock and Lehman Brothers, anyone?

Were the hopes and aspirations of a Westminster packed exclusively with Muslim MPs expected to have 'em rolling in the aisles? That, mind you, in a speech liberally decorated with invocations of Insh'allah! I wasn't aware Allah had much of a sense of humour about achieving a global caliphate, or that good Muslims used his holy name to spice up their jokes.

Or was Malik merely being funny with the aside about journalists being present?

Whatever, it was a story which didn't earn him many laughs but perfectly illustrated the problem he kept banging his head against – the temptation, nay necessity, of currying favour with one community by both words and actions that flew at odds with his public proclamations to another set of voters.

That day when we met in 2004, I took Shahid Malik's renunciation of 'Paki Politics' as specifically meaning he would not indulge in such divisive politics. We would have numerous heated conversations about my unwillingness as an editor and publisher to ignore what he saw as simple expedience and I considered duplicity. His default position remained that what went on in 'his' community was none of mine or my readers' business

But that, in microcosm, summed up so much of what was

wrong in the town. Whether Shahid Malik underestimated the high price of winning votes in a town like Dewsbury, or a local newspaper's insistence of holding him to account, the bottom line was the continued decline of community relations. Maybe he just didn't understand what he meant himself by his description of 'Paki Politics'.

4 – FROM PROUD TOWN TO POUNDTOWN

TO UNDERSTAND the various woes a town of nearly 60,000 people can find itself mired in, it's important to relate it to the handsome profile it once enjoyed. It would be an exaggeration to portray the place today like Tombstone or Deadwood, a western-style landscape of banging saloon doors with no one to hear them and drifting tumbleweed – although one area of town earned the nickname 'the Bronx' for a while because of its lawless nature.

That changed, ironically, when the dissolute young white drug addicts and criminals found themselves displaced by the expanding immigrant population. Not that it solved the problem – it just moved it on.

Dewsbury in 2011 is defined largely by its poverty, high indices of poor health, its declining employment opportunities, crumbling physical infrastructure and its crime and politics – all of which I believe share a common if uncomfortable denominator, at least to the social engineers playing games with people's lives. It wasn't always so.

When Paulinus brought Christianity to Dewsbury in 627AD it was the dominant ecclesiastical centre across a large swathe of the old West Riding of Yorkshire. Indeed the town retained this status throughout the Middle Ages collecting tithes from as far away as Halifax into the mid-14th century. Later John Wesley would visit the district on numerous occasions in the mid-18th century.

The Reverend Patrick Brontë, the father of Anne, Charlotte and Emily Brontë, was rector of the parish church – the Minster – from 1809 to 1811. In Charlotte Brontë's novel Shirley, Dewsbury features as 'Whinbury'.

The town's market had been established as long ago as the 14th century for local clothiers although outbreaks of the plague in 1593 and 1603 saw it closed down until it was reopened in 1741, around the time the district's economic fortunes were being transformed.

In 1770, a branch of the Calder and Hebble Navigation Canal was completed, linking Dewsbury to the main canal system, notably the Leeds-Liverpool, providing access to burgeoning trading centres in Manchester and Hull.

For many years the district had distinguished itself in the manufacture of fine woollen goods – a cottage industry these days but one which lives on through a handful of family firms. But by the time of the Industrial Revolution Dewsbury was the global centre for the 'shoddy' and 'mungo' industries – the recycling of old woollen items by mixing them with new wool and making them into heavy blankets and uniforms. The world's armies famously marched in and slept under Dewsbury and Batley cloth.

With a plentiful, fast flowing water supply from the Calder descending out of the Pennines, the proximity of numerous coal mines within the County Borough boundaries and the arrival of the railways in 1848 (the town would eventually have four stations making it a significant industrial hub, now reduced to just one) its vitality and wealth was notable.

The 19th century saw a huge increase in population, rising from less than 5,000 souls in 1801 to around 30,000 by 1890, a rise fuelled not insubstantially by the masses of Irish migrants flooding to England to man the wheels of the new industrial era. Not that the town's rapid expansion and industrialisation was entirely without its problems.

In the early 19th century Dewsbury was a centre of Luddite fundamentalism with numerous local examples of violent protest and destruction of new machinery. In the 1830s Chartist agitation gained a foothold and in August 1838, after a speech by Chartist leader Feargus O'Connor, a mob of between five and seven thousand people besieged the Dewsbury Poor Law Guardians in the town's Royal Hotel before being dispersed by troops.

When violence again erupted in 1840 and radical protestors occupied the town, troops were once more called in and this time stationed here to maintain public order. Dewsbury's proud tradition as a haven for 'the awkward squad' isn't an entirely new phenomenon clearly. Indeed it was reflected in the election of the town's first MP – Sergeant 'John' Simon, a Jewish lawyer from Jamaica and a Liberal. Over the years, we've had all sorts, and not half.

The town had been incorporated as a municipal borough in 1862 and the 1867 Reform Act constituted Dewsbury as a parliamentary borough. Its wealth is evidenced by the still plentiful examples of magnificent Yorkshire stone buildings that ring the town, some of which have been transformed from the derelict mills they had become by the 1970s and 80s, into handsome apartment buildings, and which stand impressively for the casual observer, passing through the town on the regular Leeds-Manchester trains.

The jewel in the crown is the fine Victorian town hall built in 1886-89, but despite its recent refurbishment it is rarely used for more than occasional committee meetings in the Mayor's Parlour, the twice yearly Collegians' am-dram productions and the odd private function. It's a shame.

TV production companies sometimes use the fabulous old courtroom for filming – the one in which Yorkshire Ripper Peter Sutcliffe famously appeared.

Not all our wonderful edifices have survived intact however. Some like the imposing Pioneer building, home of the town's Co-operative Society, is an enduring blight on the town, boarded and scaffolded up, the subject of a tug-of-war between the Council and a private London developer who brought big ideas to town but sloped off leaving eyesores and more than a few broken promises.

The woollen reclamation industry – the rag trade – still thrived in the 1950s and 1960s when the first wave of south Asian migrants arrived to provide much needed manpower. Some 2,000 had settled here by the mid-60s, ironically about the time that the advent and mass production of man-made fibres hastened the decline of the textile trade.

Most of the women of my family, my mum and grandma, aunties and older cousins, worked as rag sorters and rippers for long, back-breaking hours, for many years in the mills. It's an industry whose time has now largely passed.

Likewise the coal mines that once ringed the town – Thornhill Lees and Combs collieries, Shaw Cross, Gomersal, Flockton and Denby Grange – have long since ceased production. The seams are probably still viable, the politics and economics not.

In 1974 responsibility for local government passed to Kirklees Metropolitan Council, with its headquarters in Huddersfield and it wouldn't be too cynical to mark that date as significant in charting the decline of the town's general fortunes.

Dewsbury's retail centre was redeveloped along the lines of the 'precincting' that was sweeping the country and with it went many of the characterful old family-owned businesses that had served local people so well for so many years. The high street names that either replaced them or existed alongside them haven't proven so redoubtable.

Marks and Spencer bailed out, what remaining quality independent shops we had inexorably followed, while many more half-hearted attempts have been and gone. Dewsbury used to have two of its own family-run department stores, cultural jewels in the retail landscape, but J&Bs and Bickers too are both fading memories.

Such as we get good news, WH Smith were desperately talked out of hightailing it this summer.

Shop occupancy is among the very worst in the country and it isn't just the boarded shop fronts, it's the nature of the trade that remains. You can cash cheques and weigh in your grandmother's gold on virtually every street corner.

Charity shops abound, as do Asian legal practices touting for immigration business; we have discount and 'pound' shops by the score. If it's cheap you want, cheap Dewsbury has, in abundance.

Town centre regeneration is probably the issue that exercises local people and politicians above all others but short of a magic wand – or the multi-millions Kirklees can always find for Huddersfield projects – it's an uphill battle.

And actually, when you stop and consider the town centre customer base, it really should not be a surprise. The retail and business profile will inexorably change to reflect its users' needs and this is simply not a Marks and Sparks town any longer. We just can't get used to that reality.

I can recall the 1970s and 80s when probably 20 town centre pubs, several working men's clubs, eight nightclubs and half a dozen restaurants thrived within a ring road whose diameter is probably less than 400 yards. Today one 'underground' nightclub remains and just four or five hardly salubrious pubs – the number fluctuates as one closes and another briefly opens.

It isn't as though the town has gone tee-total, but those young partygoers who don't look to the far brighter lights of Leeds and Wakefield have migrated a mile or so out of town onto the arterial corridor of Bradford Road that links Dewsbury and Batley, a 'golden half-mile' of trendier bars and clubs, Mick Ingram's Legends, the Frontier – the former Batley Variety Club – and others.

Apart from anything else, in that quite defined neighbourhood of pubs, bars and clubs, they are safer from loitering gangs of young Asian men, or others who cruise the district in their cars occasionally pouncing randomly on anyone unlucky enough to be in the wrong place at the wrong time, or to have wandered into a neighbourhood where they aren't welcome.

My teenage nephew fell into the former of those categories – he was on a main road, not too late in the evening, when a car pulled up alongside him and four Asian youths/men piled out, kicked him senseless, stole his mobile phone and just one of his new training shoes.

When the police visited my sister to take a statement they removed some of Tom's clothes for DNA samples – at least they made a bit of an effort, I suppose. But the family never heard anything more. They didn't even get his clothes back. Arrests? There so rarely are. And on that occasion there wasn't.

A few weeks ago an ex-rugby pal of mine was walking home from the pub when again about four of them jumped him from behind. They didn't take anything, just gave him a good hiding. He ended up in hospital. When I asked the police why they hadn't made news of the attack public, they explained that they didn't think an 'appeal for information' would yield any worthwhile results.

A light briefly dawned in the Chief Superintendent's eyes when I said that was the basic difference between us – the police are in the business of creating an illusion of public safety, journalists in the business of telling people what is going on in their midst. The two are not compatible.

I think he 'got' it, but it won't change anything.

We have a ubiquitous McDonalds in town, but even it bears a sullied reputation. Heroin addicts used to go into its toilets and shoot up – until two of them were found dead, overdosed, in a toilet cubicle.

I don't recall that making the 'news' either.

The kebab and chicken takeaways apart, the sum of the town centre's restaurant trade is two Chinese and a solitary Indian, tucked away outside the town centre. Don't bother dressing up in your Sunday best.

Dewsbury used to have three or four cinemas and even a variety music hall. They are long gone.

As I write the future of Dewsbury Little Theatre, based just a half mile or so outside town, looks in jeopardy. It's in a woeful state of repair and its owners, Kirklees Council, say there's no money to preserve it. There never is, unless it's for something in Huddersfield. Bitter? You bet.

There's not even a bingo hall in the town centre any more, unless you count the concrete Mecca beyond the ring road in what passes for our out-of-town retail district. There's a Halfords and a JJB Sports, a Matalan and a Sainsburys there at least, and a few hundred yards away a B&Q, Wickes and Curry's.

And that's it, there really is nothing else to do or see at night inside the town centre, unless your requirements run to one of the two brothels that have been quietly 'servicing' the local community for many years – one of them since 1974, as it proudly used to boast on its website.

It's ironic that the arrival of the *Sunshine Supertan* massage parlour (now known as *Stilletoes,* based opposite the train station) coincided with the formation of Kirklees and the civic heart being ripped out of the town.

Dewsbury, screwed, every which way.

A few years ago a building just up Leeds Road, as it climbs out of town, was discreetly converted into a gay sauna. Cosmopolitan, or what?

It's progress of sorts, I suppose – at least if you're wearing the pink-tinted glasses of the equality brigades.

5 – MIGRATION & IMMIGRATION

THE PICTURESQUE setting of their Thornhill Hall estate, nestled in the hills two miles south of Dewsbury town centre, would have been the last thing on the minds of the resident Savile family, that fateful week in 1648 when Cromwell and Fairfax's soldiers came visiting.

The Saviles, one of the West Riding of Yorkshire's most powerful – and loyal – royalist families, would more probably have been pondering the wisdom of building their ancestral home at the top of one hill leading out of Dewsbury, but at the foot of a yet steeper hill, atop which sat Fairfax and Cromwell's Parliamentarian cannon.

Their handsome moated hall, despite its three-feet thick walls, was under siege, and their lovely landscaped parkland was heaving with very hostile soldiers. As places to defend in battle go, it was as poorly chosen as was their devotion to the flickering cause of the royal Stuarts.

Political change was coming, and for good. Or at least so it appeared to the people of Dewsbury in the 1640s. The history books tell us little about the physical detail of the Battle of Thornhill Hall – it was a minor skirmish in the greater scheme of things – save that the Roundheads' siege was ended when the Savile yeomanry emerged from the moated haven alongside what is today a pitch and putt golf course, and got their royalist backsides well and truly kicked.

The house itself went up in a bang that would have been comfortably heard down on the river plain adjacent to Dewsbury town centre subsequently to be known as 'Savile Town' so-called after the many and various Lords of that name. The cause of the explosion which laid low Thornhill Hall was reportedly an exploding gunpowder magazine. Its ruins still stand there today.

Thus, ironically, were the roots of the world's first great Parliamentary democracy further sown in a place where 350 years later a man or woman's vote would be reduced to a religious token, a chitty to be demanded and traded based on caste, colour and the call of the mosque.

It's doubtful whether any of the honourable Saviles lying in a family crypt across the field from the old hall at the beautiful Thornhill Parish Church, would be spinning in righteous indignation given their anti-Parliamentary stance.

The Third Baron Savile of Rufford died in 2008 at the grand old age of 89. As one of the last of the PG Wodehouse landed-gentry type characters to inhabit the 21st century House of Lords, George Lumley-Savile was reputedly a charming eccentric and every inch a gentleman, hunter and despite being a lifelong bachelor was reputed to have an eye for the ladies.

He was described in one obituary as "the enthusiastic friend of Barbara Cartland's daughter Raine, later Countess Spencer and stepmother of Princess Diana".

His heir to the title was a nephew, John Anthony Thornhill Lumley-Savile, who, living in Cornwall, is even less likely to visit the Dewsbury estates, let alone the eponymous Savile Town.

The public credentials of the 4th baron are yet to be witnessed but as benefactors to this part of Yorkshire since the 1370s – and George was fervent in his commitment to his Yorkshire roots – it must surely have rankled that modern perversions of democracy in and around the family seat are so brazenly carried out under the flag of another nation, Pakistan.

The Savile estates hereabouts have diminished in physical presence over the centuries, but in Savile Town – a tightly enclosed district of mills and terraced houses in the loop of the River Calder directly to the south of the town centre – the family name has been sadly traduced. Savile Town has become a bastion of Islamic fundamentalism, home in the first decade of the 21st century to sharia courts and fledgling terrorists.

It's become a place where policemen tread very lightly – and rarely – where elected white councillors can be attacked by Muslim rivals in broad daylight, and where the kingpins of the drugs trade thrive largely without fear of sanction.

Dewsbury was a wealthy town in the 19th and early 20th centuries – at least it was if you were an owner of one of the scores of mills lining the banks of the river Calder. Even today the town boasts some fabulous Victorian buildings, a handful of working mills still producing quality woollen goods and some handsome converted mills.

The Saviles aren't particularly well known by the wider public amongst the modern British aristocracy. Indeed any list of Dewsbury's famous sons and daughters could be comfortably scribbled on the back of a fag packet, regardless of the large-type warning of imminent death by cancer emblazoned on your 20 Silk Cut or Benson & Hedges.

One of our 'celebrities' was Wallace Hartley – who? – the bandmaster who stoically played on as the Titanic went to its watery grave. I understand Stan Laurel might have passed through the town on his way to meeting Oliver Hardy, while of more recent Hollywood 'stardom' Captain Jean-Luc Picard of Star Trek's USS Enterprise – Patrick

Stewart – is held forth as a local, though in truth he came from a few miles up the valley. He worked on the Mirfield Reporter newspaper, although he would have been based in the Dewsbury office. That serves to qualify him as one of 'ours' in the celebrity fame game.

Baroness Betty Boothroyd, the first female Speaker of the House of Commons, is a bona fide Dewsbury lass. 'Our Betty' grew up and went to school in the Eastborough district on another edge of the town centre and itself now a predominantly Asian enclave, and she occasionally returns to open a new building named after her. But rarely.

Similarly Baroness Betty Lockwood – no relation – a scion of the female Labour movement, despite taking the suffix 'of Dewsbury' in acknowledgement of her roots at least, probably hasn't darkened our doorsteps for decades; she's certainly not wandered the market looking for a bargain or popped in for one of the excellent lunches at Bailey's Cafe in my 18 years as an editor here.

If she's interested, tell her Cross's pork butchers on the market still does the best pies, black pudding, mucky fat and belly pork on the planet. Bar none.

Dewsbury is also a Rugby League town, that greatest of northern working class sports, and the first 'star' of the sport in British broadcasting was Eddie Waring, perhaps better known wider afield for his execrable It's A Knockout double-act with Stuart Hall, and his cameo appearance as a dancing sailor in the classic Morecambe and Wise Christmas Show skit of 'Nothing Like a Dame'.

Eddie was a journalist who managed the town's professional rugby league team but once he found fame and fortune with the BBC he left Dewsbury behind, returning only rarely. Like Betty Boothroyd, and another well known former Labour politician Sir Marcus Fox MP, Eddie hailed from the working class Eastborough area. His legacy continues however.

Today rugby league broadcasting is the domain of Sky Sports and their top pundit Mike 'Stevo' Stephenson will go down in history as one of the town's all time greats – though with respect not necessarily for his skills behind the microphone.

'Mike Stevo' was known as 'Mick Stivvy' to locals in 1973 when he captained Dewsbury to the Premiership crown and still spoke with a thick Yorkshire accent, as opposed to the pseudo-Aussie twang of today. He was probably the best 'hooker' in the game, anywhere in the world, at the time.

Indeed, Penrith Panthers paid a world record £20,000 for our hero when they whisked him off to Oz following that triumph. Back then Stivvy had been a jobbing plumber at Beaumont and Blackburn's, whose works were next door to our offices at the Dewsbury Reporter – as close as Mick came to journalism back in his formative days.

Savile Town was the ancestral home of the Stephenson family although by the time Stivvy had become Stevo, his mum and dad had moved to the new council estates atop the Thornhill escarpment to the south.

From there they literally overlooked their former home, where young Stephenson grew up amongst soot-blackened terraced houses with outside toilets, scraping his knees on the cobbled streets and local playing fields.

Whichever way you look at it, none of Dewsbury's famous sons and daughters have felt patriotically inclined enough to hang around for long once the sun of celebrity shone upon them. At least in his defining moment Wallace Hartley courageously conducted his band onward and downward – as opposed to upward – as the Titanic sank. Some of us know the feeling.

Stevo's Savile Town even of the 1960s bore many resemblances to its modern manifestation. There was a tangible sense of community. Children could play safely in the streets, wander from friend's to neighbour's to auntie or uncle's house; everyone knew each other's name, and people stopped in the street to exchange pleasantries and the day's gossip. It was, in all the ways we can describe one, a community of largely like-minded people.

It still is, but the colour, language and conversation is literally a world apart today. I still go into Savile Town occasionally to shop at the excellent Mullaco's grocery store, with its teeming stores spilling out into the pavements and the most wonderful range of fresh fruits, herbs, vegetables and spices and – my favourite – huge, imported frozen Tiger prawns. In daylight hours at least, it is the epitome of the friendly, family-based community.

It is centred upon a support network of tight-knit family and friends and – more importantly these days – shared values which might not be 'ours' from a white British perspective, but which are the cement that binds places like Savile Town together.

I honestly envy the people of that community, especially when looking at our broken homes and sink estates of single teenage mums and an entire generation of NEETs – Not in Education, Employment or Training.

The multi-cultural social engineers of local and national government remain intent on fragmenting places like Savile Town for some reason against all its residents' wishes. They occasionally stigmatise it with the 'ghetto' adjective, but it is difficult to see that desire or description being shared from within. If only the social housing estates of 'white' Dewsbury could enjoy such a sense of community.

Savile Town was perfectly positioned in the loop of the Calder for the mass of terraced housing that sprung up to house the mill workforce which remained largely white working class until the rapid influx of migrant workers from the sub-continent in the 1950s and 60s. Unfortunately for political integrationists, it also created quite a geographically self-contained settlement.

As aspirational white working class families moved away from their old terraces to the new council housing estates springing up around the district, they were replaced almost exclusively by migrant families. Savile Town is now to all intents and purposes an almost exclusively south Asian community.

It is also, from anyone's experience I've encountered, a community quite happy with the status quo. Multi-culturalism and integration are, after all, buzzwords of the white liberal middle classes, not of the people they are patronisingly intended for.

Savile Town figures poorly on all statistical analyses of social deprivation. Educational attainment is lower than average but far better than in most of the town's white council estates.

Health issues are considerable too and many of those are not addressed properly because of the cultural background of inter-marriage that lies at the root of them.

It's an ironic statistic that in a settlement where most of the households are on benefits – over 52% of all Asian 16 to 65-year-olds were classed as 'economically inactive' in Kirklees Council's most recent analysis – Savile Town also has the highest rate of home ownership in the district and quite probably more millionaires than the rest of the district combined.

Tens of millions of pounds of public money were thrown at Savile Town and other Asian neighbourhoods across the town in the 1990s when the Conservative government's City Challenge and SRB (Single Regeneration Budget) funds were being targeted specifically at ethnic minority communities.

New central heating systems, double glazing, roofs, plumbing – all targeted at areas indubitably in most need, but also by nature predominantly 'immigrant', whether 1st or 2nd generation.

As you can imagine, that caused more than its share of resentment in poor white working class neighbourhoods excluded from the bounties. The crass lack of foresight in pursuing these policies has much to answer for.

The people of Savile Town, with their own GP surgeries, dentists, community centres, schools, mosques and madressas (Markazi is by far the biggest but there are numerous other mosques within half a mile) appear content with their lot.

It has taken time, it has taken both cash persuasion – Asian men turning up at white folks' doors with bags of money offering to buy their houses – and violent insurrection (more on which shortly) but Savile Town today is as exclusively Asian as any district of Islamabad.

IT WAS to a settlement and streets very much like Stevo's Savile Town and Betty Boothroyd's Eastborough that my parents, Jimmy and Kathleen Lockwood, took me home from Moorlands Maternity Home in the winter of 1958.

My first home was Sackville Street in Ravensthorpe, a two-up, one down, back-to-back terrace with an outside toilet down a cold and dark 'ginnel' – passageway – behind our neighbours' house. My uncle Bill and auntie Kathleen lived next door to us; uncle Joe and auntie Joan next to them. Ravensthorpe was another terrace-lined service community for the mills, running parallel to the Calder on the west of Dewsbury, back up the valley towards Mirfield and Huddersfield.

The area is dotted with them – Westtown, Scout Hill and Batley Carr. My family's roots are in a migratory influx too – the Irish, who came to work on the Leeds-Liverpool and Aire & Calder canals, the railways, and of course the mills and the mines of West Yorkshire.

Our immigrant stories are remarkably similar. The first

Catholic community of Irish immigrants gathered predominantly in the Westtown area, across the banks of the Calder from Savile Town. That's where my mother was brought up before marrying a Batley man, Jimmy Lockwood, and when they found their first home it was in close proximity to members of both their families. The patterns are familiar across the world.

Ours wasn't the only immigrant gathering either – the Second World War and its aftermath had brought significant numbers of Polish visitors but they, like the Irish, were Catholic and the communities lived comfortably side by side – generally right smack bang at the bottom of what it is now fashionable to call the property ladder. We were all just about clinging onto the bottom rung.

With work and some prosperity and the creation of more habitable social housing, so our families dispersed. Like Stevo's family the Lockwoods moved to Thornhill.

An asthma sufferer from when I was just two years old, I was six when our family doctor decided the pall of smog still sitting poisonously over the mills in the Calder valley wasn't doing much good for my tortured little lungs.

My illness was a passport for our family – my sister Julie having joined the ranks – to also be granted one of the impressive three-bedroomed council houses in Thornhill.

Luxury, sheer luxury. An inside loo and no more tin baths in front of the fire; we had gardens on three sides, my own bedroom (!) and literally across the road, miles and miles of open countryside which did then, and still does, stretch unblemished out towards the Pennines to the west and Peak district to the south, with only the massive edifice of the Emley Moor tv mast to 'spoil' the view. Fresh air, 365 days of the year for this wheezing little asthmatic.

"He'll grow out of the asthma soon enough," assured Dr Percival. I never did. At 52 I doubt it's likely now.

And in the wake of us all, as our immigrant-descended

white working class families escaped the barely habitable slums of the old mill housing, the influx of south Asian families flooded in to take our places, their desperate fingers replacing ours on that tentative property rung.

Today's social engineers of liberal England have for some reason seen it as their life mission to disperse what they term ethnic minority ghettoes and force integration, be it in the workplace, the school, or even the neighbourhood.

The fact that neither white nor Asian community is comfortable with this concept doesn't seem to occur to them as being anything other than a racial hang-up – with the label of blame firmly strung around the white community's neck. It doesn't bear any kind of intellectual scrutiny, but then it is so rarely subjected to it.

Colonisation is a simple migratory social fact which goes back way beyond Pakistanis, Poles and Irish. It's as old as mankind. I'm sure the same models of community were prevalent among Angles and Saxons and Normans alike here in our isles, and a sight more bloodily established too. But they have valuable historical lessons to teach us regarding the battle of languages and cultures, even religions. That defines much of English history.

More recently the USA is a massive melting pot established on exactly the same social science. Jewish, Italian, Irish, Polish, German, Dutch, Spanish ... pick a new world country, any country, and find, even hundreds of years on, pockets of settlement that proudly identify with a distant land.

Where countries like American and Australia as examples differ, is in the default attitudes of the arriving migrants. Generally speaking, they stepped ashore at Ellis Island or Botany Bay, and while clinging proudly onto their heritage for spiritual solace and their countrymen for a ground-support network, they quickly subscribed to the founding ethos of those countries.

They may have been instrumental in forging those new societies and their values at times – and not always painlessly – but the new nation state was the beacon they all gathered round.

English was the language that was required in order to contribute, to progress. And later, when Chinese and Asian and other migrant communities arrived under whatever guise or necessity, whatever went on within their specific community remained there. On the outside, the rule of the new homeland's law wasn't challenged or usurped.

Indeed, study multi-cultural states around the world – and I use that term to describe identifiably separate cultures, not our British happy-clappy social soup – and a clear pattern emerges.

Where peaceful co-existence is the norm, the domestic culture dominates, largely unchallenged. Hence you can have Christian communities in Muslim, Sikh, or Hindu states. But they know their place; the price for peaceful co-existence.

Where the tribal or religious balance rests uneasy – and Shia versus Sunni, or Muslim versus Hindu in south Asia are the most obvious examples – then frequent bloodshed becomes part of the national tapestry.

You can draw similar parallels in Darfur, in Palestine, and in the Balkans during the 90s where political self-determination, twisted by self-justifying religious dogma, can lead to the most horrific outcomes.

But where new cultures are integrated successfully into an established nation state, the willingness of the migrant community to subscribe to the new values, or at the very least respect them, is a common thread.

That's the foundation my Irish forefathers built their new lives on; they kept their Catholic churches and social clubs and rugby teams, they drank their Guinness and sang beery songs in weepy nostalgia of the homeland, but they bought into English life and opportunity with zeal.

In essence, there wasn't a choice about it. Britain was a much less tolerant place then. There was anti-Irish prejudice, for sure, but once the bog-accents had passed within a generation or two, the differences were hardly noticeable, and there were actually relatively few of them.

That, however, is where the new wave of Muslim immigration has differed. It has taken root in much the same model of settlement, but has markedly not been asked or expected to remotely respect our ways, our values, our beliefs.

Whether deliberate or not – I suspect it is, given the anti-British nature of the left-wing social scientists indulging themselves in their nation-changing agendas – the migrant culture trumps the hosts', at every turn.

So much about our lifestyle and culture is despised by Muslims, be they traditional old school or militant and young (and they may well have a point), whether that comes as a result of mosque teachings, misguided wars in Iraq and Afghanistan, or simply the distasteful sight of semi-naked drunken white girls heaving their guts up after a night on the lash.

But just as characterising everything Islamic as radically anti-western is both unhelpful and unfair, so is elevating it onto a superior pedestal and trying to buy its friendship at the cost of alienating the people who are paying its board and lodging. And that is the realpolitik in Dewsbury.

Whether modernist second or third generation Muslim or newly imported non-English speaker, it is no wonder there's not the slightest reluctance or guilty conscience about embracing the 'benefits' (both financial and rights-based) of an entire social/economic structure that appears tilted significantly in their favour.

The state-sponsored sense of privilege and entitlement has become an absolute fact of public perception, even if it is on occasion either exaggerated or rooted in urban myth.

The bottom line is that this two-tier system clearly does exist on many levels and that nothing is done either actually, or even philosophically, to give the barest impression of trying to balance the scales.

That is what causes most of the deep-rooted resentment in Dewsbury – a mixture of unquestionable appeasement and favouritism. That is why relations between the two communities have never been further apart, with an inexorably widening gap.

6 – NUMBERS

SAVILE TOWN was the bulkhead of the Asian migratory influx but has been literally 'full' for a long time and the old mill and migrant communities of Ravensthorpe, Westtown, Scout Hill, Eastborough and Batley Carr are now predominantly Asian too, some of them overwhelmingly. The seepage has tipped over into Thornhill Lees and Dewsbury Moor, taking with it all the usual and easily predictable problems.

Best current estimates on the Asian-white population ratio (ahead of the results of the 2011 census being published in 2012) put the figure between 35%-40% Asian, with the numerical concentration of ethnic minority population being higher the closer you get to the town centre. The community's influence is certainly greater than the simple numerical weighting, and it grows year on year.

Visitors arriving on the main arterial routes of Huddersfield Road and Bradford Road that follow the line of the Calder valley and the smaller waterway of Batley Beck, can be forgiven for imagining that 35-40% figure is severely underestimated.

As the side-by-side mills of the textile industry packed along the riverbanks, so the social housing built to accommodate their workforce hemmed in the town centre. As each migrant community has arrived, that's where it has taken root, though clearly none on the current scale or with comparable outcomes. Where the Irish and the Poles were (fairly rapidly) assimilated both geographically and culturally, the new migrant wave has displaced the sitting population and replaced the culture with its own.

The facts underpinning this rapid population growth are easily enough explained – the ethnic birthrate is massively higher than the indigenous one, while the importation of husbands and wives, not just often but usually close family members, continues relentlessly. The cost in human misery of this practice is huge, whatever the defensive myopia of national politicians unwilling to face up to it.

I took my car into a garage recently. Opposite me, on a doorstep fronting onto the main road, sat a young Asian girl the locals call 'Nibbles'.

The child is physically and mentally handicapped. She sits there watching the cars go by, and she gnaws at her bandaged hands. They have to be bandaged because she eats her fingers. Not her nails, but her fingers – hence the 'Nibbles'. It isn't meant cruelly, just as her entirely preventable condition wasn't meant cruelly.

The practise of inter-marrying is meant primarily to keep wealth within the family, predominantly by tying first cousins together, the health risks of which are commonly understood. Where the problem is then compounded is when the habit becomes generational and the genetic dice are even more dangerously loaded.

Where Nibbles lives, entire ranks of streets of more than a thousand people can trace their roots back to the same couple of villages in Pakistan.

And still the relatives come, still they marry, local men to imported girls who are often barely more than children, not speaking the language, producing a child every year or so, some of whom are healthy – even if those children's own genetic time-bomb only sits ticking for a while longer.

At other times it might be a male cousin from the sub-continent, to a 'Yorkshire' bride – very much like Sayeeda Hussain, now Baroness Warsi, the most powerful Muslim woman in Britain – and work will be found for him within the community, in one of the bed factories, at the wheel of a private hire car, or in the kitchen of a curry house. The emancipated young Muslim women like Sayeeda and her sisters give a form of integrated hope on the one hand, but they are very much in the minority.

There is a burgeoning professional class even in downtrodden Dewsbury, and Muslim law and accountancy practices are possibly the one white collar growth area in recent years – but their economic focus is still very inward-facing, towards servicing 'their' community. On all of their windows, Asian legal practices trumpet their expertise in immigration law.

When the Muslims Against Crusades called for their emirates to be founded in Dewsbury, Bradford and Tower Hamlets, and for trade to be 'withdrawn' from the wider (white) community, they were stating no more than the bleeding obvious to most businessmen trying to make a living in a town like ours. That is quite simply how the local economy already works – except where necessity and expedience dictates, obviously.

Occasionally the Daily Mail will highlight the case of a Muslim supermarket worker refusing to handle packs of bacon or sell alcohol, or indulge in some other imagined anti-Islamic activity. It's complete tosh of course. Across our district you can buy sausages and bacon and enough booze to float the Titanic, all day every day, from hundreds of shops run by hard-working Muslim businessmen.

But such as the economic traffic is predominantly one-way, it isn't a two-fingered, up yours stance, certainly not that I can detect. It's people keeping business among their friends and family and like-minded souls, wherever practical. It isn't too much different from what Freemasons have been doing for centuries, or what Jewish communities have stood accused of down the ages.

It just isn't good for overall local economic stimulus, that's all. It's especially not good when, having done business together, so many members of one particular community don't like paying their bills and all kinds of imagined service issues are dreamt up, or haggling over a fixed, agreed price is suddenly thrown on the table.

That's another problem and a frustratingly common one for anyone trying to do cross-community business. The money is usually forthcoming eventually, but it is so draining and repetitive and, frankly, an unnecessary strain on cultural understandings and relationships.

THE INCIDENCE of mental and physical deformity in the Asian community is already a huge financial and health service burden, and it shows no sign of even being formally acknowledged, let alone tackled. The institutional fear of giving offence means senior public service figures might acknowledge it, but show no appetite for addressing it.

It's probably 15 years since the phenomenal rates of diabetes in Dewsbury's south Asian community was openly admitted by the local health authority as a substantial drain on resources. However with the point being made, there was then little subsequent stomach to combat the root causes. Why? Again, at the risk of giving offence most likely. Health service professionals are on a career shortcut to a dead end when they put their heads above the parapets on such subjects.

Consider some of the numbers. Across all of Kirklees in 2010 there was an estimated Asian population of around 48,000 in a district population of 408,000 – around 11% of the total.

Of this gross population just under 63,000 were schoolchildren – but more than 15,000 of the schoolchildren were Asian, accounting for nearly a quarter of all children in education. Within a few years those children will all have children of their own, again at birth rates far exceeding the local norm. Where are they going to live?

While there are pockets of Asian population in a couple of Huddersfield urban districts, the vast majority of those 48,000 are in Dewsbury and Batley, just as the predominant Afro-Caribbean population (around 6,500 people) resides in Huddersfield.

Between 1971 and 2001 the population of Kirklees increased from 371,000 to 389,000. That's an increase of what might be considered a sizeable 18,000 in 30 years, given the declining indigenous British birthrates.

However in the last 10 years that number has increased already by nearly 20,000 and it is estimated that within another 10 years that the Kirklees population will be approaching 450,000 – a massive jump in population numbers, almost exclusively due to continued immigration and the birth-explosion in the south Asian communities.

Those aren't the only numbers that help to explain why Dewsbury at least is on its knees economically.

In 2007 and 2010 a national Index of Deprivation* study was carried out measuring various indices of poverty based upon a range of factors including crime, education, unemployment, health and housing.

The exercise didn't just look at a town, or even a settlement like Savile Town, Thornhill or Ravensthorpe, but broke those down even further into what were termed 'Super Output Areas' of a few hundred homes.

To look specifically at an Asian area like the heartland of Savile Town it is easy, predictable even, to see where the

* Index of Deprivation 2010, kirkleesmc.gov.uk/community/statistics

social problems lie. It's in the UK's worst 7% in respect of 'income deprivation' – lack of money.

In respect of access to and uptake of education, skills and training it's in the worst 9% and in terms of the quality of domestic environment, the bottom 4%. Overcrowding is a major issue in that respect, although again that is a cultural norm. It's bad, but there are a lot worse.

However in the same period four specific 'white' areas of Dewsbury sank to some of the worst levels of deprivation in the entire nation. They were all roughly ranged around the council estates my generation populated when we 'escaped' the back-to-back terraces of what are now the immigrant communities – these four black spots were centred on two estates in Dewsbury Moor, one in Chickenley, and one in Thornhill.

The settlement in Chickenley is in what is colloquially referred to as the 'tin village' – part pre-fab post-war council housing. That small area ranks as the 27th worst place for educational achievement, skills and training levels in the country, out of more than 32,000 – in the bottom 0.1%.

The Moorside and School Lane area of Dewsbury Moor, where kidnapped schoolgirl Shannon Matthews lived, was the 50th worst for crime in the nation, again in the very bottom percentile ranking. I suppose the drugs have to be paid for somehow. That doesn't necessarily reflect on all of the people living there, many of them hard working and house proud. It just shows how likely they are to be victims of casual crime from the deadbeats they have to live in proximity to.

In many instances the deprivation ratings of typically white working/benefit class areas in educational attainment and financial poverty are far below the 'improving' so-called Asian ghettoes. This is despite the fact that 52.8% of all Asians aged above 16 are classified officially as "economically inactive" compared to 31.2% in the white community. Breeding is clearly not recognised as a career choice, even if it pays reasonably well. The black market of cash remuneration and drugs doesn't figure at all.

This figure is made even more stark when considering there are relatively few retired Asians (just 4.2% compared to 14.3% in the white population). That social burden is yet to hit the economy although a positive aspect of how important and close the family-unit is, is that the elderly tend to be cared for within their community.

Evidence of that is revealed by only 20.5% of local Asian men or women being in full-time employment, with 19.5% designated as looking after the home/family – this compares against a figure of only 5% in the white community.

Again much of this is explained by the number of imported spouses who are unable to contribute through a lack of language, and the cultural concentration on breeding large families. I wouldn't pretend to possess specific knowledge that this amounts to any kind of formal strategy of Islamification dictated by the mosque (although it may well be, and would be no more unusual than the tacit encouragement by the Catholic church to procreate heartily during the Irish migration).

A rather more simple and uncontroversial explanation is that it's an obvious by-product of our willingness to both allow continued mass migration, to fund unemployment as an acceptable way of life, and childbirth as a divine and cost-free right.

If it is fashionable in an increasingly right-leaning Britain to frown upon single-motherhood as a career option, it is no less a ticking time-bomb to encourage migrant communities to pump out state-funded families that are double or triple the numerical size. That's what has happened, and continues at breakneck pace, here.

If the British state is stupid enough to not only allow but encourage this, how can we blame people for taking advantage? This is the Promised Land!

You can see why 'Poundtown' is so popular for a growing number of Dewsbury people, who if nothing else know all about being thrifty and living within limited means. The town's founding fathers would turn in their graves.

THESE troubling statistics apart, the fact remains that the Muslim community has outgrown its constricted geographical bases like Savile Town, but the manner of their colonisation of other areas contributes to the schism in community relations.

The sheer weight of numbers makes the dispersion inevitable, but it's often the manner of it that creates difficulties. It begins with one house being bought on a street. Then another and another. Again, there's nothing radical about this social reality.

As I described, my mum and dad's first house was next door to my uncle Joe and auntie Joan's, and their back-to-back terraced house was attached to my auntie Kathleen and uncle Bill's. Why wouldn't people want to live near their friends and family?

Where the problems arise are in the ever-present cultural differences. It clearly isn't considered an issue by these new tenants' friends when they put pressure – quite explicit pressure – on white residents in a neighbourhood to sell their houses and move out.

No matter that there isn't a For Sale sign at the end of the garden path, or that the elderly lady has lived there for 50 years and always thought she'd eventually pass away in her own family home.

Knock, knock, "you sell to us". And knock again. And Again. No isn't taken for an answer. And if the resident is steadfast, then day-to-day life can all too often be made unbearable, in small but hectoring ways.

This isn't just anecdotal, it's a fact of Dewsbury life. And if you're of a patronising nature, belong to the liberal elite that can smile benignly at this simple 'rudeness' that indicates nothing more than a cultural misunderstanding, then I'm wasting my time trying to explain how much ill feeling it can cause. It's particularly distressing as I said for elderly residents who thought themselves settled for the rest of their days only to find a domino effect of white flight leaving them isolated in a community that suddenly often doesn't even speak their language.

Then comes the inevitable knock at the door and a cash – almost always cash – offer to buy the property. And generally at an insultingly low price as well, although the offence is neither understood nor cared about. There's nothing illegal to this – it's simply one more 'difference' – but as exercises in social harmony go, it's counter-productive. And never do we hear a word of formal criticism of it, let alone recognition that it is tacit harassment.

In the mid-1990s as I married and started a family, I was selling a terraced house of my own in the Staincliffe area, sitting on the border of Dewsbury and Batley. The purchase eventually went through to a young local couple, but not before I'd rebuffed three or four knocks at the door and cash offers generally 25% below the (fair) asking price.

Refusing the offers wasn't a problem for me, but for elderly people the mere intrusion often is.

Across the road from that former house of mine was a social club which had been bought out and was in the process of being turned into a mosque and madressah. As modest enough a terraced house as mine was, it remained a 'des res' for one part of the community.

In general the would-be Asian purchaser might shrug his shoulders and wonder what the fuss is all about – he's just trying to buy a house, to live as close as possible to his recently moved brother/sister/cousin, but ignorance of the cultural sensitivities involved doesn't prevent what soon borders on harassment and, naturally, more ill-feeling between white and Asian communities.

The unfortunate consequence of that form of colonisation and ensuing resentment is that often purely aspirational Asian families who move out of the immigrant heartland – like Savile Town for example – and become the first family in a predominantly white street or neighbourhood, can be and often are exposed to rank bigotry and abuse.

In 2007, a year before my family left Dewsbury, a young Asian woman moved with her child into a smart, large three-bedroomed private semi on an adjacent street. My driveway faced hers. The problems that arrival caused went far beyond her personal experience.

For starters, the white family who sold her the house were suddenly at almost violent loggerheads with their neighbours, wary of exactly the type of colonisation I have described.

It was a salutary lesson in such events. Mark and Michelle and their three children suddenly announced one day they were upping sticks and moving to East Yorkshire.

They were at no small pains to point out they'd had enough of the town Dewsbury was becoming, with specific reference to the growing Muslim influence. People understood, as people do.

They were a popular young couple and their youngest daughter had suffered terrible health problems. They left with everyone's blessings – but it then transpired they'd sold the house to this young Muslim woman, causing massive friction with their immediate neighbours. They left sharply and haven't been in the habit of returning to visit.

I found the new resident a quite pleasant young woman for the first couple of months and always said hello, or waved, while secretly wondering how someone who was little more than a girl (and single mother) could afford nearly £200,000 for a house quite patently far larger than she needed. I popped a Christmas card through their letterbox, as I did with our other neighbours.

Then one day this attractive, smiling young mum was replaced by someone clad head to toe in her black burkha and niqab (full face veil). I stopped saying hello and waving for one simple reason – and it wasn't in the slightest way based on any racial prejudice. I just hadn't a clue who was walking in and out of the house, her, or a female friend or relative. Think about it – recognition is simply impossible.

Was she smiling at me from behind that black mask, or mouthing a profanity? And more importantly, why, all of a sudden? Was it pressure from the occasional men who paid a visit to the house?

Either way it was such a shame, because her face veil drew a symbolic veil across any hope she had of interacting with the rest of the neighbourhood. Ours was a generally familiar and friendly couple of streets, with a long-time resident Sikh family among our neighbours, but her hopes of joining that community was gone the minute she decided to don that militant costume.

Still, her colonial outpost had been established, her flag was in the sand, and it is a process that continues apace as the ever-increasing Asian population bursts out of its overcrowded settlements – and has more and more money to spend.

7 – THE GAME, LOST

THE COLONISATION of large swathes of the residential district by the migrant community was as predictable as it has proven turbulent, but in illustrating the social and cultural schism it has caused, we need to consider other everyday examples of a town's life.

The events of June 24th 1989 marked the effective end of a damn good boozer in the Scarborough Hotel, a very public and visible 'western' affront to the Savile Town community that was probably 90% Muslim by that time. Two other pubs stood as decadent western symbols in similar, if not quite so provocative localities on the fringes of Savile Town.

It took a little longer before the Savile Hotel, like the Scarborough, became unviable as a business and eventually a private residence, as drinkers became less and less willing to venture into the neighbourhood, while the other pub, the White Hart Inn, which once boasted the town's most affluent clientele of doctors, Masons and Rotarians, was destined not only for last orders and private ownership, but to become the home of Dewsbury's sharia court, headquarters of the Islamic Institute of Great Britain, and the chillingly-named Paradise Primary School.

'Paradise'. Irony indeed give that just down the road Mohammed Siddique Khan would plot his own path there. When the Paradise opened in 1998 it was a small private establishment with just eight pupils. It has since outgrown the former pub and its 200 or so students are now taught at premises back in the heart of Savile Town and directly under the forbidding gaze of the Markazi mosque.

As I write, the Paradise and its backers are busy trying to defy planning law by finding a way to prevent the building of a critically needed access road to an industrial site. The Paradise outgrew its home at the old White Hart and was transferred lock, stock and barrel into the heart of an industrial estate knowing full well the implications of such a move, but that appears to matter not.

Militant Islam isn't just about suicide bombs and terror threats; it's also about challenging mainstream authority at every turn. The outcome will be interesting, but in these parts the community's track record in getting its own way is pretty impressive.

So far the race card has only been played lightly on this one, the muted suggestion from the Paradise supporters being that a reluctance to send dozens of HGVs through the tight back lanes of a completely residential area of (white) Earlsheaton across the river is blatant (racial) favouritism.

That apart I wouldn't attempt to attach any overt conspiracy theories to the demise of the pub trade in and around Savile Town. That isolated mob attack on the Scarborough aside, there was probably more a case for their demise because of local drinkers not fancying patronising pubs in a part of town where it simply was neither safe nor comfortable to be wandering about late at night.

It's also necessary to acknowledge the general overall decline in the pub trade anyway; clearly, as a community fills up with non-drinkers – Muslims – there is going to be less and less local trade for licensees. One pub does persevere quietly in the locality, the Leggers, a small waterside establishment servicing the picturesque canal basin with its community of barges, wedged between the river Calder and Savile Town. It potters along quietly.

Riots were not required to do away with the Savile Arms and the White Hart, just the inexorable colonisation of the area, the march of time and the general demise of the licensed trade. Where the Muslim community spreads, pubs and clubs close down. It's economic and social common sense, if you think about it.

Up on the Westtown hill across the Calder, the closure of the Methodist chapel where my sister married in 1988 (she wed a divorcee so the ceremony at that time couldn't be at our family's St Paulinus Roman Catholic Church) coincided with the opening of a grand new mosque nearby.

Where not long ago the traditional Westtown Boxing Day charity Fancy Dress parade used to take in eight pubs and working men's clubs on 'the hill' now only three remain. I'm not certain exactly how liberal the colonial politics of four-time Prime Minister William Gladstone actually were, but a mere 20 or so yards away from where my sister married, the former Gladstone Liberal Club too is now a mosque.

Its teaching scholar is mufti Zubair Dudha, a smiling and softly spoken man, who nevertheless tells parents that allowing their children to mix with the kuffar – us – is an evil that is "bringing ruin to the holy moral fabric of Muslim society". I can't imagine the local Methodist preacher or Catholic priest would get away quite so blithely with such a pronouncement, but no one so much as remarked upon it when he made that public statement.

I await the day when Khalid Hussain, his successor at the Kirklees Race Equality Council, Jamal Akhtar, or their 'race police' friends step forward and report a Muslim organisation/figurehead for inciting racial hatred. Or is it really a one-way street?

In Ravensthorpe the Station Hotel is an Islamic cultural centre; the eponymous Ravensthorpe Hotel has gone the same way. Other examples abound.

However if the battle for local pubs was lost by apathy

and consumer choice, far more starkly and unrepentantly hostile was the takeover of the jewels in the crown of Dewsbury's sporting facilities, coincidentally located directly adjacent to Savile Town.

Opposite the Scarborough pub, across the busy, arterial Savile Road which links Dewsbury with the hillside communities of Thornhill and beyond, stood Savile Town cricket field, its adjoining football, rugby and hockey pitches, and the unobtrusive Savile Town sports and social club, complete with its bowling green populated almost exclusively by elderly gentlemen and a few ladies, of a very sedate nature. There was also a little OAP's drop-in centre on the site. Was.

The main recreational area, the cricket field, once home to Dewsbury CC, hasn't seen a game played on it for many years. In its distant heyday it actually hosted Yorkshire County Cricket Club games. For Yorkshiremen, that affirms its sacred place in our history but it is no longer recognisable as ever having been a cricket field, unless the circular nature of the grassed area lends a clue.

I remember the Dewsbury club's home as having a handsome pavilion and covered stands, the best cricket ground of all in a district with no shortage of them, but in the early 1980s the tenancy of the Dewsbury Cricket Club was becoming a persistent thorn in the side of the growing migrant community.

Their children could hardly play in the streets of Savile Town as Mike Stephenson and his contemporaries had done a generation before. Cars were scarce commodities in those 1960s days, but playing in any street in modern Britain is for a child to take its life in its hands. Especially children, unfortunately, generally taught no road-sense because most of their mothers do not speak English or are unfamiliar with busy traffic areas.

Other recreational areas existed around Savile Town and

still do, but none quite so spacious as the fields which housed the town's main cricket team, the Dewsbury and Savile Ladies Hockey Club, the bowling club, and a marvellous natural amphitheatre on an adjoining piece of land which staged all of the town and the district's major amateur Rugby League competitions.

My dad played for the Dewsbury & Batley Boys under 18s rugby team against Wigan in the early 1950s and a crowd of 3,000 people lined the bankings around the Savile Town field. Those really were the days.

By the mid 1980s however the cricketers had gone. Their pavilion and stands had been burned down around them, literally; the cricketers who remained soon got tired of running the daily and weekly gauntlet of hostile youths.

Women fared no better. Abuse of the hockey ladies, both verbal and physical, saw them desert their long-standing home.

In September 1993 the ladies hockey team were moved to ask for police protection at their games. Ironically, their call came after a game in which they were playing a police ladies' team. Apart from verbal abuse from gangs of Asian youths, bricks and stones were thrown at them, and there was even vandalism while the game was in play, with their nets being sliced open with knives.

When they returned to their field after a game it would be to find the holes for their goalposts filled in.

Mr Farooq Bashir of the Savile Town Community Centre said publicly that "we deplore this type of incident". He supported the call for the police to get involved.

Inspector John Mason of Dewsbury police replied that "we cannot give protection but officers on patrol can keep an eye on things."

And what do you think happened? Arrests? Young people taken to their parents and cautioned? The hockey ladies played on and lived happily ever after?

Of course not, the police tacitly wanted them – and their provocatively enduring presence – out of that place. So eventually they went and as they moved out, the young people of Savile Town moved in.

Down on the rugby pitch however, the sporting tenants were to prove a tad more resilient. For a while at least.

During those years throughout the late 1980s and early 1990s I played in numerous pre and post-season rugby tournaments, district finals and representative games on the Savile Town field. What started as mischief – I'm being generous – soon became criminal malice and one of the first occasions upon which the police displayed their true colours and flew the white flag of the shape of things to come.

Occasional acts of vandalism soon became the norm. Before every game the teams, players, supporters and officials had to comb the pitch, inch by inch, to uncover and try to remove the shards of broken glass and bottles, pieces of metal even, embedded deep in the ground, their intention so transparently being to cause maximum physical damage to anyone unwise enough to attempt to play rugby there.

The rows of neat and well kept terraced houses surrounding the field were almost 100% Asian, the rugby players exactly the opposite.

In May 1992 one player, Dean Booth, required 17 stitches in a massive gash down his leg suffered while playing in a charity Rugby League match. Notably, even before kick off in that game, five bags or containers of glass had been collected from the field by players and fans.

One observer at the time described it as resembling a police hunt for a murder weapon as men and women walked, shoulder to shoulder, heads down, scouring the surface, looking for hidden dangers.

I recall from my own experiences that some of the most viciously concealed shards and spikes would be embedded on the try-lines where players might be found sliding or tumbling across to score. Easy meat, cheap victims. The message from the locals couldn't be clearer, while the non-attempts to combat it by the police or local authority couldn't be more craven.

At the time of Dean Booth's injury a spokesman for the managing Heavy Woollen League, which ran local rugby, spoke defiantly about not giving into the vandals. Indeed the rugby league community persevered with the resistance for several more years, putting the occasional cost of gashed legs and arms and torsos down to defiant experience. But the problems worsened, rather than subsided.

People would return to their cars to find wing mirrors smashed, paintwork scratched and all the while a police force simply not interested in such acts of petty vandalism.

There were other rugby fields elsewhere not so provocatively within such an overwhelmingly Muslim enclave. Go use them, was the unspoken but heavily hinted response from council and coppers alike.

Savile Town's playing fields for many years now have belonged to the locals. Quite literally.

Indeed the story of how the Muslims of Savile Town came to physically own the playing fields is salutary in itself, a symbol of the amateurish early attempts by mainstream political parties to play the race card.

We white men can play Paki Politics too – we're just not very good at it, as this example proved.

On this occasion it was the Conservatives, as so often in Dewsbury awakening rather late to the possibilities of the mass-manipulated Muslim vote.

Ann Taylor had been sending sacks full of Eid cards to her Muslim constituents for years before the Tories, as their fortunes failed rapidly through the John Major years, were roused from their torpor.

The Savile Town playing fields were held in local trust for the good of the townsfolk by the trustees of the eponymous Savile Estate and when one of the said trustees passed away, the two remaining – both local Tory grandees as it transpired – decided that a piece of political opportunism was marvellously to hand.

Rather than keeping the gift of this recreational jewel in crusty old trustees' care, what if they magnanimously handed it over lock, stock and barrel to 'the community'? And 'the community' in this instance was right on the doorstep – the Muslim community.

In an effort to package touchy-feely new Conservatism with rank political opportunism the remaining trustees decided it was a good idea to bequest the sports fields to the people of Savile Town.

The obvious problem was that there was no actual separate governance of the Muslim community per se, no central authority to pose for a publicity photograph gratefully receiving this magnanimous gift.

And so, with the Markazi mosque being the largest single institution of note in the area – at least physically – and despite its own management being as outwardly silent about what went on behind their imposing walls as a monastery full of Trappist monks, the Tories granted the Markazi a 999-year lease on the land for a token sum of £1.

As vote-winning strokes of genius went, it was an unmitigated disaster. In the days pre-September 11, 2001 and the full outbreak of declared Islamic war on the western world, and despite all the racial tensions I've so far outlined, I don't think anyone in Dewsbury would have highlighted 'religion' per se as being a radical cause of discontent.

There were cultural issues, certainly, territorial ones too, but despite the first Gulf war and the troubles in the Balkans, the tensions in Dewsbury were not overtly religious, Islamic vs Christian by nature. Not at all.

It was about culture and community, far more. Indeed I

can barely recall seeing Muslim women wear the full face niqab back in the 1990s. That degree of marked separation was yet to come.

The problem for the meddling Conservative trustees of the Savile Estate was that the Markazi, despite dominating the landscape and much of the high-brow Islamic radical agenda worldwide, had much less to do on a day to day basis with the common or garden Muslims of the area, specifically in Savile Town where at the time there were another half dozen smaller mosques.

The Markazi's weighty influence is more profound now as the religious divide between Islam and secular British society becomes more tangible, more pronounced. But certainly back then while it attracted worshippers, preachers and religious students from far and wide, on a day-to-day basis it was far from being the dominant theological or social institution it is today. Local Muslims were far more likely to attend one of the other mosques in their neighbourhood than the Markazi.

In hindsight, and of all the custodians the meddling, gerrymandering Tories could have picked to bequeath the town's sporting crown jewels to, none were more unsuitable a beneficiary as the Markazi.

The white majority of Dewsbury were incensed as you would imagine, especially as this all came at a time when the failing Conservative Government was coincidentally throwing millions at deprived – mainly ethnic – communities through its City Challenge and Single Regeneration Budget initiatives.

New roofs, windows, heating and plumbing systems were very worthily funded in row upon row of (privately owned) terraced homes, almost universally Asian.

Demographically as previously mentioned they were the most needy, the least likely to be in employment, with the most critical health needs, ergo that's where the majority of the money went. Socially altruistic, no doubt.

But while it might make sense in the cold light of the day's physical needs it didn't, and still doesn't, play well with the inhabitants of all those failing white estates across Dewsbury and Batley. The resentment still lingers. And then right on the back of that, suddenly the district's prime public sporting facility was being handed over to 'them'.

Not only was ill feeling promoted outside Savile Town, the Muslim majority who worshipped elsewhere – and were most likely to want to use these public spaces – were hugely annoyed by the Markazi's good fortune. It's difficult to imagine a means by which the plot could have failed more miserably.

As sporting own goals went, the Conservatives' patronising efforts had none of the desired, but all the predictable effects that wiser observers might have seen coming. Wisdom and politics don't necessarily make comfortable bedfellows however.

Even after 30 years in the town the shadowy figures who run the Markazi don't do 'public' and they have certainly never done 'gratitude' in any form that I have witnessed.

There isn't and never has been any attempt or desire to engage with the wider community outside the Markazi walls – not here in Dewsbury and not even nationally when their influence has fallen under the news spotlight for the activities of some of their followers.

The Markazi's mullahs don't condemn those of their devotees who try to blow up American passenger planes or succeed in murdering ordinary users of the London transport system; they merely stand serenely behind benign philosophical platitudes of upholding "peaceful" religious goals – and they stand more literally behind concrete walls bearing all-seeing CCTV cameras, alongside dire warnings to passers-by that taking photographs of the Markazi mosque is expressly forbidden.

They certainly don't do 'thank-yous'.

While we were researching our defence case for the Malik trial I took our barrister Jonathan Crystal along South Street in Savile Town and parked opposite the forbidding Markazi gates, ringed by walls, wire and cameras, and those ubiquitous 'no photography' signs.

I wanted to take a photograph as part of our evidence, to portray the kind of place Savile Town was. I could point my camera at pretty much any building on any street in the kingdom – sensitive military installations apart, perhaps – but the lawyer seemed worried about the forbidding signs, so my co-defendant Jonathan Scott rang the Chief Superintendent and asked his advice.

"Can we take photographs?" he asked (I'm paraphrasing slightly).

"You can but I wouldn't."

"Why not?"

"It might cause a problem ."

"What if we were attacked?"

"I would send a couple of officers out. Are you being attacked?"

"No – but we're certainly being watched!"

"I can't do anything about that. Attacked yes, watched no."

The advice was to write to the mosque elders asking for permission to photograph the building. Not that it would ever be given, or the request acknowledged.

I've taken a few pictures of the Markazi over the years, but in enlightening our London lawyer it was a point worth making.

The locals, the ordinary residents of Savile Town meanwhile, had seen the richest and most aloof organisation in their midst given control of a facility it neither cared nor had use for. If any debates have taken place within the Savile Town community regarding this issue, they have never being aired publicly outside it.

New playground areas have been built for the local youngsters and the former cricket field is a series of soccer pitches.

The only organised sport that has taken place on those prime acres in the intervening 15 or so years is local league football, down on what was the old rugby pitch, and even that has forged a controversial and fiery history.

Immediately the rugby players departed, the malicious glass-planting miraculously ceased, but there have been more than a few incidents of matches between the local footballers and their visitors becoming 'overheated'.

The resulting conflicts have often witnessed scenes reminiscent of the Michael Caine film Zulu, where hordes of attackers miraculously appear atop the surrounding bankings and descend upon a besieged and rapidly retreating band of suddenly very isolated (white) brothers.

There is only one narrow entrance/exit to the amphitheatre and it is easily blocked when local youths have a mind.

The police always play things down and will do until someone is killed – hospitalised isn't generally enough – and the Serious Crime boys are called in to mop up. Blood and damaged property and cars has been the occasional outcome, followed by the police force's liberally applied no-publicity blanket draped over the incident and few, if any, held to account.

Savile Town FC, the current home club, eventually left the local competitions and now play in division three of the Huddersfield League. Whatever the standard of football, competing against teams from outside the immediate area probably makes for a far more peaceful pastime.

With effective ownership of the playing fields and the closure of the Scarborough, Savile Hotel and White Hart pubs, the Muslim community of Savile Town had effectively enclosed itself pretty much against outside interference.

If a ghetto existed, as liberals fancifully saw their mission to be the 'curing' of, it was self-imposed and the people within it were more than comfortable with their situation. I don't think the residents of Savile Town do, or ever have, recognised the patronising description of it being an 'Asian ghetto' as applying to them. It's their home, their community. What's not to be happy with?

With just one arterial road running through the district – one which could be closed on the community's whim, as would be very effectively displayed – Savile Town was on its way to becoming a no-go area both in culture and in attitude.

Some years later when local drug gangs clashed with interlopers from Bradford on its streets, complete with a stabbing and gunshots, one (Muslim) Savile Town councillor described it as a case of righteous local youths resisting the attempts of a Bradford gang to infest their neighbourhood with their evils.

As risible as that embarrassing tripe was, there was never a shortage of local authority and senior police officers happy to swallow it. After all it made their lives far easier than attempting to disprove the rubbish, let alone deal with its consequences.

The message was becoming increasingly clear through the 1990s. These are our streets and what goes on here is our business, you keep your noses out of it.

Everyone does, mostly, and especially after dark – but trouble isn't the exclusive domain of darkness as my co-libel defendant, Councillor Jonathan Scott, would find out while campaigning for re-election in 2006.

8 – THE AUTHOR

ONE EXPRESSION has become a staple within the immigration lexicon when debating relationships between indigenous and ethnic communities in Britain generally, and in places like Dewsbury specifically.

The conversation inevitably starts thus ... "I'm not a racist but ..." and what follows is a predictable monologue of either plain frustration or outright antagonism. The eloquence of articulation – or the plain and simple curses – all depends on the company you keep.

Earlier in 2011 Baroness Warsi landed herself in hot water when she spoke about hostility to Muslims "passing the dinner table test", whatever that was supposed to mean. She was roundly criticised for it but, despite being no fan of Warsi's any longer, I think I know what she meant. Those dinner table conversations, I guess, would generally begin with "I'm not a racist, but..."

That simple qualification – "I'm not a racist but..." – isn't always so politely offered depending whether you're at a dinner table or sitting at the bar. Many are the pub tap rooms or Working Men's Clubs where simple, blunt bigotry is proudly espoused on a daily basis over a pint of Tetley's or John Smith's bitter, Carling or Fosters lager.

After all at the 2005 General Election Dewsbury delivered the highest BNP vote in the UK. At the time Kirklees Council had several BNP councillors among its ranks, all from our end of the valley.

I've long argued that not everyone who votes BNP is a de facto racist and that they are the ultimate electoral protest vote, but nonetheless it would be facile not to acknowledge that there is a tangible and growing mistrust, dislike – yes, even unvarnished hatred – in many quarters, and not all blue collar either.

The current Prime Minister David Cameron chose Dewsbury in which to launch the Conservatives' local election manifesto of 2008 and I sat listening to his glib, patronising bullshit in the Mayor's Parlour at the Town Hall. Looked good, sounded slick, said nothing – and this observation from a man who not long afterwards (me) would find himself being fast-tracked through the Conservative candidates programme and on the verge of standing for MP in the 2010 general election.

Why that unlikely prospect never came to fruition will be explained later, but on that occasion, when we came to the Q and A session with the future Prime Minister, I asked Cameron what his party would do to deal with the issue of towns like Dewsbury delivering growing thousands of BNP votes.

"We must listen to the message of people on the doorsteps," came the condescending candy floss reply.

I couldn't believe he had stepped into a seething cauldron of barely contained racial hatred like Dewsbury's armed with nothing better than that. I tried again, I got the same brush off. It said pretty much everything I ever needed to know about David Cameron's politics.

There was no strength of conviction here, no real appetite for rebuilding broken parts of society – why shore up the crumbling wall when a coat of emulsion would suffice to mask the damage for now?

But in trying to paint a picture of the issue beguiling and bewildering a melting pot like Dewsbury, it is important that as its author I make my own politics and beliefs clear.

True, I would almost comically make it onto the Conservative Party approved list of candidates in 2010, but I am no more a natural Tory than a mouth-frothing Communist. What am I? A 'caring capitalist' comes as close as I can manage in just a couple of words.

I was actually working as a window cleaner (a part-time moonlighting job – I was also working as a journalist and as a nightclub dee-jay) one day in the late 1980s when Margaret Thatcher's motorcade swept through the town centre. I didn't see Maggie herself, but dropped my squeegee and put down my bucket in order to offer twin-fingered vee-signs of 'welcome' to Yorkshire.

Its history with textiles apart, this is an area steeped in the mining industry though the pits have all shut down now. But many were my rugby pals who had fought the bitter battles of the miners' strike. You couldn't be a 'proper' Dewsbury bloke and like anything about Thatcher.

As a businessman more than 20 years on I see things markedly different, but as someone who almost wept when awakening that Friday morning in 1992 to find Neil Kinnock had failed so dismally to unseat John Major, and who jumped for joy at the ascension of Tony Blair in 1997, I am walking, talking testimony to the life theory that we live and learn; that there's no fool quite like a fool who wants to believe.

On the day of the July 7th 2005 bombings I was trying to get back into England from a week's holiday with an American pal, Phil Sarris. Phil's family own a home on the Greek island of Lesvos and we'd been out there with his folks. The massive queues trying to get through Manchester airport were a puzzle – staff on strike? Tea-break? – and only as we emerged into the northern afternoon did we learn the horrific details of the bombings that had claimed 52 lives in London that morning.

The image of the double decker bus with its roof blown off is iconic of the moment still for me. And then it emerged that Mohammed Siddique Khan had masterminded the atrocity from Dewsbury. From my old home street in Thornhill Lees. It was surreal.

The edition of The Press that we published in the wake of July 7 was key to The Press, my little independent local rag, being named the Yorkshire Weekly Newspaper of the Year, against the might of the country's biggest blue-chip publishers, and also the Newspaper Society's free Weekly Newspaper of the Year for the North-East, North-West and Yorkshire.

Someone thought we were publishing responsible journalism, but not everyone. I hadn't been long back in the office in the wake of July 7 when a colleague alerted me to a posting on what was the highest-read journalists' website of the day, Hold The Front Page.

It was then owned jointly by my rivals' publishers Johnston Press, plus Trinity Mirror, Newsquest and Northcliffe – the four largest regional publishers in the UK, owners of probably 90% of the country's local newspapers. The website had a section for biographies of British journalists and media figures and my name was among them.

That morning, just days after the London bombing, I checked my listing and was alarmed to read that it attributed Danny Lockwood with having been the secretary of the BNP since 1993.

Someone had either hacked the website or supplied malicious information which hadn't been adequately checked. Either way, the potential damage not just to my professional reputation but to the safety of my family was massive. It would be bad enough in any town or village in middle England, but here in Dewsbury, the 'home' of the worst terrorist atrocity in the nation's history? I was livid.

The website responded accordingly, shut the whole thing down while it put its house in order, apologised without (much) delay and paid a nominal sum in damages – nothing like as much as you'd imagine. The lawyers probably earned a tenner for every pound I got.

But what the incident did was affirm the antagonism the professional 'left' had for a newspaper like The Press and for me in particular. I don't know who was guilty of that malicious prank, though I have a reasonable idea and he is stunningly, to me at least, still working in journalism. And yet the thought of anyone seriously accusing me of being racist seemed ridiculous and still does.

Without getting too autobiographically maudling, I hope this anecdote goes some way to explaining some of my core values. And why I still get myself in trouble.

I went to St Paulinus, the Roman Catholic primary school in Dewsbury, and don't mind admitting I had a pretty lousy time of it there. I was quite a sickly kid, growing up with asthma at a time when there were none of the treatments of recent decades, and our family GP, Dr Percival, thought the best way to 'treat' my oft-tortured lungs was to prescribe an anti-convulsant sedative, Phenobarbital, to try to get me through the night.

But certainly until I reached my teens, rare were the nights when I didn't have an asthma attack of varying severity and my poor sainted mum was to be found sitting helpless sat my bedside.

I loved sport and playing out with my mates, especially when the family moved to the open spaces of Thornhill, but the asthma was an obvious drawback. I can still recall sitting wrapped in an eiderdown but with my head hanging out of the living room window trying to get some cold, fresh air into my lungs.

My pals would come to see if I was playing out and, if not, could they borrow my ball. I usually had one because my dad was a window cleaner and had a funny old sense of respect for property; if people left footballs and rugby balls lying about their gardens and wouldn't look after them, then Jim would.

If I was a bit of a weed it did nothing to stifle my own sense of justice – an unfortunate social trait I see in my own 15-year-old son – and a mouth big enough to get me into all kinds of trouble.

I can bring to mind dozens of playground fights before I was my son's age. I even remember winning one, a rarity. And with a choice of keeping my gob shut or bringing down the wrath of the gods, it would generally result in black eyes, bust noses, and as often as not my running away from my persecutors. I could run a bit, asthma or not.

In my last year at St Paulinus my class teacher and the school deputy head Mr Cooper banned me from the annual camping trip to the Yorkshire Dales. Even when the head, Sister Leonardine (these were still the days of the nuns in Catholic schools) pleaded my case, Mr Cooper was determined that he had no intention of chasing Lockwood across Ingleborough, Whernside or Pen-y-Ghent.

In those days you had an A and a B class in each school year. Mr Cooper took the A stream, so, deprived of the Dales visit, instead I was sent with Mr Harris and the B class on a three day trip to Cliffe House, an educational/recreational outdoor centre up the valley in Huddersfield.

I still remember being sat on a rope swing, and a gang of fellow pupils coming up with a meek kid and instructing me to get off the swing, otherwise they'd make him hit me.

I won't embarrass the lad by naming him, but he was even more terrified than I. Obviously being a stubborn loud-mouthed little git I refused to budge, so they made him hit me. I gave him a whack back predictably, as you would, and a gang of 11-year-olds fell about me at which point – déjà vu – I legged it.

I was eventually corralled up a railway banking by the pursuing Cliffe House staff and teachers in the nearby village of Honley. Maybe Mr Cooper had a point. But I still hated him.

Of the 39 pupils in Cooper's class 36 of us passed the 11-plus exam in 1970 and went to attend Cardinal Hinsley Boys, or Margaret Clitherow Girls, a pair of twinned Catholic Grammar schools 10 miles away in Bradford. So much for the hindrances of class sizes, eh?

Of the remaining three pupils one left to go to a private school and two still did well enough to earn a place at Dewsbury Technical School – an educational halfway house between the 'failures' (ie the B stream kids) who went to secondary schools, in our case St John Fisher Secondary Modern, and the grammar system.

If I didn't like St Paulinus, I hated every living breathing day at Cardinal Hinsley's, a brutal, repressive regime, one of those places of which its survivors often remark "a good old slapping/caning/whipping/beating never did me any harm!"

I don't physically recall being on the end of corporal punishment from any of the staff – I was sufficiently cowed and terrified as to never step out of line. But that situation was more than made up for by my peers, essentially the exact same group of boys I had been schooled with for the past six years at St Paulinus.

A few years ago I had a heated exchange with a schoolmate from back then, on the terrace at the Houses of Parliament of all places, and he clearly thought my memories of the lousy times I experienced at Cardinal Hinsley's were at best exaggerated, at worst completely fabricated. I must confess to being tempted to throw him in the Thames, but he had something of a point. I doubt that any child's individual recollections are widely shared, not necessarily even by its parents.

I see it in my own children's flights of emotional fancy – a world in black and white, of unbounded joy or dark fear. So I'm sure there were periods of calm in between the dramas and the playground bullying I experienced at Cardinal Hinsley's, but I still clearly recall what I was often called by my 12-year-old peers – "Paki lover".

In grammar school at least, our young minds were being introduced to formal strands of education and history wasn't just about William the Conqueror, Henry VIII, or the World Wars, but British social history too.

Long periods of time off school or unable to play outside with kids on the estate because of my asthma, plus my natural passion for books and knowledge, meant that I was probably very well read for my age.

I understood the economic reasons for mass migration from the Caribbean and the Indian sub-continent. I knew all about the British raj, about colonisation, the reach of empire, the development of Commonwealth, the rights of the Queen's overseas subjects to seek a better life here and our obligations to them.

During school holidays as a youngster there generally wasn't anyone at home so for weeks on end I would accompany my mum to the mills where she worked as a rag sorter. What an adventure that was – diving in and out of bales, making swings and slides in the warehouse. All that dust and muck. Great for a kid with wheezing lungs!

But even by then, in the mid-60s, much of the labouring work, shifting the bales, lugging the sorted rags about, was being performed by Asian men. I can still picture 'Sam', one genial, lanky Pakistani man who was part of the fixtures and fittings at my mum's mill. I understood the economic dynamic of migration.

And as ever, there was that big, fat, smart, trouble-finding mouth of mine. In class and outside in the corridor and the playground, I argued, probably quite eloquently for a 12-year-old, in defence of immigration and its philosophies, at least in theory.

So I got the shit kicked out of me. Paki lover. Big puff. Whack, kick, punch. Kids are a funny lot, cruel and vindictive in their persecutions. I recall another occasion on the long bus trip back to Dewsbury from Hinsley's.

My mum had bought me a fashionable Parka coat for winter, one with about a dozen pull strings with plastic toggles, loads of zipped pockets, and a fur-trimmed hood.

It was no mean feat given our straitened financial circumstances. Mum didn't earn much and dad washed just enough windows to source his week's beer money and pay his £10 a week board – a sum that never increased up until the time we left him for good in 1976.

I don't know what it is with kids and this particular tactic, but my antagonists again found an unwilling stooge who they coerced into coming up the bus from the back seat and hitting me. I hit the lad back, having long before learned that the shame of backing down was far more painful than the blows of physical defeat – and so again I found myself with a few lumps knocked out of me, but also tied inextricably to the bus seat by all the toggles on my new Parka.

It was there, all alone, the bus having emptied, and crying quietly at my predicament, that the bus conductor finally found me. I can laugh when telling the tale now, but it was massive at the time. The final straw was soon to follow.

It was another 'Paki lover Lockwood' incident, this time on my 13th birthday just before we broke up for Christmas. Usually I could outrun my pursuers if the odds were too great, but on this occasion they trapped me in the toilets.

I got the 'bumps' – thrown in the air 13 times by the gang, traditionally caught in the birthday prank, but instead my fate was to be let drop on the tiled toilet floor and given a half-hearted booting, before being picked up and thrown again. Then there was the head flushed down the toilet stunt, just for a 'laugh'. Hilarious.

That was it. I went home from the hellhole known as Cardinal Hinsley Grammar School that day and never went back. My mum took me to see Dr Percival, explained my predicament, how it was affecting my asthma (my mental health wasn't holding up too well either!) and I started the January term at Dewsbury Technical School, in the same group as my two former St Paulinus classmates, Tommy Keane – my best friend for years to come – and Mick 'Ratty' Routledge. That move of schools changed my life. Probably saved it, actually.

But my sense of justice regarding the obligations of British governments, the economics and social responsibilities of immigration, were pretty well formed. The left-wing critics who today report my every word that's perceived as being critical of ethnic or religious minorities, haven't a clue about the educational journey I've taken in forming those views.

Some years later, in my mid-20s, I was standing in my mum's second floor council flat in Westtown, about 400 yards from my old Dewsbury Technical School, which coincidentally shared an extended campus with the town's Catholic secondary modern school – St John Fisher.

What a stroke of genius it was to lump those two side by side, especially as one of the schools is now almost exclusively Asian. Every summer is a pitched battle, though hardly newsworthy except for the occasions when a pupil is hospitalised. And that happens often enough.

Anyway, I had declined the opportunity to go to St John Fisher's when leaving Hinsley's, because in 1970 they only studied for the lesser CSE exams, and the Tech did O levels and CSEs.

The Tech was renamed Westborough High during the

comprehensive cataclysms of 1974 and by the time of this incident – the mid 1980s – it was already a predominantly Asian school. A group of its pupils, aged about 12 or so, were walking past my mum's flat minding their own business, when a bigger white kid came hurtling out of a nearby flat and laid into one of the lads.

In a flash I was down the stairs, had pulled the aggressor off the Asian boy he had attacked, and sent him packing with a half-hearted clip round the ear. I might not even have made contact with him.

However by the time I had despatched the group of boys safely on their way and made my way back upstairs to my mum's flat, it appeared to all intents and purposes – and to the rapidly growing crowd in the street – that I had been guilty of a major assault on a small child. His dad came storming out looking for vengeance for the poor injured little mite.

To compound matters the dad was a rugby teammate of mine – and a bloke a lot stronger and tougher than I was. But what can you do? Much to my mum's anguish I went down to face him and we ended up grabbing each other by the throat, him threatening all kinds of revenge, me trying to calmly explain what had happened, how his son had been bullying the other boy, and how I had only been doing what any responsible adult would.

"And what kind of Paki lover are you then?" came his response, or words to that effect.

No physical damage was done. We were decent pals before that incident, and would be subsequently, once tempers had subsided. But it was symbolic in so many ways. No Paki lover, nor hater. Just an ordinary bloke with a decent sense of social justice. Colour and creed doesn't – shouldn't – come into it.

But it certainly clouds matters. And of course as I was to discover ad infinitum once I was in a position of quite measurable editorial influence, starting at the Dewsbury Reporter in 1993 and later at The Press, people see what they want; they perceive whatever suits their agenda, regardless of the truth. It isn't just vulnerable children who are guilty of that.

9 – THE EDITOR

IN ATTEMPTING to establish my credentials as an appropriately, or even sufficiently, dispassionate narrator of the changes this town has witnessed, one incident will, I hope, assist in setting the stage. This isn't about race – it's about right.

This happened in about 2005, a few years into the life of The Press at a time when I was still the Publisher and the editor on a day-to-day basis. I used to be invited along to address a seminar staged by a UK-wide group called Common Purpose, a well-intentioned organisation with a real value and role to play in areas like ours.

One of its main goals is to bring together people from diverse backgrounds to foment greater understanding and widen their perspectives on an impressive range of issues. This isn't about putting bolshy kids in a classroom and telling them to get along, it's an exercise in bringing together influential adults from a wide variety of professional and social environments.

I can't speak for other quango-based projects but I never found Common Purpose a goody-two-shoes attempt at social engineering; it was far more practical.

For instance on each of its courses there might be half a dozen senior managers from the local authority, the health service; inspectors or even superintendents from the police, executives from major employers in the private sector, plus men and women running local charities or other public service organisations, all of whom could benefit from knowing more about not just each other's roles, but a wider understanding of topical issues.

In towns like Dewsbury and Batley, race and religion are fundamental to so much and one of the modules of each Common Purpose course featured the 20 or so delegates coming face to face with people giving representative views from various communities. Hence there might be an Islamic scholar, an Asian councillor – who at least had a foot in the secular political camp – and the voice of the great white unwashed, typically me.

I wasn't quite required to play Mr Angry, the spokesperson of the silent majority, but it was always good fun – from my perspective – to get up the noses of the delegates I typified in print as lily livered, liberal sweethearts, feeding handsomely off the public tit and playing expensive games with our lives.

Common Purpose groups always had a healthy proportion of Kirklees Council, NHS, and Social Services managers who all saw themselves as cultural engineers; they made their ample livings patronising ethnic and social minority groups, all the while determined to make the other 95 per cent of us accept them as our own personal burdens; the price of Britain's Imperial conscience, mixed with a big dose of guilt for us being white, employed, and having any kind of nationalist affinity for the Union flag.

I despised those people then and I still do; they are far more dangerous to our nationhood than any closeted bunch of terrorist nutters determined to blow themselves and a few innocents to pieces.

I enjoyed the combative nature of the exchanges and I still would, except I don't get invited back to Common Purpose any longer, I suspect for a misdemeanour I am still troubled by. The sessions run under the auspices of the

Chatham House rules, meaning everything you hear and learn can be repeated, but not its source, to protect the confidence of people in often highly influential positions.

I fear that in my excitement at one revelation I mentioned the person who said it. I was and still am deeply embarrassed for that lapse of etiquette. When I tell you this story you'll understand why.

On this particular Common Purpose session we had broken up into groups, each of the three speakers having smaller sessions with each set of delegates in turn. The challenges to me were always pretty predictable.

"Why is The Press a racist newspaper? Why are you a racist editor?" would be typical, usually from a Kirklees Council diversity manager or maybe an equal opportunities executive. My answers were well practised, depending on the specific angle of the question – they would usually be armed with a recent story to illustrate their point.

Although the headline might seem race-oriented, quite often the subject below the waterline was drugs. So I explained, as oft times before.

After an enjoyable few years at Dewsbury Tech/ Westborough High School, I had a dismal set of 'O' level results and, dispirited, went off to work in the warehouse at John Menzies, not writing newspapers but packaging and delivering them. By the end of that sunny summer of 1975 I knew the job wasn't for me and wrote to the editor of the Reporter telling him what a brilliant journalist I'd make if only someone would give me a break.

He wrote back advising me to make my own break – beginning by going to finish my education. I enrolled on two A level night school courses but never made those stick, so I took the editor, Jack Gowers, at his word.

After what had effectively become a working gap year, I got a place at Wheelwright 6th Form College, re-taking my 'O' levels and sitting my 'A' levels which I subsequently passed. At the second time of asking, I got to see Mr Gowers having fulfilled my part of the deal, he was good to his word and gave me a chance and the rest, professionally at least, is history.

My best friend during those years at 6th Form, and for some time afterwards, was an immensely bright and talented council estate lad like myself, Michael Preston.

Mick was the best looking lad in the place, the best footballer, cricketer ... you name it. He could charm the birds out of the trees and regularly did. And he was a natural academic talent too.

Mick died at the age of 33 from a heroin overdose which he took in the company of his elder sister Karen who, like Mick and their younger sister Melanie, was a heroin addict.

He left a baby boy, Max, by his German girlfriend. Karen and Melanie's saint of a mother, Beryl, has played a large part in bringing up various of their children at different times, but Beryl isn't alone in Dewsbury.

I have five friends – at least – good people, hard-working people, caring parents, who have all lost their children to heroin overdoses, several of them finding themselves in their 40s, 50s and even 60s suddenly faced with raising their grandchildren.

If those deaths were gun crimes, knife attacks, teen suicides, there would a public outrage and demands for action. And those are just my personal acquaintances. Multiply that unacceptable death toll 10-times, 20-times, and much, much more, because they are there – it's just the shame of it that keeps it in the dark.

In the mid-1990s I was attending a Dewsbury Rotary Club luncheon and the guest speaker was a gentleman whose name escapes me, from the national drugs charity Lifeline. He explained, to our absolute astonishment, that proportionately Dewsbury had a worse heroin problem than inner city Glasgow, Liverpool or London. I recall vividly his statement that "the main difference being that Dewsbury's addicts are on average three or four years younger than those in large metropolitan inner cities."

Our kids were being poisoned before us, and not only was no one explicitly aware of the depth of the problem, no one was doing a damned thing about it – and certainly not the police. The fact was then, and remains now, that the drugs trade in Dewsbury – or at least the heroin trade – was almost exclusively the domain, the cottage industry, of the Asian, specifically the Pakistani, community.

Since then the criminal enterprise has spread well beyond the heroin trade into cannabis, ecstasy, cocaine and more – but heroin's the big killer.

If validation was required it came from one of our own Rotary Club members, community pharmacist Bob Dunkley, who proceeded to outline the sheer horror of his daily routine, with addicts taking their methadone outside his pharmacy and exchanging it for wraps of heroin; of him trying to remonstrate with addicts and dealers alike and having his premises vandalised and his well-being threatened. Bob ended up a nervous wreck.

The town, it transpired, was a living, breathing drugs den. I confess to having been surprised by its rapid growth and how wide its tentacles were. I'd left Dewsbury in 1981 and although I came back for periods of a year or so on more than one occasion, I spent much of the next 10 years in America or Australia.

When I was home I was working hard and wrapped up in my own rugby activities. I was ignorant of the spread of the drug culture. Sure I knew about the odd spliff here and there, one local amateur rugby team was renowned for taking to the field with half the players 'whizzed' up, but innocently, naively, that was as much as I was aware of.

And suddenly as an editor there it was in front of my eyes. In the young men of no visible means driving flashy

BMWs and Mercs round the town centre, all of them, virtually without exception, Asian. They were dealing from car windows by the park gates, outside the college, on the corner of every street ... it was rife.

Early in the life of The Press I got a tip-off about a bloke with one of the best known cars and private number plates in the district, who could reputedly be found selling drugs from the self-same vehicle on Friday and Saturday nights – in a car park directly behind the police station. I passed by one night and sure enough, there he was.

We passed the information on, but I've still seen him regularly over the years, in a newer car but the same number plates. If he wasn't untouchable, he was as close to it as I could fathom.

There was a spell of a few years when for no accountable reason a firework – a rocket – would go off, not at Guy Fawkes night, November 5th, but the middle of January, April, June or July even.

"That means there's been a delivery," I was told, though it seemed a bit of a crude form of communication in the age of mobile phones and texts. No one could come up with a better explanation though.

The problem from my perspective – and the police will understandably take exception to this – was that there appeared no concerted attempt, or even will, to tackle criminality within that community. The consistent barrage of cries of "racists!" were as predictable as they were plain wrong. But on the face of things, they seemed to work.

In our town the experiences of 1989 and the Salman Rushdie riot had changed the policing dynamic it seemed. The revelation from the man from drugs charity Lifeline came at a time when the politics of ethnic minority appeasement were in full flow here in Kirklees, even though we were still a long way off the race riots of Oldham, Burnley and Bradford in 2001 that themselves pre-dated the September 11th al Qaeda attack on the Twin Towers. But appeasement was already a fact of life.

As long ago as 1992/93 when I had been working as a news reporter on the Yorkshire Evening Post in Leeds, the-then police officer responsible for fighting drugs in West Yorkshire, Det Chief Insp Richard Blakeley, had furnished me with an exclusive story about the impact of and relationship between drugs and crime. He said that drugs were responsible for a massive proportion of all crime, whether directly in its trade, or indirectly in soaring burglary and car crime to fund the abuse of drugs.

I seem to remember Dick Blakeley being shot down in flames by at least some senior constabulary sources at the time but within a matter of weeks Home Office figures were published showing the problem was every bit as serious, and worse, than he had said.

I'd known him since my very beginnings as a journalist at the Reporter, when he was an up and coming young detective winning a Churchill scholarship to study crime fighting methods in the USA. We're still close. And when I launched The Press in March 2002 and we began the life of our new paper with a series of in-depth investigations into the local drugs trade, it was to the then-retired Dick Blakeley that we went to for an authoritative analysis of the depth of the problem in Dewsbury.

Our stance as a newspaper was that drug crime – any crime – should not be about race, whoever was behind it. It was about crime. But if race or religion was being used as armoured protection behind which crime prospered, and if the police and local authorities were effectively complicit in that by a reluctance to upset ethnic sensitivities, then it was time that someone who cared stood up and shouted about it.

At The Press we cared, we shouted.

We ran stories about gun-point robberies in the heart of

our town in which the police ridiculously played along with the fiction that they were about anything other than drugs. They all involved the 'usual' casts of characters.

One businessman who had a bullet put into the car seat alongside his head and who was relieved of £30,000 in cash said he had been collecting monies for bed sales – as I mentioned, where textiles once were king, the Heavy Woollen district has become the UK's centre of bed manufacture.

Asked about such a huge amount of disposable notes, he lamely replied "Muslims like to deal in cash..."

Indeed it was an excuse trumpeted out by our own MP Shahid Malik some years later as he bobbed and weaved and tried to explain his very lax financial arrangements surrounding his questionable MP's expenses.

Malik's dodgy landlord, Terry Zaman, when approached by the national media made out that Malik was paying buttons for his rent, thinking that would help his patron's case, except it didn't. Quite the reverse.

What followed was a murky backtracking of stories and explanations, of non-receipts and 'cash payments' to paper over the cracks of two badly askew stories.

Ah, we're Muslims you see, we like to deal in cash, don't trust the financial authorities. It goes against Islam. Except when it suits of course – but that warped logic, that self-perpetuating lie in fact – is never, ever challenged.

It is a default excuse within their community and in my experience at least it's generally a cover for criminality or tax avoidance. I'm happy to be proven otherwise, although I'll tell you a story about a character who appears and is named elsewhere in these pages. I won't join the dots, just in case...

I was phoned by an Asian contact and told about one of this bloke's money laundering wheezes. Drugs being as big a business as it is, a considerable problem the industry has is making the cash legitimate. This valley has more takeaways than it probably sells curries on some nights. Cash businesses, you see. Cash businesses are everywhere you look. But once the cash is banked, that's only half the problem. The next one is moving it out of the banking system without lumping 40% to the Revenue.

I can't testify to this, but I will say my source was about as rock solid as you'll get; a pillar of the Asian community, though at war with other factions within it. Those conflicts very rarely surface in public by the way. It's not 'our' business – we just come in handy when they want to put the surreptitious boot into one another.

He described a well known character as occasionally going to one of his banks and making a cash withdrawal of anything up to £100,000, explaining that the cash was needed for a transaction which was acceptable under Sharia. No credit, no interest, no western 'usury'. And the bank complied.

That money was then transported to another country where it was duly salted away and our man/men returned to the UK. Cue the bank's client to return to his branch with £100,000 in cash and an explanation that the deal had fallen through and he needed to pay it back in.

A different 100k, a dirty 100k, but mission accomplished. Voila! True? I don't know, but the millionaire Muslim businessman who described it to me, with names, dates and destinations, obviously thought so.

That was several years ago though and the authorities nationally have tightened up on money laundering scams quite impressively. The impact of that scrutiny has been felt often and painfully in our town in recent years.

Back to the streets of Dewsbury. Less than 100 yards from my family's local social club, the Irish National Club in Westtown, and past where my mum used to walk my children to school at St Paulinus at the time, two gun-toting

Asian youths poured bullets into the front of a curry takeaway as their prey fled in through the front door and out the back.

A mile down the road in Ravensthorpe an immigrant lorry driver was shot in the leg and robbed in broad daylight by Asian youths. Up the valley two miles in Batley, a petrol bomb was thrown into a snooker hall, famously, openly a hotbed of drugs trading. A running gun-battle took place in nearby Staincliffe, straddling the border of Dewsbury and Batley.

But here's the 'news': not a single arrest was made in any of those cases. Not one. The BBC's Look North or ITV's Calendar cameras? Nowhere to be seen.

Coincidence, convenience or conspiracy? You decide.

But it has to be said in defence of the law enforcement agencies that complaints were rarely made by the injured parties or witness statements given. And if the victims won't give evidence, in truth, what chance do the police have? It's easy for me to say they were turning a blind eye, but even the harshest critic would have to confess that they were quite often literally between a rock and a hard place.

It didn't make it right, though. Not for honest, ordinary, hard-working Dewsbury people. Whatever the colour or the ethnicity of the criminals.

I KNEW of the social impact of drugs first hand, and I also knew that it was not an exclusively Muslim/Asian industry from a dealing point of view. Theirs was mostly but not exclusively – certainly as time, drug fashion and opportunity passed – a heroin-based enterprise.

But bigger urban areas, cities like Bradford and Leeds, were the more likely sources for cannabis, ecstasy or cocaine. In 1992, the year before I got the editor's job at the Dewsbury Reporter, while I was working on the Yorkshire

Evening Post in Leeds, I lived in a council flat opposite my mother's flat in Westtown, just outside the town centre.

My young upstairs neighbours – on the third floor, I was on the bottom floor – were wont to come to life about 3am and party until daylight. They didn't work and they didn't have carpets down, so the noise of their partying was loud and clear. God knows how the bloke in the flat directly between us coped. Days and weeks of increasingly fractured relations, of pleas for common courtesies and an attempt at discretion, ended about 5.30 one Friday morning in summer when in a desperately sleepless state, I'd had enough.

I'd been upstairs to their flat about 3.30am and asked politely for them to quieten down, but two hours later I stormed up the stairs, kicked their front door off its hinges, and threatened to throw a few of them off their balcony. Sleep deprivation will do that to you.

Hoping the message had registered I went back to my ground floor flat and tried to get back to sleep. More fool me. Minutes later the beat of hurried footsteps rumbled through the building and in what rapidly transformed into a scene from Night of the Living Dead, all kinds of characters suddenly started appearing from nowhere.

One bloke came running at me with an iron bar. I grabbed a golf club from behind my front door – a pissy little eight-iron as I recall – and charged back. He disappeared down the estate towards the Irish Nash with me in pursuit, as the zombie cast gathered behind me. I even remember waving to a puzzled neighbour as he left on his way to work an early shift. The flat. The front door's open, I suddenly recalled. Bugger. I hurtled back.

Within minutes, with a crowd of nocturnal creatures outside in attendance, my windows had been smashed and I was out on the communal grass area with the golf club in hand, having it out with four young men all in various states of high excitement.

I don't think it was just adrenaline.

Apart from the broken windows not a lot of damage was done because my assailants were unwilling to get within actual combat range, preferring to back off from my occasional charges – I was reluctant to stray too far from my front door – while they picked up stones, bricks, whatever came to hand, to pelt me with from a safe distance.

It must have been hilarious to witness, though not for my poor, panicked mother who, awoken to the incident like the rest of the neighbourhood, eventually called the police when I signalled to her from the grass that I was unlikely to get a good result here. I was quick enough – and furious enough – to get any one of the bastards, but that left three to go ransack my flat, plus their pals.

The police officers attended, the zombies disappeared whence they came, and having calmed matters the police gravely informed me that they were trying to talk my neighbours out of pressing charges.

Well, I was the aggressor you see! Shouldn't have remonstrated with them so! Threatening behaviour. Criminal damage to their flat door. And this conversation was had with the three of us sitting amidst the glass-strewn mess of my little one bedroom flat.

The officers weren't daft – I have invariably had a good working relationship with the coppers on the beat – and with a nod and a wink they suggested that I bring a few of my Dewsbury Celtic rugby teammates up to 'sort the problem out'.

For some reason it wasn't even tempting, because I couldn't see a reasonable result out of that course of action. My tenure at St John's Walk was at an obvious and abrupt end but there had to be a better way than a surreptitious group kicking for these scrotes. That merely propagated the bigger problem.

So although I was working at the Evening Post at the time I got my editor's permission and I wrote a front page, first person article for the Dewsbury Reporter describing exactly what had happened, naming names and addresses.

The outcome was that I was subsequently interviewed by the Drugs Squad, to whom I gladly gave my full co-operation. The girls hosting the party were not the root of the problem, that lay with lads living in another flat within our block. Their main supplier was not a local man, but a bloke apparently of Afro-Caribbean roots, who visited from time to time in a big expensive motor, probably but not necessarily from the Chapeltown or Harehills district of Leeds. These were recreational 'party' drug users, not heavy duty heroin addicts. I'd have had a quieter life with smackheads.

A few weeks later detectives advised me to visit my mum's flat early the next morning and sure enough, at about 7am, a door was kicked in once again – this time by the police – and the cretins inside, the low-level minor dealers, were hauled off to be dealt with properly. Evicted and prosecuted.

It was a good result, I'd say, though in the process I'd earned a reputation as a grass with some of the estate and the town's low lives which, as I mentioned earlier, was something I was to get used to over the coming years.

Back to my Common Purpose appearance and I gave them an abbreviated version of this narrative as I generally did, stressing always the crime, always the cost, never the ethnicity, except when it was used as a shield or as an alibi. And I generally concluded the session with this next story – one which did have a 'happy' ending of sorts.

One morning in late 2003 I got a call from an old family friend, Malcolm Foggin, sadly dead now. Malcolm lived with his wife in an immaculately kept council house on the Manor Way estate in Staincliffe, scarcely a mile or so from both Dewsbury and Batley town centres.

He asked me to come see him which I did and we sat in my car watching a council flat across the way, at 10am, doing a brisk business in selling wraps of drugs through the ground floor letter box.

It was as blatant, as brazen, as that. Ironically, just the previous Friday, we had carried in The Press the latest inquest of a local youth dead from a heroin overdose. The victim had lived in Staincliffe, a few hundred yards from where Malcolm and I sat.

Maybe he had bought his supplies here, though there was no shortage of purchasing options. But this took the public nature of the trade to ridiculous levels.

While sat there watching a few transactions and taking photographs of the purchasers coming and going – all young, white – I was briefed by Malcolm. The man who had the flat was an Asian in his 50s by the name of Yunus Shaikh. Co-habiting with him was a young girl from the neighbourhood, barely over 20-years-of age, Sheena Kelly. Her family were terribly anxious about the girl but didn't know what to do, or who to turn to.

The retail heroin trade itself wasn't what was troubling Malcolm and the other locals, common enough as that was, but the attention it was attracting. I noticed that all of the windows of the ground floor flat had been freshly boarded up. A car on the street outside had been firebombed.

It seemed Mr Shaikh was the recipient of some earnest and rather drastic attention from local business rivals and if things carried on, there was going to be a war on the streets of the Manor Way estate in which not only the guilty might get caught up.

So I walked across and knocked on the door, then bent to peer through the gaping mouth of a letterbox which seemed to have had the flap removed with just a grubby tea-towel draped over the inside.

"Who is it?" demanded a female voice from inside.

"Danny Lockwood from The Press," I said. "I'd like to speak to Mr Shaikh please about reports of a racist attack on his property." Well, as journalistic subterfuge goes, it's quite some way of the News of the World's celebrity phone hacking. It was worth a go.

"Fuck off," came the reply. End of conversation. For then at least.

Back in the office an hour or two later I got a phone call from the friend of Mr Shaikh who said he wanted to talk to me, yes he had been the victim of a racist attack and he was willing to go public with it. Put him on, I said to the female caller. Come and see him now, she said.

By that time, and because of the nature of the journalism we were pursuing at The Press and one or two barely veiled threats I'd received from the drugs community, I had a plain-clothes drug squad undercover officer's number on the speed dial of my mobile phone. I rang him and asked if it was safe to go see Yunus Shaikh who, it became clear, was very well known to the law. The advice was that I shouldn't go, but if I did I should have the redial button on my phone handy just in case the shit hit the proverbial fan.

I can still picture every detail of the inside of that flat – once the four or five massive deadbolts had been pulled back to let me in.

Yunus Shaikh was a wizened little man, looking older than his years, clad in traditional black clothing, sitting cross-legged on the floor in front of the worn out fireplace. I was seated on a sofa between two very large, silent and menacing young men, all muscles and dirty looks.

The broken glass from the vandalism attack of 36 hours previously was still scattered all over the place. No one had even bothered sweeping it up. The place was, excuse my French, a shithole. There was what looked like blood on the carpet, on the walls and – I couldn't understand how at the time – blood splattered on the ceiling too.

Later I would be informed that this probably resulted from people shooting up and spurting blood though I admit I can't quite get my head round that scenario. If it sounds like a horror story, then it surely looked like one.

Every now and again there would come a knock on the door but a young woman in the shadows – presumably the one who had spoken to me – would tell them to come back later. I wondered if she was Sheena Kelly but it was clear she wasn't, because right then Sheena walked – staggered – into the room and I had never seen anything quite like her.

She was clearly high as a kite and even more clearly at death's door. I couldn't tell you if she had been attractive once, but this young girl was all hollowed out skin and bones. Her eyes were upturned in her head, which was arched back as she stood unsteadily before us. She wore a thin little tee-shirt with no bra, and just a pathetic little pair of tribal dugs, rather than breasts.

Her belly was exposed and despite there being nothing of the girl, the flesh was a doughy, pastry-like white, all pocked and scarred, I presumed from injections but I don't know for sure. The insides of her arms were raddled with poorly healed needle marks, what looked to my untrained eye like collapsed veins. It was truly shocking.

And amidst all of this, Yunus Shaikh proceeded in his halting English to tell me how I was right, he was the victim of racist attacks, from people who not only wanted him out because of his ethnicity – despite the fact this was a very mixed neighbourhood – but that it was because they wanted his flat!

This, my friends, was a bona fide des-res! And he would appreciate my help in getting the authorities to clamp down on his persecutors. For some reason I didn't feel particularly threatened at all, despite the lumps of muscle on either side of me. I put it to Shaikh that that was bullshit, that he was dealing drugs, that I'd witnessed it myself, and that this was nothing more than a dangerous and rapidly getting out-of-control turf war.

In turn he demurred and insisted that he was some kind of relative of respected local Batley Labour councillor Shabir Pandor, that they hailed from the same village back in the Punjab or wherever, that he was the victim here, that I had a duty to help fight his battles. I should mention that Councillor Pandor furiously refuted any connection with Shaikh, however tenuous. That was by the by. Shaikh was never going to admit his activities but at least I'd asked the question. In the best traditions of the journalistic profession, I made my excuses and left.

I will never know which part of inviting a snooping journalist inside that flat seemed a good idea to Yunus Shaikh, but I'm glad that he did.

We ran the story with a full page picture of his flat and its boarded up windows, and of a customer walking away from a deal, under the headline 'Drugs Den', and carried an account not greatly different from what I've outlined.

If I was wrong then I was in a whole heap of trouble. The paper would probably be closed down and I'd be bankrupt. But I wasn't wrong.

Before publishing however I backed up the story a couple of ways. I will not hesitate to be harshly critical of Kirklees Council and especially its paid officers in this narrative; equally I can lavish only praise on some of its elected members and former Staincliffe woman and ex-Mayor of Kirklees councillor Margaret Bates is one such individual.

When I told Margaret what was going on and my fears for the health – the life – of Sheena Kelly, she was all over the case like a rash. I also dug around within my police contacts because whatever I might say corporately about the force in West Yorkshire, there is an abundance of damn good coppers who feel as frustrated by red tape and politics as I do. They are often a reporter's best friends – and vice versa.

It transpired the activities on Manor Way were not only common knowledge to the police but a handy source to be mined as required, like so many battery hens. Well, a drug arrest is a drug arrest! Why block the dam when you're measured by the bucket full?

At that time the divisional police had a drugs task force targeted with making a quota of arrests and the picture that emerged enraged me as much as Shaikh's activities.

It was never confirmed – nor would it be – but it seemed that the people doing their 'shopping' at that flat would be harvested as and when required, identified and picked up when it suited the community drugs team to chalk a few more low level arrests, while leaving the main source to carry on unimpeded.

What importance the monitoring of Shaikh took in a wider anti-drugs strategy I don't know, but police certainly knew that Sheena Kelly was using her body as a storage facility – yes, like that – for hers and Shaikh's drugs.

If there was a bigger investigative picture around Shaikh it was never shared with me and in the meantime local kids were dying of overdoses and Sheena Kelly didn't have long left either, if I was any kind of judge.

The story in The Press moved a number of things along at a precipitate rate, including one more visit from the characters so apparently keen to take on the tenancy of Shaikh's flat. On their next visit they ripped off the council-erected boarding from the windows, got inside and kicked him senseless, putting him in hospital for a while and inflicting a fractured skull. At least that's what I was told by police contacts.

Suddenly activities in the flat were closed down and the next thing I knew about the matter was when I received a letter from Her Majesty's Prison and Young Offenders

Institution New Hall, about seven miles from Dewsbury. It was from Sheena Kelly, starting a six year sentence for her part in the drug dealing.

In her letter the young woman tacitly thanked me for helping save her life. She had been through New Hall's drug treatment programme, was off the heroin, and despite her sentence was looking forward to the opportunity to rebuild her life. I don't have to tell you how immensely fulfilling that moment was. I never heard what sentence Shaikh got, but was told he was facing 10-12 years.

After receiving Sheena's letter I went through the hoops and over the jumps that the Home Office puts in front of people like me in order to try to visit her, but by the time the permission came through she'd been moved to a women's prison in Durham and I faced having to start the bureaucratic trail again which I never got round to.

I did write a feature on New Hall and its work with drug offenders in particular, but I didn't catch up with Sheena Kelly. She'll have been out of prison for some years now. I hope the kid's managing to steer clear of the heroin.

And that, in short, is what I told the members of Common Purpose: that the heroin trade in Dewsbury is run, virtually unchecked, by the Asian gangster community. I told them that they're probably responsible for 95% of the drug dealing in the district but that the police too often are institutionally afraid of the racism card and the implicit, tinderbox threat of another Bradford, Burnley or Oldham riot, another Savile Town.

I explained that I believed this to be criminality on a massive scale which happened to be hiding behind the race card and that our police won't even pretend to tackle it, because they're afraid of the repercussions; that because the perpetrators of this racket have brown skins and are Muslim, and because there is an unwritten, unstated, but clearly understood policy of appeasement by police, local authority and national government alike, that it prospers barely checked.

I explained that that was what The Press was trying to speak up against – criminality, not the colour of the criminal. I always felt good for making that speech, even if it generally made little impression on my audience.

And then on one memorable occasion I got the predictable response from one delegate of "it's ridiculous to say that the Asian community is responsible for 95 per cent of the heroin dealing, you can't possibly justify or qualify that."

Except on that occasion someone who definitely knew the precise situation was sitting quietly in the group and so I asked what he thought of my claim.

Under the protection of that forum – the words would never have passed his lips in public – he replied: "I'd say 95 per cent is wrong. It's probably nearer 98%."

And unforgivably, some time later I let slip that man's name against all the spirit of Chatham House and, professionally speaking, I still feel lousy about it. On that specific occasion however his observation not only shut my critic up, but it elicited one of the more remarkable responses I've experienced from such a gathering.

A middle aged woman, one of the more noticeably reticent members of the group, suddenly decided that she saw things rather differently. She admitted to being in the anti-Press and anti-Lockwood camp prior to the forum.

But then she opened up and told the group about her own 20-something son, who was struggling to hold down a job because of his heroin addiction.

She was middle class, had raised and schooled and disciplined her son well – as best she could – but he'd been sucked into the nightmarish blight of heroin like so, so many others. Working class, middle class, it doesn't even start to figure when this substance is on every street corner, at every school gate, at such ridiculously cheap prices.

Her boy had stolen cash, hocked the family video, anything of value that could be moved on for the next fix. It went on and on and on and it was a living nightmare for a family trying to live with the young man's sickness.

Through all of this the poor woman had hidden the burden of her shame. She imagined that theirs was a rare predicament. She suddenly saw that it wasn't just commonplace, that there were other people in her own community who were suffering in similar ways, but it was incredibly common – and either ignored or hidden away from public eyes. She said she saw what we was doing suddenly in a rather different light.

"It's rife!" I wanted to scream at the room. "It's bloody rife! And no one is doing anything about it because of WHO is doing it!"

But I didn't scream. I just thanked them for their time and counted that one mind changed as a victory worth all the occasional public scourging.

10 - ISSUES

MY LIFE AS a journalist, any journalist's life in a town like this, would be a whole lot easier without the criminal, religious and cultural issues within the Muslim/Asian community. It wouldn't be as 'newsy' that's for sure. We rarely struggle for front page stories in Dewsbury. But in terms of the external 'political' pressure brought to bear on an editor because of the sensitive ethnic/cultural/religious issues involved, it leaves no place for faint hearts. At least not if you intend doing the job right.

A diet of cheque presentations, notices from the Women's Institute, kiddies getting a visit from the Green Cross Code man ... that's the nice'n easy life for a weekly newspaper editor. That's what my peers fancifully get away with in Oxfordshire and Dorset, isn't it – a soft-bellied 'working' retirement? Maybe not. Either way, it would be so far removed from representing our town as to make the so-called newspaper not viable. Not professionally anyway.

Whether a weekly paper or the Sunday Times, I believe journalists have a duty to news. I like to think I've brought a few good youngsters through the system too. Daniel Martin on the Daily Mail, Duncan Gardham at the Telegraph, Richard Porritt on the newsdesk of the Evening Standard – they were all 'my' trainees, hopefully given a good grounding in the job, and waved on to better things with thanks and best wishes.

There's another important distinction to make in separating regional and community papers from the big boys, especially when the big stories hit, like Mohammed Siddique Khan, Karen and Shannon Matthews, or the 48-hour wonder that was played (by the police) as a repeat of the Jamie Bulger case, and turned out nothing of the sort.

That was a case where one Det (now Chief) Supt Andy Brennan briefed the world's media outside Dewsbury police station on how a five-year-old boy was lucky to be alive having been tortured and hung, first reportedly by a gang of children, then latterly when it was clear Brennan was chasing his tail on that line of inquiry, by a wicked 12-year-old girl acting alone.

Unlike the frenzied, bottle-fed national media, we never bought the hype.

The police wanted that child prosecuting for attempted murder for the 'hanging in Devil's Ditch'. I lived 400 yards from that 'Devil's Ditch'. It wasn't a name I'd heard attributed to it before or since. It was just a few trees alongside a well used piece of recreational land.

And what had actually happened was that the girl had got fed up of this little boy from her estate following her around – he was left to wander off alone at that tender age, mind – and she apparently tied him to a branch to stop him. He then got in a tangle and had minor rope burns round his neck.

I suppose it could have turned nasty, but it wasn't exactly the act of cold-blooded Satanism the police had appeared so keen at first to make out. A local magistrate struck magnificently by a rare outbreak of common sense refused to even send it to Crown Court and made the girl the subject of a care order.

That was a big difference and the case served to illustrate the chasm between being a journalist who has to work and live alongside the subjects of his stories, and the

Fleet Street glory boys who descend like locusts – this week Dewsbury, next week Birmingham etc etc – and disappear just as suddenly, leaving nothing behind except a few quid for the sources they buy and lots of residual ill feeling about journalists.

On that Devil's Ditch case I couldn't understand how the tv cameras and a select few national journalists could ever have discovered the location of where the little boy was found before we did, with our huge network of contacts.

I'm not saying some entrepreneurial officer was getting a drink out of it – that only happens in the Metropolitan Police, doesn't it? But someone tipped the tv boys off. That's just how it works.

We local newspapermen and women meanwhile have to live with the repercussions of what we write. It focuses the mind, especially after you've got it wrong a few times. And I know I have over the years.

In terms of social criminality, as mostly vividly illustrated here, the reference is to a drugs-based black economy which I would estimate has cost far more lives in our district alone than Mohammed Siddique Khan and his conspirators took on July 7, 2005 in London. And yet it flies under the public radar, day in day out, week in, week out, year in, year out. It endures today, largely unchecked.

And then there is the religious criminality, the long-term project to subvert British democracy, to carry on the quest for a global caliphate, to Islamify this nation not with bombs or revolution – although they are handy tools of influence and manipulation, as the IRA so successfully proved – but by the creeping subjugation of our timid political leadership. That tends to be a subject pontificated on by far more esteemed Fleet Street writers than we hacks on the ground in Dewsbury.

But such as 'big' subjects present themselves within the newspaper context, like July 7th 2005, they are relatively straightforward to judge as an editor. News is news.

Where the water gets pretty cloudy is in 'newsifying' events that populate the chasm of a cultural gap between two communities with nothing whatsoever in common.

That's a journalistic tightrope and you can't not fall off occasionally.

British Islam by definition and long experience is rather easily offended and has an entire support network and race industry straining at the leash to wrap themselves in the cloak of that vicarious indignation, prod another finger in British establishment's chest, and smirk as another step backwards is taken in retreat.

But what about when the roles are reversed? When the habits, expectations and plain ignorant behaviour of the Muslim community offends our sensibilities? Who do people complain to? At least, who do they complain to that will: a) listen, or b) act upon their concerns?

The police don't want to know unless lives are lost, and even then they step hurriedly backwards to make way for the Regional Crime Squad.

The local authority, health authority, they are all institutionally reverse-racist to listen to many frustrated residents – whether those organisations recognise it of themselves or not.

I can't speak for your town or city. It seems in most places the only people willing to listen are the recruiting sergeants for the BNP and now the EDL, and that doesn't get anyone anywhere. In Dewsbury and Batley and Mirfield and Heckmondwike, for some years now people have been able to pick up the phone and speak to the local paper.

We might not be able to right their wrongs, but we can give them a voice. That's where the judgment calls on what is 'news' require an acute ability and sixth sense to separate plain prejudice from legitimate complaint.

I don't pretend to have made the right call on every

single occasion and it does not lend itself to an easy life.

In a wider context I can't for the life of me suggest how best to bridge that cultural divide other than to leave the two respective communities in peace and allow time to blur the edges; allow some mutuality of understanding and respect to grow from the roots up.

You certainly can't impose tolerance and respect, especially if your default position is to keep beating your own breast in post-colonial guilt, pretending that everything is 'our' own fault and that no blame exists in the explicitly patronised minority community.

Unfortunately for everyone in Dewsbury the social engineers of the liberal left haven't the kind of patience to wait generations for communities to learn to live with each other. And in a local authority that's as driven by Political Correctness as Kirklees Council, it has the worst kind of stormtrooper.

The message that has been shoved continually down the throats of Dewsbury's majority white populace is that it is they who must change, who must sacrifice, who must be made to concede, to respect, to turn the other cheek.

It is incredibly patronising and it is generally a volunteered favouritism of the ethnic community rather than an elicited one – but it is a measure of the self-righteousness of the liberal left that they don't even see the condescending irony. It has also, after many long years in existence, bred a level of expectation and self-entitlement among the migrant community that I don't think can be undone.

No cash price has been too high for initiatives aimed at buying the favour of the ethnic minority, no blind eye too blatantly applied to unacceptable behaviour on so many levels.

Let me give you a simple example of how tolerant, ordinary citizens' heads are turned 'racist'. How people arrive at the dinner table or the public bar and start with "I'm not racist but..."

My wife is not from Yorkshire, let alone Dewsbury. She was born in the south-east and raised in north Wales, then spent most of her adult working life back in London, moving to my home town after we married and before the birth of our son.

When our second child was due two years later my wife, being a mum approaching 40, was advised to take the amniocentesis test to check on the well being of the foetus which she duly did.

We had a boy, and for whatever reason my wife decided she would like to know the sex of her second child which a regular scan might not definitively reveal, but which the tests she'd subsequently had certainly would.

We were told by the staff at Dewsbury District Hospital that it was against their corporate policy to impart such information. When we asked why, we were told that it was because the tests could not be 100% accurate and they were not willing to take that chance.

You're not taking that chance, we are, we insisted. We wish to know. My wife was uncharacteristically furious. It is my body, my child, the tests are on my body. I wish to know. Back came the patronising shake of the head.

Except the small risk of an inaccurate scan was not the reason this information was withheld, not at all. At least it wasn't if the nurses and doctors who worked within the Health Trust and who had told me the reasons behind the policy were to be believed.

In the south Asian community, female births are valued much less than male births and there was compelling anecdotal evidence within this health authority that the diagnosis of female births led to an inordinately high proportion of 'unsuccessful' pregnancies and terminations.

Again, my own re-telling of this is by its very nature

anecdotal because it was tacitly impossible to get anyone within the health trust hierarchy to even discuss it. If it wasn't true, no one in authority would take the opportunity to disabuse the public notion of it.

In the instance of my wife's scans and the dogmatic stance of the health professionals I demanded to see the hospital chief executive Roger French, a man I knew and liked through our professional dealings. I also knew that he was in his office – I'd seen him a little earlier. He duly came over to the maternity unit to speak to us.

What followed was an uncomfortable – for him – five minutes during which I voiced my theory about the unofficial reasons for non-disclosure, my wife insisted she cared sod-all about that but wanted to know about her pregnancy, and he hummed and ahhhd and shuffled his feet before deciding on a means for a possible get-out.

He couldn't, wouldn't, change hospital policy, but if our GP rang the private company in Leeds which processed the tests for the NHS, then they could pass on the information. We subsequently discovered she was expecting a healthy baby girl.

But the fact that we were in Dewsbury Hospital's maternity unit at all was due to my long-suffering wife's tolerant nature, given her experiences during the birth of our son. That the little mite made it to full term was testament to his neo-natal doggedness in itself. We nearly lost him several times in the early stages of the pregnancy when my wife was in the care of King's Hospital in South London – she was still working at the Daily Express.

When his time came the little feller wasn't leaving the warmth of mum's tummy so after an inducement and 20-odd hour labour, and with signs of the baby's heartbeat becoming irregular, an emergency caesarian was swiftly and expertly carried out. We both have nothing but the highest praise for the medical care involved.

The maternity wards at Dewsbury District are never less than busy and it is a matter of cultural fact that the proportion of Asian deliveries was and is far, far higher than within the indigenous population.

I read in the Sunday Times a while back that between 1991 and 2001 the Indian population in Dewsbury increased by 25% and the Pakistani by 60%, a combination of prolific birthrates and imported spouses and relatives. That growth rate has not diminished in the intervening years and the pressure on the health service is immense.

After the birth of our son my wife was on an open ward and the mother in the next bed was an Asian woman. Witnessing the differences in approaches to new motherhood was instructive in itself but dispiriting in the context of this work. We were doting parents, fascinated by every coo and cry of this little miracle. Visiting times were awaited with eager anticipation, the hospital rule of no more than two visitors per bed strictly adhered to.

It became quickly clear that the mum in the adjacent bed had neither care nor concern for her own child. Its cries were ignored, there was no attempt to feed or change it – the nurses were regarded as hired help to assist this infant through its first days while the mum got some rest. But that was something and nothing really. Not our problem.

More galling was the total disregard for any hospital rules by her family – a situation we saw was incredibly common, and simply tolerated with a resigned shrug by the hospital staff. Her visitors, always and exclusively men it seemed, turned up whenever they wanted, in as many numbers as they cared to see fit. Two to a bed? I saw six on more than one occasion.

But it was this habit of turning up when they wanted, sitting there silently round the bed, that eventually caused the greatest offence.

My wife, like most new mums, wanted to feed her child

herself and, like many, had struggled initially to get her baby to 'latch' onto her nipple, but she persevered and succeeded and took great pride in this most natural of acts. And then one afternoon – out of visiting times so I wasn't there – as she fed her son, she became uncomfortably aware of furniture being moved.

She looked up from her baby's face to find the host of men round the adjacent bed had brazenly turned their chairs round to enjoy the sight of a white woman's exposed breast. I'm not saying that was their sole reason for being there – the opportunity to ogle other women's breasts – but I couldn't tell you why they did visit, and at such inopportune times. I never heard them speak to the mother they were visiting. The child was generally in a side room being cared for by nurses. If anyone has a better explanation I'd be glad to hear it.

My wife couldn't get out of that hospital fast enough and it's probably a good job that I wasn't present when the peepshow incident occurred, but then again if I had been, or if any other father had been, I severely doubt that it would have happened at all.

We complained to the hospital staff, as you would expect, and we received the default, disconsolate reply that characterises all such incidents across the entire landscape of cultural exchanges in a town like Dewsbury – that familiar shrug of the shoulders, raised eyebrows and cursory "what can you do?" or an occasional "we've mentioned it to management but we're told to be tolerant to avoid being called racist".

As so often, the default position, the creeping retreat from a culture with alien values to ours, was maintained and strengthened not by its own proponents but by the gutless white, liberal management class of middle Britain.

If you don't tell a child its behaviour is unacceptable, if you don't then demonstrate and enforce the rules within its environment, you cannot expect it to learn what is and isn't acceptable. And you certainly can't complain when you find you've brought up a monster.

Not by any massive policy campaign, or high philosophical commitment, but by a thousand tiny acceptances of unacceptable behaviour, of a thousand tiny steps backward that translate eventually to a fully fledged rout, has this irreconcilable division in a town been created.

For too many otherwise 'reasonable' people that's the corner they find themselves backed into – passing harsh comment about the unacceptable behaviour of people who do not share their civilised sensitivities and worse, regard them with scorn.

That isn't simply what's happening in towns like Dewsbury. It's too late. It's already happened. That is one relatively minor example of why the divide between cultures is widening, but there are hundreds. Every single day.

When Sayeeda Warsi says that Islamophobia has passed the dinner table test, I believe she has neglected the wider point – that the tentacles of this foreign culture has impinged so far on their lives, and offended their sensibilities, that it's become commonplace to discuss it.

Whose fault is that?

11 – STREET POLITICS

IT IS TIME to introduce new characters to the subplot of the Islamification of Dewsbury, most of them of Pakistani or Indian Muslim heritage, many of them characters I consider good people, well meaning people.

Most were born overseas but have lived here for the majority of their lives. Through them can be witnessed many of the issues which beguile anyone trying to make sense of the mass of contradictions that are interwoven within what Shahid Malik termed 'Paki Politics'.

In the summer of 1989 at the time of the Dewsbury riot, only one of the nine elected councillors representing the town, part of the 72 in total who made up Kirklees Council based in Huddersfield, was of non-British origin and he was an Indian Hindu with less in common with the burgeoning Muslim population than the local Rabbi – not that I think the town has one.

If respected local GP, Dr Hanume Thimmegowda was a 'token' councillor, he couldn't have been much less representative. He was also an early casualty in the political power game. I wouldn't mind hazarding a guess that some BNP candidates actually received more Muslim votes than Dr Thimmegowda at times. And yes, you would be amazed how many ordinary Asian people subscribe to the BNP stance on immigration!

For the very many who consider this 'their' country (even if not sufficiently to fly the Union flag) the recent influxes of displaced Iraqis and their middle eastern cousins, then economic migrants from eastern Europe, has brought nothing but trouble.

Why aren't the government doing something about it, they regularly call. You have to smile, when their appeals, like others' before them, fall on multi-culturally deaf ears.

So many of my Asian/Muslim friends cannot understand what our (British) problem is with enforcing our laws and standing up for our traditions, our culture. In the meantime however they'll happily and quietly continue to benefit from our munificence, our institutionally patronising weakness. More fools us, they conclude. But not in public of course.

Observing the strategies and events that characterise the growing Islamic influence, both with a large and small political 'p' says much about the changes we have witnessed.

The role of spokesman for the Kirklees Black Workers Group, arguably the faction indirectly responsible for the violence on Saturday June 24th 1989, was a hitherto largely anonymous man by the name of Khalid Hussain, chairman of the group. Hussain's platitudes in response to criticisms of the public meeting were very politically adept. He said the Dewsbury 59 Defence Campaign was not a pressure group to subvert justice, but merely an attempt to invite helpful witnesses to come forward. Barely plausible, but hardly inflammatory.

And Hussain himself was playing a far longer game than Councillor Jack Brooke could foresee from his position atop the local authority's Equal Opportunities Committee whose remit was admirably woolly.

That body was eventually replaced 'independently' by the Kirklees Racial Equalities Committee (KREC), complete with substantial new local and central government funding

– a response not just to any civil unrest but also a marker of the new age of Politically Correct 'equality'.

Khalid Hussain would emerge first as member, then director and ultimately Chief Executive of this quietly powerful and – for my money at least – dangerous quango; dangerous not in its apparent purposes, but in the nature of the people who effectively controlled it from a decidedly biased political perspective.

KREC was intended to be a voice of moderation but became the blunt instrument of the left-wing race zealots. At least that was my experience, if only from the times they attempted to have me prosecuted or censured for publishing stories that did not meet their approved agenda.

With that first show of Islamic militancy in any kind of organised fashion in Dewsbury in 1989, a tone had been set. Furious accusations of racism against police and politicians, despite an absolute absence of evidence to support the criticisms, would become the day-to-day norm, the default response.

Notwithstanding words from people like Geoff McGill that resonated with most reasonable people's thinking, local Muslims were on the march, and not just metaphorically.

The predictable, but effective, wailed cry of 'racist!' while not exactly a part of the daily call to prayer across the town's mosques, became the mantra of Muslims' social and political bartering. It was that crude, and that simple – and it worked.

Angry young men involved in a variety of either criminal or merely anti-social enterprises accused the police – accused anyone in a form of authority – of racial harassment. It became the virtual shield of Dewsbury's rocketing heroin industry, almost exclusively owned, managed and laundered by the Pakistani Muslim population.

Certainly the police and Labour MP Ann Taylor (until

she resigned in 2005) never visibly took on the 'community' again after 1989, though for vastly different reasons. For Taylor it was a starkly political expedient. The Muslim community, as compact and internally malleable as it was, was one huge reservoir of voting power to be tapped almost en bloc.

From the political heights looking down it also appeared at the time to have a natural working class (and benefits class) affinity for Labour, though years and experience have shown that its loyalties are influenced less by economic factors than racial/religious influence.

Certainly 'party politics' as most of us understand that concept doesn't come much into consideration in manipulating the Muslim vote. It's the main reason why the naïve Shahid Malik, however well intentioned he might have been, couldn't possibly avoid being dragged into 'Paki Politics'.

Under any social indices you cared to measure, from health to education to unemployment, the south Asian community was plum bottom of the list at that time.

The Irish had probably fit the same profile in their day, the difference being that in the 19th century there hadn't been such a sophisticated means of identifying and communicating with such a targeted part of the populace.

There probably wasn't the central means to publicly bribe the Irish vote with social funding and favours and, given their background and history, it is no surprise anyway that Dewsbury's Irish Catholics developed a long and proud tradition within the Labour party.

But towards the end of the 20th century the south Asian community could be manipulated into voting almost en bloc with the mosques crucial to the strategy. In this instance Labour got the jump in Dewsbury, at least initially, on mobilising the Muslim vote.

The Tories and Lib Dems were not far behind however –

with at times almost comical outcomes. The democracy founded in part on the fields of Thornhill Hall 300 years before by Cromwell's Roundheads was set to enter a disgraceful, discredited age.

For the police, a policy of non-confrontation would ripple ever outwards as a central theme, even before the Stephen Lawrence sea-change when the service became paranoid with the idea that it might be institutionally racist.

West Yorkshire got its fingers burned in 1989 with the Rushdie protests, but by the time of Oldham, Burnley and Bradford's civil disorder a dozen years later, the police had already been scared witless when it came to policing large scale Muslim enclaves. From the summer of 1989 the bodies of authority, political and judicial alike, were on the back foot. Certainly in our neck of the woods

In any study like this, it is difficult for the author to appropriately discern whether the adjective 'Muslim' or 'Asian' is most appropriate, let alone Pakistani, Indian or Bangladeshi, or even Hindu/Sikh. There are few Bangladeshis in our district and although the Pakistani/Indian split is around 3:1 the Indian population tends to be from the predominantly Muslim region of Gujarat, which shares its north-west border with Pakistan.

I lean towards the Islamic description because in my experience it has been the influence of religion that has increasingly dictated the groundswell of activism, and which most fittingly reflects the background of the people involved. It's also a description which has become more valid in recent years as Islam has become more of a self-definition from within the community itself.

The increasingly Muslim domination of all aspects of life in Dewsbury would never prove to be solely or even expressly political in nature. It wouldn't even appear recognisably co-ordinated, on a day to day basis. The realisation of where we've ended up only dawns when the sum total of events are regarded from a distance.

My starting point has been taken from June 24th 1989 and from that day it has been a gradual accumulation of influence and concession. No huge earthquake this, but a thousand tremors; no master plan that I could describe, just an inexorable forward march with no opportunity missed to put the ever-retreating, always appeasing authorities on the defensive.

This became an attitude which would pervade every aspect of Dewsbury life, from commerce, law enforcement and politics to sport; from the freedom to write criticism of it, to the freedom to walk certain areas of the town in safety. By the time that one or two sensible, reasoned voices emerged from Savile Town's Pakistani community, calling for an end or at least a curtailing of the Politically Correct madness that had paralysed any rational debate, the damage would be well and truly done.

There were and are such voices and I'll celebrate them in due course, but they are largely voices in the wilderness.

KIRKLEES Council reduced its number of councillors from 72 to 69 with a ward restructuring a few years ago. Dewsbury is still represented by nine councillors in three wards; Dewsbury East, the redoubt of both working and middle class white families, which has three Labour representatives, two white men and a white woman, currently all Labour.

It had a BNP councillor for a while but Colin Auty, a hugely entertaining bloke and a thoroughly good amateur football and rugby player in his day, had a massive fall-out when he tried to challenge the national party leader Nick Griffin, was on the metaphorical end of a good old National Front-style kicking, and subsequently resigned his seat.

I recall the election count at Dewsbury Sports Centre

when Colin, to his astonishment, found that he had been voted in by the people of Dewsbury East, ousting a popular Labour councillor. I was up on the viewing balcony and took a photograph of Colin.

"What now?" I asked. He raised his palms and shrugged his shoulders and eyebrows, struggling not to laugh at the absurdity of it all. "Lord knows!" he replied.

Colin, a self-employed painter and decorator, hadn't canvassed at all during the election campaign. "I don't need to," he explained. "The other candidates are doing my canvassing for me with the tripe they're spouting."

He described himself as "completely non-political" and "certainly not racist" telling me on one occasion in our office reception, "I'm just the bloke standing at the end of the bar, pissing and moaning about the mess we're in. And I just decided that instead of complaining in the pub all the time I should stand up make my voice heard."

I don't think Colin ever really considered himself typical BNP fare, hence his eventual fracturing with them, but as a nice bloke who would help a Muslim constituent every bit as readily and wholeheartedly as anyone else, he never did come to terms with the rank hatred he experienced not from the ethnic minority, but from fellow white mainstream politicians and their bureaucratic affiliates.

He saw himself as an ordinary bloke trying to stand up for anti-PC common sense and in protest at a town being taken away from him and his family. He was nonplussed when virtually everyone else within the world he entered was interested only in painting him as a Nazi thug.

Colin's moments in the public spotlight reached their zenith in March 2007 when he wrote a song for his Irish band, Red Claire. The song sniped at the perceived loss of British ideals and berated the Savile Town community particularly as a place rife with "smack" and even hinted at paedophilia within its streets.

As a result MP Shahid Malik accused Auty of being guilty of deplorable behaviour and complained to the local authority watchdog, the Standards Board for England.

Malik claimed the choice of song was akin to that of a preacher of hate, saying: "The straightforward message behind the lyrics is that Savile Town is populated by foreigners who do not speak English. That it is a place where residents openly sell heroin and that these people are paedophiles."

He added: "As an elected member, Auty is in a position of responsibility, trust and authority and by writing and performing lyrics such as these he is bringing his position and suitability into disrepute and question.

"Councillor Auty has fallen so far beneath the required mark that I felt it was my duty to refer the matter to the Standards Board to investigate."

The local BNP organiser Nick Cass, now long estranged from Auty, defended it thus: "It has come to our attention that Dewsbury MP Shahid Malik has contacted the Standards Board and submitted a press release to newspapers and radio stations about a song which was printed in the BNP's newspaper the Voice of Freedom, written and produced by BNP Councillor Colin Auty. The song is a generalisation of what has happened to Dewsbury and the rest of Britain in the wake of mass immigration.

"It points out how British culture and the British way of life has been replaced in certain areas by another culture from another country. It is about how mass immigration creates a country within our country and replaces our ideals and heritage. We make no apologies for this song as every word in it is true, and can back up with argument any of the points raised within the song. If Mr Malik would like to contact us we will even sing it to him."

In fact in what probably wasn't the smartest move he ever made – at least in the cause of a peaceful life – Colin

Auty and a pal went to video themselves singing the song across the road from Shahid Malik's constituency office in Dewsbury town centre – a mere 30 yards from The Press offices.

The fall-out included Malik's staff describing how they cowered with fear, intimidated by this race-hate act of provocation – a claim frankly hilarious to anyone familiar with the geography or the characters involved.

Malik's office has, or had, just a small hatch opening onto the public area. It was a surprise his staff were even aware of the two men and video cameraman across the street.

Even so, Terry McKay, a Socialist Workers Party and anti-fascist activist with a long and proud history of running battles with the BNP and National Front, and a public order conviction of his own, hardly fit the bill of being a trembling victim.

He became socially rehabilitated as Malik's PR man, though quietly basking in his pseudo-anarchist credentials as 'Tegs' McKay. I still see McKay most weeks and he clearly models himself on 'Citizen Smith' of the 1970s sit-com starring Robert Lindsay. Bit of a tosser is McKay, if you must know.

Neither the typical 'victim' was Paul Moore, Malik's right-hand henchman who he brought to Dewsbury with him from Burnley, another staunch anti-BNP activist who lived midweek in Malik's 'second home' in the town – one of the various second homes Malik flipped for expenses purposes in the space of one term in Westminster. The Standards Board eventually dismissed the complaint about Colin Auty as he had been acting in a private capacity.

When Colin and the BNP's ways finally parted the seat reverted to a Labour representative. The far right party did try to defend it through the BNP's district organiser Nick Cass but he fell well short. The point I took from the process was that Colin Auty had been a well known local bloke who people could relate to. Electing him hadn't been about a radical shift to the right, but opting for a trustworthy carrier of the protest vote.

It is to the BNP's frustration, and possibly bewilderment, that having seen three councillors voted onto Kirklees Council during a purple patch around the time that Shahid Malik came to Dewsbury, they have all lost their seats and their aggregate share of the popular vote has dropped.

Such as an explanation for that could exist, or one of many, may be witnessed via the thoughts of my pal Pat Kane. Pat and I used to stand and have a natter in the playground at St Paulinus school, me picking up my two children, he awaiting his granddaughter.

Pat liked to have a drink in the Flatt Top pub in Thornhill and – perhaps surprisingly to some readers – the regulars used to sit around and talk politics. Many of these men were ex-miners, some still carrying the scars of the fateful 80's strike. And a group of them made a 'policy' decision on which way to vote, to influence local issues as best they could.

In 2005, when the BNP in Dewsbury recorded the highest vote in the UK, these men had decided they would show their displeasure by casting their en bloc vote to the BNP. None, I would hasten to add and certainly not Pat Kane, were what you would describe as typical right-wingers; all of them more Labour voters if we're trying to apportion a stereotype.

Some time later, looking ahead to the next General Election of 2010, Pat intimated that his de facto voters' club was likely to change tack. They despised what Shahid Malik had brought to the town but their protest vote of 2005 had been to no avail, real or imagined, so it looked like they would be swaying behind the blue rosette of the Conservatives.

However you measure their influence, they got the outcome they sought. And eventually, my views on the protest-rooted qualities of the BNP seemed to come to pass. Early in 2011 the rump of the Dewsbury and district BNP membership resigned en masse and went off to join the fledgling English Democrats party.

They had had enough of Nick Griffin's vile bile, and the local electorate had had enough of them. They'd hung around long enough to see off their bete noire Shahid Malik, but in Dewsbury and Batley at least, the BNP were a spent force. 'White' Dewsbury East then, has three white Labour councillors.

THORNHILL and Thornhill Lees lie in the electoral ward of Dewsbury South which includes Savile Town and now has three Muslim councillors, one Labour, one Tory and one who was Tory, switched to Independent and who has since reverted to the Tories. Dewsbury West, which includes the heavily Muslim populated districts of Scout Hill and Ravensthorpe, also had three Muslim councillors, two Liberal Democrat and one Labour, until the local elections of May 2011, when a white member of the Irish Catholic community, and son of a former Mayor, ousted a Lib Dem Asian councillor.

Although still a minority population in the town the Muslim community has had a disproportionate impact on the political landscape over recent years. Their influence will only continue to increase as the years pass, not just through population numbers but assisted by the ability to mass-mobilise the community's vote.

Their turn out is regularly (and admirably from a sense of exercising your franchise) higher than in other wards. This is a factor the politically-active within the Muslim areas are acutely aware of and adept at manipulating.

Of those six Muslim councillors at the time of the last general election only two represented Labour, and yet in an express example of how this manipulation works, the ethnic vote came out overwhelmingly for Labour's Shahid Malik.

Democratic? Yes, even if not in a party-political way that we would prefer or expect our Parliamentary system to be characterised. Local affiliation to Lib Dem or Tory – or in the case of a major local political character, Tory-turned-Independent-turned-Tory councillor Khizar Iqbal – counted for nothing when Malik was trying to win the seat after replacing Ann Taylor as candidate in 2005.

It was the same again in the General Election of 2010 when he faced the white Conservative candidate Simon Reevell, local Lib Dem businessman Andrew Hutchinson, and newly Independent candidate Khizar Iqbal. The ethnic vote fell in four-square behind Malik on both occasions because the politics of race and religion trump those of notional secular interests every time.

As Malik himself described it, 'Paki Politics' – but only in its mildest sense. There is nothing wrong with mobilising a section of the electorate that I'm aware of, at least when the tactics are within election law – although that isn't always the case.

Khizar Iqbal is one of the longest standing councillors to emerge from the midst of the Muslim community and he was, until the run up to the 2010 elections, a staunch Conservative. Well I say staunch. That he held a completed Labour Party application at the time he opted to become a Tory is not shocking, at least not in local terms of political reference.

A character like Khizar – a man I consider a personal friend and a thoroughly good ward councillor – has a currency in a town like ours akin to a Wayne Rooney or a John Terry in football. Chelsea (Conservatives) and Manchester United (Labour) will barter for his valuable services based not on his political principle, but on his personal sway in 'the community'; the replica shirts he can sell, to maintain the metaphor.

The only thing you can count on is that he won't be signing for Norwich City (Lib Dems) who might be good for a council seat in the areas where their influential personalities hold sway – Scout Hill, Ravensthorpe – but will never break through to the Champions League of Westminster candidacy. Lib Dems have finished as low as fourth behind the BNP in Dewsbury in general elections, however well they have fared in the local council seats.

Khizar opted for the blue rather than the red ticket, just as his former friend and political protégé Baroness Sayeeda Warsi did some years later. The Baroness, anointed as Conservative Party chairman and Minister without Portfolio in 2010 by David Cameron, is a chapter all of her own in Dewsbury's murky political story.

She too, like Khizar, angsted over which way to jump before entering politics in 2003, before wisely – for her career at least, if not the good of the town she so publicly espouses love for – choosing blue over red.

Khizar Iqbal was a crucial character in the libel trial of myself and The Press against Shahid Malik, both as a witness to the events that took place during campaigning for the local elections in Savile Town in 2006, and as the one councillor with far and away the most popular public support in Dewsbury – and not just amongst Muslims either.

If the common-sense white majority needs a vociferous champion it need not look so far to the right as the BNP – in fact no further than mild-mannered Khizar Iqbal. In 2003 Khizar stood up in the Kirklees Council chamber and made a speech which virtually brought the house down.

He received that rarest of things in such a generally petty, factional and always combative and tribal political arena – a standing ovation from members of all parties.

Scathing of the influence and indeed the existence of bodies like the Black and Ethnic Minority Police Forum, and with his then-Tory colleague Imtiaz Ameen critical of the very existence of second-language assistants in classrooms (they wanted English-only spoken) Khizar voiced a stand for social and fiscal common sense, but also a courageous truth.

He told the council chamber that if a white councillor stood up and spoke his words they would be denounced as racist. He declared that it was time this absurd political correctness, this fear of addressing the tough issues of the day, stopped. That it was damaging, not mending, community relations. It was a masterstroke for his personal political credibility, if nothing else.

Our newspaper The Press acclaimed Khizar as a hero for real, progressive modern politics, of drawing a pathway for improved community relations, of a leader to show everyone in the town the way. We re-printed his speech in full over two pages. It was brave, it was timely, it was certainly populist and, if you will pardon my French once more, unfortunately it was pissing into the wind.

The vested interests of the race industry, the massive neo-political machinations of an entrenched liberal bureaucracy, were never going to be diverted from their self-promoting causes so easily, so casually.

There was and is too much money and power involved in the multi-cultural project. The voice of one man and his friends against cynical party machines and vested interests compounded the size of an already Herculean task. Khizar remains a good man nonetheless.

To this day I hear of few people, of any colour or creed, who speak much of a word against Khizar Iqbal. He wanted desperately to stand against Shahid Malik at the 2010 general election after Sayeeda Warsi had tried and failed dismally for the Tories in 2005.

As she sagely remarked afterwards, Dewsbury might be ready for a Muslim MP, but certainly not a female Muslim MP, nor two Muslim candidates.

Warsi experienced at first hand the inherent deceits of her own community. Her closest friends effectively lied to her face. Members of her own party, at least those of her own ethnic background, were the worst.

They campaigned with her – on the face of things – but many did not even vote for her. Emancipation is some way from being reality for the Muslim women of Dewsbury notwithstanding the Baroness's personal milestones, although there's little sympathy from my perspective.

A woman I would once have called 'friend'. Not now.

Warsi would later petition the grandfather of the UK's youngest ever convicted terrorist for a Sharia divorce, in Dewsbury's long established Sharia court. She was cute enough at quietly playing the Muslim community game when it suited her needs, but in politics the odds of success in such a male-dominated culture were stacked massively against her.

The Tories picked Warsi to run in 2005 because they naively imagined she might split the ethnic vote, while benefitting from the rank unpopularity of Labour among the white community in general in 2005. And even though Muslim, she was 'our' Muslim, born and bred in the town. That had to count for something too, didn't it? They were wrong on all counts.

With Warsi suddenly plucked from the ignominy of electoral failure into the senior Tory hierarchy – and later elevated to the House of Lords – by Michael Howard and David Cameron, both eager not to lose the wider public benefits of an intelligent and articulate Muslim woman, the door was open for a new candidate back home.

Khizar Iqbal got nowhere in trying to win the

nomination for the Conservatives for the Dewsbury seat, even when in late 2008 the incumbent Prospective Parliamentary candidate, Kevin Hollinrake, had to stand down for personal reasons. The rush was on to find a replacement and Khizar desperately wanted it.

However like so many first generation south Asian politicians, he is occasionally let down by either his verbal or written grasp of English. Twice he took the Tories' Parliamentary board exams, and twice he failed. A campaign grew to get him special dispensation.

Pleas were entreated to Baroness Warsi herself, at the very summit of the Conservative hierarchy, to pull a couple of strings and let Khizar loose on Malik – with his local links and his massive support within Savile Town he could hole Malik beneath the waterline.

That was the perception in some quarters, if not widely shared in others, but then again the importance of the mass-Muslim vote had taken on an inflated life of its own. The pleas fell on deaf ears. Whether personal or not, Dewsbury men were not getting any kind of a helping hand from Sayeeda Warsi in the battle to unseat Shahid Malik, where she had failed.

In light of that Khizar, closely advised and supported by my libel co-defendant, ex-Dewsbury South Tory councillor Jonathan Scott, decided to give up the Tory whip, go Independent on Kirklees Council and further to stand as an Independent at the general election.

Several theories abound on their motivations. Khizar felt let down by the Tory hierarchy, but perhaps also overestimated his local influence. Scott was undoubtedly ill-favoured towards Malik and although I doubt that he imagined Khizar could unseat him, if he could keep his own popular Muslim vote, traditionally massive for him in Savile Town, then he would damage the incumbent MP's campaign, possibly fatally. That was clearly what Malik surmised to be their agenda, in the aftermath of his defeat.

In contributing to the ousting of Shahid Malik, Khizar succeeded at least nominally insomuch as his 3,813 votes could be construed as being the difference between success and failure for Malik, whose 17,372 votes fell short of matching the white Tory candidate Simon Reevell's mark of 18,898.

Equally, it could be analysed that as a popular Tory, and given the rancour of shenanigans within the local Conservative Party which subsequently saw most of the executive disintegrate, Khizar may even have been taking hardcore Tory votes away from them, rather than Malik.

I suspect the latter to be true, evidenced by the distraught look on Khizar Iqbal's face at the election count, where box after box of Savile Town votes piled up overwhelmingly on behalf of Malik.

Khizar's people had promised him their support to his face. As with Sayeeda Warsi five years previously, they lied. My only surprise was that Khizar was surprised; as someone who had benefited in the past from such flighty and malleable allegiances, he should have known better.

Jonathan Scott had been Dewsbury South's last white councillor until losing his seat in 2006. It was in that campaign when he and Khizar Iqbal were publicly accosted by one of Malik's closest allies – the uncle of a convicted terrorist – while campaigning.

It was on that election day that Scott stood helpless on the streets of Savile Town and witnessed overt corruption at the polling booth; that day when he was threatened and intimidated in the street by young Muslim men, that the seeds were sown of our libel battle with Malik.

THAT LEAVES the third local ward of Dewsbury West. Muslim candidates first stood in Dewsbury in 1992 when the Lib Dems put up two for local elections to Kirklees in Mohammed Razaq and Fiaz Baig. Both failed to win a seat but in a precursor of what was regularly to come, Razaq was promptly 'poached' by a much-travelled Labour councillor and local Mr Fixit, David Beetham, who seized on the opportunity to manipulate Razaq's standing in the smaller, more compact Muslim community of Scout Hill.

Thus equipped with the red rose and a brazen political expedience that has come to characterise his countrymen's approach to politics, Razaq was elected onto Kirklees Council with a Labour ticket for Dewsbury West.

His wasn't to be the last flight of political principle in a local elections, or of either candidates or councillors having a change of mind mid-term and jumping from one party to the other, seemingly on a whim.

Selection processes for candidates at both ward and constituency level became characterised by mass membership applications for the local party, handily ahead of a council candidacy coming up for grabs – usually from large extended families and their friends.

The ambitious applicant would duly be swept in on the popular vote over and above the claims of long-standing white councillors. Then the 'new' party members would disappear into the woodwork never to be seen again.

It isn't new, it isn't revolutionary and it isn't illegal either. It was simply that easy to transform the political landscape in Dewsbury.

The shady practices that have subsequently infested the actual contesting of elections is not so above board or straight-forward however. In the late 1990s the politicking of Labour's David Beetham, who had poached Mohammed Razaq from the Lib Dems, was looking likely to split the local Labour party as traditional, long-serving members like Labour's Jack Brooke were edged towards the exit after sometimes decades of public service.

It wasn't just Labour. In Dewsbury West the Lib Dems' Keith Oldroyd's position came under immense pressure from younger but completely inexperienced candidates, all of whom turned out to be Muslim. They key was the newcomers' ability and promise to deliver a large block vote.

One by one the old guard of long-serving white councillors fell or were pushed. In the mid-1990s the town had been represented by eight white and one Hindu Labour member, as unrepresentative of the actual electorate as the radically transformed version by 2006, where only the stalwart three white Labour representatives of Dewsbury East stood flying their solitary flag, one of them BNP.

Council elections in Kirklees like many places typically attract a low turnout, often down around the 30% mark, so despite there still being white voter majorities in all of the wards, the fact that the disinterested majority was often careless about turning out at all gave disproportionate muscle to the malleable Muslim vote.

With the increase in influence however came an increase in problems during campaigning and at the poll. Shahid Malik's idea of 'Paki Politics' always spoke to me of manipulating/appealing to one specific voter community in a completely different manner to the larger, wider electorate.

One message from candidates to get 'them' to the polls supporting you, a different message for 'us'. Nowhere was that better illustrated than by the high feelings surrounding the Iraq war, though for a while at least Malik managed to tiptoe around the bald fact that he supported Tony Blair on every single piece of Iraq war policy and vote in the House.

However what began to raise its head in Dewsbury from the late-90s onwards was far more reminiscent of good old fashioned third-world voting corruption; elections where plain and simple violence, fraud and intimidation were the order of the day.

In Dewsbury West Mohammed Razaq had been the breakthrough Labour Muslim representative but he was soon followed by a close rival in Lib Dem Karam Hussain, who still serves on the council. I think it was during the local election campaign of 1998 or 1999 that Karam went public over a physical attack which left him nothing worse than badly shaken, but which he claimed was politically motivated in the run up to the local elections.

Then came claims and counter claims that people were being coerced and intimidated at the polling booth and on the doorstep, of fraudulent practices whereby individuals not even in the country somehow managed to vote.

With the advent and growth of postal voting the claims of fraud went through the roof and incredibly inventive some of them were too, but time and again the then-returning officer at Kirklees Council, Chief Executive Tony Elson, poured soothing oil on the waters. Reports and investigations were commissioned and nothing happened.

The only tangible outcome was that each year before voting, candidates would be sternly reminded about their legal and moral obligations. Then the starting flag would go up and all hell would break loose.

Democracy? If you say so. And it was not the sole domain of one political party either, rather one ethnic community.

Karam Hussain, who emerged as the senior Lib Dem figure in Dewsbury, is an interesting character who typifies many of the contradictions I've observed over the years. A genial enough chap, he sent his Muslim children to the local Catholic schools – my own St Paulinus – to better foster their integration into British society. Over the years I have given journalistic work experience to a couple of his sons, Kamran and Ednan, grand lads both.

From St Paulinus the boys went to the St John Fisher

RC High School and one incident involving one of them created quite a poser. Being an Asian/Muslim pupil in any white-dominated school would be tough enough, but on this occasion Karam rang me to complain about something which would infuriate any parent.

One of the school toughs had rubbed his son's blazer in dog excrement and he felt his complaint to the headmaster wasn't being taken seriously – a situation compounded by the fact that the alleged bully happened to be the son of a teacher at the school.

As then editor-in-chief of the Reporter group of newspapers I'd personally had something of a hit and miss relationship with St John Fisher High School despite belonging to its same Catholic community. They weren't always as switched on in public relations as they could have been and on this occasion I spoke to the headmaster and advised an urgent and serious response to the incident which was duly forthcoming.

Councillor Hussain however was not mollified. He wanted to see this incident all over the front page of the paper. He wanted his voice heard and very publicly too.

Ultimately, and despite the easy allure of a provocative local story, I prevailed upon Karam Hussain to spare his son the public humiliation of running with it. He didn't like it, but as I pointed out, he wouldn't be the one left having to live with the recriminations of it.

I couldn't countenance contributing to the ordeal of an already isolated child by making his difficulties so widely known among his peers. What chance would he have for the rest of his school days? The other kids would make his life even more hell than it already was.

I don't know if it was the right call as an editor, but I certainly felt it was right as a parent.

But then again Karam Hussain has never been backwards in coming forwards with complaints, specifically about voter fraud. Just last year, in Karam's ward, a group of Asian men arrived at the polling station and said they didn't have their voting cards, but gave their names and addresses and were allowed to vote.

Two hours later a group of men turned up with voting cards from the same addresses. Not a year has passed in the past decade that elections both local and general haven't been plagued by these, and far worse incidents.

To highlight just a few, in 2003 and on the back of the decision to invade Iraq, there were dirty tricks allegations from the Dewsbury Labour Party after anti-war leaflets telling people to vote Lib-Dem were circulated in Asian communities – this time the accusations made against Karam Hussain's political allies.

The leaflets said that to vote Labour or Tory "was to sanction the massacres of millions of innocent citizens".

The leaflet was handed into police by Karam's arch-rival Mohammed Razaq. Meanwhile during the same campaign his Labour colleague and Dewsbury East councillor Paul Kane accused the mosques of militarising the electorate against Labour.

"If the Lib Dems aren't responsible for these leaflets they should be committed to finding out who is," said Councillor Kane at the time.

"Far be it from me to say people shouldn't vote. I would like to see 80 or 90 per cent turnouts and if I lost in those circumstances, so be it. But this simply isn't democratic. I was receiving phone calls at 7pm on Thursday (election day) telling me there were suddenly floods of Asian people turning up to vote Lib Dem.

"This is a wake-up call to everyone. One of these days the indigenous white population is going to be waking up with someone they neither want nor deserve because these antics are not democratic."

That year the Dewsbury Divisional Superintendent,

police chief John Cocliff reported that the elections passed without public order incident despite the increased number of BNP candidates.

The year after it was a slightly more overt form of fraudulent behaviour in an election where Kirklees was one of the British local authorities to experiment with an all-postal voting system.

In the militarised Muslim communities the sharp practices reached epidemic proportions with complaints flying left and right. This time the police mounted extra patrols after reports of gangs going door to door collecting postal votes – on one occasion three Asian men claiming to be from the Conservative party, at houses in Eastborough, a Labour (Dewsbury East) stronghold.

The police were called in by a once again indignant Councillor Kane who said: "This type of politics stinks and has no place in a modern democracy. If these allegations are proved I want these people charged so the community knows this kind of behaviour is totally unacceptable. I will not let this lie."

Mrs Nazia Bi, whose husband Arshad Hussain speaks poor English, reportedly answered the door to three men speaking Punjabi. She said: "They were three Asian men wearing suits who asked in the Punjabi accent if they could take our ballot papers. My husband said we had not filled them in yet but they said it did not matter, they would take them anyway. My husband said 'my wife speaks English but she is not in'. Then they left. My husband said he did not recognise any of them."

Mrs Bi said Asian women especially were confused by the new style ballot papers.

The dirty tricks allegations continued to fly. A Lib Dem flyer attacking Tory candidate Martyn Bolt in neighbouring Mirfield had no printer's imprint or publishers' details, against election law. The Lib Dems denied all knowledge, predictably. Then, following his own complaints, Paul Kane had to defend his own decision to 'doorstep' people and offer to deliver ballot papers to the election booth for them – this time within the guidelines, as he and his team were offering to deliver signed and sealed postal votes if the individuals didn't want to go in person, but again a tactic at the very least on the margins of being above board.

Despite it being a postal vote, people could still deliver their signed forms in person. Councillor Kane accepted that the practice could be open to abuse but said "there's a big difference between delivering signed and sealed ballot papers, and collecting blank ones" which he "knew for a fact" had been going on.

In the greater scheme of things, and in a new age and environment where mass manipulation of the Muslim vote was becoming a tolerated norm, these issues were barely 'news' any longer. Certainly protestations to the respective chief executives at Kirklees Council were kicked into the long grass. Just so long as mass violence didn't break out a few dozen – hundred? thousand? – corrupt votes were a small price to pay.

Sorry, but I believe one is too many. You get the hundreds and thousands when you refuse to prevent the one. The controversy over manipulation of the Muslim vote was to come to a head on Thursday May 6th 2006 in the heart of Savile Town.

JONATHAN SCOTT was elected as a Conservative councillor for Dewsbury South in the all-out elections of 2004 when the entire Kirklees Council elected membership stood in re-drawn wards. Generally only one of the three ward councillors would be up for election in each year, by rotation. On this occasion voters got a 3-2-1 choice for candidates.

Scott benefited from his association with the popular Khizar Iqbal and another urbane young Tory Muslim candidate Imtiaz Ameen, who would be selected the following year to contest then Labour Home Secretary Jack Straw's Parliamentary seat for the Conservatives in the General Election.

Iqbal finished first in the vote, Ameen second, and Scott third – all Tories – comfortably ahead of the highest placed Labour candidate Masood Ahmed. Finishing third meant Scott was first to face the electorate in 2006 when he again came face to face with Masood, representing Labour.

During our libel trial in November 2007 much was made of the phenomenal 50% swing from Tory to Labour in Dewsbury South's voting of 2006, this at a time when the Labour government's policies over the invasion of Iraq had been largely discredited.

There was a groundswell of Muslim antagonism to Labour both nationally and locally – especially in Savile Town and Thornhill Lees, home of suicide bomber Mohammed Siddique Khan, the Markazi mosque and the target of regular visits from the anti-terrorism squad, one of which resulted in the arrest and imprisonment of the schoolboy grandson of Islamic scholar Yakub Munshi.

But while nationwide there was a seismic shift away from Labour candidates, there was not in Dewsbury South where, all too critically, MP Shahid Malik had taken a very personal interest in the local authority election campaign, not generally regarded as a duty of the Member of Parliament.

There was much argument in our subsequent trial over exactly how involved Malik was – from running the entire campaign as we claimed that he boasted, to merely lending moral support, as he modestly admitted. Certain facts were incontrovertible however not least the massive and unexpected swing against the standing councillor, Jonathan

Scott, flying in the face of all possible political logic.

What became clear to Scott and Khizar Iqbal on the doorsteps of Savile Town was that as much as they liked their most popular councillor Iqbal and disagreed with Labour policy pretty much on all levels, they would still be voting for their "Muslim brother" Masood Ahmed. That's just the way it was. No claims of anything untoward, simply the way it was.

Scott was understandably frustrated, not least at the misleading volumes of disinformation being circulated about him and the Tories by the well organised Labour party machine. He and Khizar redoubled their leafleting and canvassing efforts and were in the heart of Savile Town, near the Mullaco's general store – very much a social heart of Savile Town – and just a couple of hundred yards from the Markazi, when they were confronted by another Labour activist and sometime candidate Abdul Hai Munshi, just a few days before voting.

Abdul Hai is the son of Sharia court senior cleric Yakub Munshi and uncle of Hammaad Munshi, still the UK's youngest convicted terrorist, jailed for his plotting. The family were very close to MP Malik.

I've had dealings enough with Abdul Hai Munshi over the years and don't hesitate to describe him as inhabiting the outer fringes of what I'd consider sanity. Barking, mouth-frothingly mad works as a description too.

During the Tory canvassing on behalf of Scott there ensued a confrontation between him and the teenage son of Khizar Iqbal who was helping his dad. Khizar intervened on behalf of his son and there was some pushing and shoving before onlookers intervened.

Immediately afterwards Abdul Hai Munshi rang Malik and told him he'd been assaulted by Khizar Iqbal – remember that in Savile Town, Jonathan Scott's slender hopes of being re-elected rested heavily upon his association with Khizar – and Munshi urged Malik to use his influence with the police to have the other man arrested for assault. Malik duly rang Chief Inspector Keith Hallas, who had major responsibility for community affairs in the Dewsbury division, and pressed him to take action against Iqbal despite not having witnessed the event himself.

This would lead to interesting scenes in the Royal Court of Justice in London but for the moment went nowhere. Chief Insp Hallas wisely investigated, but quietly.

No action was taken for reasons which would later become clear.

On voting day Scott and Khizar did the rounds of their ward but spent it mostly on Orchard Street outside the Savile Town polling booths. It was there that Scott watched with astonishment as Labour party activists stood at the entrance to the community centre urging voters to select "ake" – or number one in Urdu. Masood Ahmed was number one on the voting slips.

People coming to vote were being stopped and greeted by the Labour tellers like the old friends that they probably were, but in contravention of every rule in the book regarding accepted practice in the vicinity of a polling station.

Scott complained to the deputy returning officer about what was going on and words were said to the Labour activists, but to no visible effect – at least not sufficiently to the Tory councillor's liking.

During this time he also saw Shahid Malik on the scene, often on his mobile phone, before occasionally disappearing for a while on his round of other polling stations.

At one point Scott started to become uncomfortable at the attention he was receiving from young Muslim men who were circulating the polling station in what he described as flash cars – not a rare sight in Savile Town.

But he was on the end of what he described as "thousand

yard stares" as they slowed down to cruise past him. He had witnesses who testified to one such young man stopping, getting out of his car and telling him "remember this face – you'll be seeing it later."

At that he phoned Chief Inspector Hallas to voice his concerns on a number of levels, not least his personal safety. A permanent police presence was put on the Orchard Street polling station for the remainder of the day.

Despite the widespread swing against Labour that day across the country, the three Dewsbury wards produced surprise results. Firstly in the 'all-white' Dewsbury East ward, popular and long-serving Labour councillor Eric Firth was unseated by the BNP's Colin Auty.

In Dewsbury West where the Liberal Democrats had enjoyed a clean all-Asian sweep of the three seats in 2004, they unwisely fielded a white candidate in 2006 and Labour's Mumtaz Hussain came out of nowhere to win the seat. And, in Dewsbury South, Jonathan Scott's healthy majority over Labour from 2004 evaporated, Masood Ahmed garnering 2,322 votes to Scott's 1,568, just ahead of the BNP on 1,457 (the 'white' Thornhill vote). The Lib Dem candidate received a paltry 293 votes.

Having mulled over what had happened to him, Scott wrote a considered letter about the tactics he experienced and it was printed, almost word for word, by both The Press and the Dewsbury Reporter. They edited out just one line from his letter. At The Press we always considered ourselves a serious paper on local politics and we followed up with an interview of Scott the following week in which his experiences of the election were discussed.

It was, in hindsight, no more controversial coverage than a hundred other previous examples. I didn't even consider it overtly critical of Shahid Malik, though he obviously did.

He complained briefly by phone, but refused to address the debate in print and we hung up on good terms. Or so I thought. A few weeks later on the anniversary of the July 7 bombings Malik even penned an exclusive article for us to carry. He continued being held to account, especially in our letters pages by members of the public less and less inclined towards him, but just as often he was held in a positive – fair – light in our pages.

I don't think I've ever disagreed with the suggestion that Shahid Malik was a hard-working Member of Parliament.

But then some 10 weeks later, out of nowhere, he issued a libel writ for what Scott had written and we had published. The writ was taken out against us, the small independent newspaper, but not the big, blue-chip owned Dewsbury Reporter.

I should have backed down, but I didn't. It's been a long-time failing of mine.

12 – MUSLIMS AT WAR

WHAT I FELT strongly from the first receipt of the letter-before-action from Shahid Malik's lawyers, was that this was not merely about Jonathan Scott's words after the 2006 local elections, or the follow-up article in The Press. I believed it was about a far larger and actually more crucial point in terms of British democracy and freedom of speech – of shutting The Press up. Of shutting me up.

That's what I felt at least. I judged – wrongly, it transpired – that the threat of legal action was probably meant as a shot-across-the-bows from which a compromise accommodation could have been reached at little cost to either party (at least financially to us, in light of what it would eventually cost in pounds, shillings and pence).

I judged that if I shouted back at Malik's lawyers as aggressively as they had at me, and called their bluff, that the whole issue would disappear. Bad call.

Malik was fed up of his enemies firing pot-shots at him via the local media generally, but The Press specifically as we gave far more leeway to our correspondents than our counterparts at the Reporter.

Much of it was barely veiled, politically motivated spite from the family and friends of Sayeeda Warsi, the Dewsbury woman Malik had defeated at the 2005 General Election. Much of that became clear as the case unfolded.

Just before the libel writ was served I received a furious

phone call at home one Saturday morning from Malik. He was raving about another letter from a Muslim reader sniping at him who, he informed me, was one of Sayeeda Warsi's four sisters.

'Right of reply' I said to Malik as I always did in traditional editorial fashion. 'Fair criticism'. 'Broad back needed in politics' etc etc.

He was having none if it and reminded me that he'd issued libel proceedings against an impressive number of editors who had crossed his path over the years. I ought not to think that he wouldn't do it to The Press.

There was no mention of the Jonathan Scott letter on that occasion which was a dim and distant, but soon to be revived memory. I can only think that Malik gave his solicitors our recent files and the Scott letter was the one thing they found which they could make a bit of a complaint to beat us over the head with, by way of ramming home how serious he was.

It probably didn't help either of our cases ultimately that Malik's solicitors were the Labour party's (in London) pet solicitors, human rights specialist Bindmans.

'Sir' Geoffrey Bindman had recently been knighted by Tony Blair for his presumably heavily discounted services to miscreant Labour MPs. Certainly they were representing Malik on a no-win, no-fee basis and like every solicitor you've ever experienced, they eschewed any notion of diplomacy opting instead for a big fuck-off battering ram of threats of death and destruction.

This is lawyers' bog-standard opening gambit in dealings with what the generally consider to be knee-trembling weekly newspaper editors. No one likes libel cases, except perhaps Ian Hislop at Private Eye.

Boards on the bigger newspaper companies which dominate the publishing industry invariably back down eventually. Unfortunately (for both parties) I didn't have the luxury of such back-up. And so, in turn and in typical fashion, I sent them a lengthy letter invoking multiple colourful versions of the rather simpler Anglo-Saxon epithet of 'go fuck yourselves'.

The battle lines were drawn and, to all our cost and like the trenches of northern France in 1916, they barely moved an inch from first to last. Just more blood, more victims.

It was ironic indeed that it had all been prompted by the arms-length poison of Malik's hated rival Sayeeda Warsi's family. I hadn't written a word of the coverage complained about, but as editor I was personally responsible.

And I stood to be ruined, not only in business, but in losing the roof over my family's head.

Strange as it may sound and as I've intimated, I've always found Shahid Malik a personable chap. But, as I warned him at that first meeting in 2004, if he played silly buggers we were in for a stormy ride and given the characters he'd aligned himself to – Terry McKay, Terry Zaman, the Munshis – that was always likely.

He played the down-home Burnley-lad card with the calculated aplomb of that proudly Lancastrian bigot Bernard Manning. The difference was that Manning remained an unrepentant Manchester lard-arse until his dying breath, while for many a year, by the time 2004 rolled around Shahid Malik had long been the London liberal elite's pet Muslim, conveniently trading on his working class northern roots.

It worked for him and probably will for years to come. Nothing wrong with that, people get along as best they can, with whatever tools are at their disposal. That's his (r)ace card because in my opinion at least it certainly isn't his intellect.

He's a bit of a chameleon in that regard is Shahid, slipping easily into the required role of the day. It's a gift in some ways for a politicians, but not – as he found – when it brings such combustible interests into conflict.

When the cameras are rolling you can't wear two faces at once though I've witnessed it live on the BBC's Newsnight. He seemed to find ways to take about three different positions on a single divisive topic, with nary an attempt at joined-up thinking. Even the other guests looked at him aghast.

I mentioned earlier how yesterday's truth didn't necessarily bear any relation to today's in the south Asian culture. With Malik, he could speak out against anti-Iraq protestors in one breath and support their argument in the next without seeing the contradiction. It was always going to be his downfall, or at least create difficulties.

'Dewsbury jobs for Dewsbury people' proclaimed the banners in his constituency office window – before he had to explain why he'd sneaked his Burnley-resident dad on the public payroll as a "case worker" for a constituency more than an hour's drive away.

We just weren't supposed to notice. In the very same vein he saw no conflict in lobbying for millions of pounds of central funding for a new college facility in Huddersfield, even as Dewsbury College was effectively being ground into the dust. Joined up thinking simply didn't apply.

He wriggled out of those minor embarrassments, as he mostly did his other expenses 'difficulties' with nerveless aplomb and vocal indignation that we dare question his propriety. Some of Shahid's explanations about those multifarious expenses claims have still not been sufficient to satisfy all interested parties.

Things he said in witness statements and on the stand at our trial proved incompatible with other public proclamations. I don't think he ever saw the problem in that however. Certainly his political paymasters didn't appear to.

The fact was that, like Warsi, he was deemed a valuable

modern Muslim by the party infrastructure, at a time when the political elite decided such individuals were a rich source of association to be mined.

Malik seemed to be conveniently forgiven a number of gaffes which might have ended other careers – not to mention the attention of the courts when considering breaches of expenses rules and indeed questionable testimony in our trial.

But things like putting his dad on the payroll, before the full weight of the Westminster expenses scandal, were only a symptom of what has always been his underlying drawback. In my view he just isn't very clever and suffers from that dastardly malaise – Muslim memory. What was convenient yesterday doesn't have to maintain today.

Yes, Shahid Malik was also, and probably still is, an affable, plain-speaking man who, for a while at least, had me believing that he could make a positive difference. But even if I suspected there would be tears before bedtime from the moment he rolled into town, it was clear that Dewsbury had long needed a modern British Muslim to drag the mad mullahs of Savile Town and the manipulative 'community leaders' into the 21st century.

He had a chance of making that happen, of being a uniting, not dividing figure, but the danger was always of trying to play both communities as separate entities, with separate value systems. The town required someone with the courage and consistency to say and stand for very difficult things.

It proved to be a quality he did not possess, but it was also probably an expectation too high from people like me.

Unfortunately the portents for a troubling outcome were writ large the moment he addressed the gathered masses at the polling station in Dewsbury Sports Centre after winning the election in May 2005.

It might have seemed a smart idea at the time, but he

chose to begin his acceptance speech with a greeting in Arabic, the translation of his first words being "I am a Muslim." He did that in the general election where the BNP in Dewsbury had their highest vote across the UK. Talk about pouring petrol on the flames.

Vanity or stupidity? Probably a bit of both, but the gathered Muslims went frantic, in the style of a crowd of 1962 Beatles fans. Their messiah had arrived, if not quite Dewsbury's. It was an annunciation which chilled a lot of hard-working and well-meaning born and bred local folk, but which heralded much of what was to come. I hope the idiots in the Dewsbury Constituency Labour Party cringed when they heard it, but I doubt it.

In hindsight, we should have half expected something so inflammatory, judging by the campaign that preceded the vote.

Standing vanquished in the public shadows in our sports centre that night, but not for long in the national psyche, was Sayeeda Hussain-Warsi. As it worked out, losing that election was the best possible thing that could have happened for Sayeeda, soon to be Baroness Warsi of Dewsbury, a title and name she still uses out of convenience, though she has since divorced her cousin/husband and remarried.

If Malik had partly charmed me when he rolled into Dewsbury, the far more cunning and flirtatious 'modest' Muslim mum had me eating out of her hands.

On the morning that David Cameron announced his first coalition cabinet, the beaming Sayeeda waltzed along Downing Street in her traditional shalwar kameez Muslim garb, draping her coat over the railings of No.10 to pose like a Hollywood /Bollywood siren for the adoring cameras. Star attraction. Attagirl (I almost reached behind my back upon witnessing that, to see if I could still feel the scars from the Tories' stiletto I'd had slipped between my ribs).

It was a mercurial journey for the former immigration solicitor and seemingly left-wing member of the Rowntree Trust. Her election efforts having ended in comprehensive defeat, Michael Howard, the then Tory leader, needed a presentable Muslim and was blessed in finding one who also ticked the boxes of being a woman, very clever, extremely ambitious, and attractive.

The cameras tend to put a few pounds on Sayeeda, but she possesses a charming, attractive and flirtatious nature when she wants to switch it on.

Michael Howard phoned Sayeeda and offered her the job of Vice Chairman of the Conservative Party. She was a relative party newcomer but you don't have to be either brown or from the sub-continent to play 'Paki Politics' as Howard proved on that occasion and David Cameron hammered home when his turn came, spiking a Labour government reshuffle by announcing Warsi's elevation to the House of Lords on the same day.

One of the very first people Sayeeda contacted upon receiving Howard's offer to move to London was me. It was a rainy late afternoon in West Yorkshire and my car was winding down the hillside between Dewsbury and Batley.

I was doing the school run. I pulled into the car park of an old mill as she told me excitedly of Michael Howard's offer – party vice-chairman.

Why had she rung me? To understand that, you have to understand the opportunism of our new political brethren. We first crossed firmaments when she rang me to take exception to an editorial piece I'd written in 2003. I invited a rebuttal and Sayeeda wrote an exceptional piece of political/social analysis.

From thereon I encouraged her, offered advice, counsel, and when she suddenly 'turned' party political just the year before taking on Malik in the 2005 General Election, I was, I believe, a valued media foil. I was probably also a bloody fool, easily flattered as a middle aged journalist, in the presence of an artful, attractive and calculating woman.

Sayeeda plumped for the Conservatives ultimately but I'm reasonably content that that was only because it was where the immediate local career openings lay.

Her history in typical 'New Labour' human rights fields had her marked bang to rights as a typical liberal leftie, but even now, five years on, I don't think I've fathomed the depth of Baroness Warsi's 'small p' political philosophies – if indeed there are any.

She really could be the first Muslim Prime Minister of the United Kingdom, although it's equally clear she's made her share of enemies at the Tories' top table.

But that afternoon, when she was catapulted from failed Dewsbury candidate into the frontline of international politics, I was honoured that Sayeeda trusted my judgment sufficiently to ask advice. I'd met her husband – an arranged marriage from Pakistan, a man removed by far, far more than those mere miles from his attractive wife and their young daughter.

"What about Aamna?" (her daughter) was my first observation. "You'll be in London almost full-time and I don't think Westminster is for her."

But the Hussains have a very strong family. Sayeeda's mum and dad are lovely people. Her four sisters are just as impressive as she is, on every level. There would be no lack of strong support at home.

"And your marriage?"

There wasn't a hope in hell the culturally contrived marriage would endure this pressure although Sayeeda had previously espoused the virtues of these arranged relationships in print and on a national stage too, saying they worked for her and husband Naeem.

But ultimately it didn't. For Sayeeda I suspect the bindings of that marriage were as much an incentive for the career jump as anything, though she would never admit as much. The girl was off and running.

Later, when she was made Baroness Warsi of Dewsbury, she rang just as I was walking into my mum's council flat just outside Dewsbury town centre. It was raining again. This time she confessed she'd rung to tell her dad first, but that I was the second person to know (I have subsequently learned that there was at least one other 'second person to know' – there are probably others).

Still I was hugely flattered, to the point of hopefully disguising my anger at a shameful system of governance which allowed our Prime Minister to throw elected democracy in the toilet and wipe his backside with it, in the name of contrived ethnic-political expedience.

Malik might have won the 2005 General Election but Sayeeda Warsi was the winner in the long-run, although she hadn't felt that when the election count revealed that the Muslim vote had simply deserted her and gathered behind Malik. She was left battered and bruised from a campaign which had seen no holds barred fighting from both sides.

Malik went ballistic when it was discovered that the Labour peer Lord Ahmed, a friend of the Hussains, had appeared in Dewsbury (at an ethnic event, no whites invited naturally) to support the Conservative candidate, Sayeeda. It is as clear and concise an example of that community's radically different allegiances as you could possibly ask for.

You can't blame Malik for his frustration at that, although he would not have hesitated to play the same card. He'd just been trumped on that occasion that's all.

Just how close Lord Ahmed and Warsi were was further revealed when they jetted off together on a mission to save the British 'teddy bear' nanny Gillian Gibbons from Islamic justice in Sudan. She had unwisely agreed to a child's suggestion to call the teddy Mohammed, if you recall.

Back to the campaign and Warsi was in turn aggrieved when Malik touted powerful political figures from Pakistan round the community centres and mosques backing his claims that he – Malik – would be the better candidate in terms of helping the folks back home. Home as in Pakistan, of course. Not much mentioned there about the voters of Dewsbury.

Malik took the offensive when he attacked the Tories for politicising a community Eid event attended by 2,000 people in Savile Town.

The event was organised by local businessman and Malik's landlord – both personal and of his constituency offices – the aforementioned 'colourful' Terry Zaman. The event was sponsored unwittingly by the local HSBC bank, completely out of their depth in these murky waters.

It was rich that Malik should go public first over that, because when the Tories and Lib Dems found out that only he of the candidates was on the guest list they wangled invites from the bank, much to the future MP's chagrin.

On the day, when Sayeeda and her family arrived at the function she was stopped at the door by Malik and told: "No women allowed in this hall. Women downstairs."

If it is remotely possible for a supposed modernist Muslim politician to be more overtly sexist and insulting, then I can't imagine how. Warsi ignored him and marched inside which, paradoxically, might even have cost her votes in that closed, male-dominated culture.

It was almost hilarious afterwards when, in support of Malik, his little henchman Zaman said: "This is all Asian politics which should be left in Pakistan. Shahid Malik was invited as a guest but the Tories were not invited."

Zaman was widely quoted saying that he was decidedly not a Labour member and had never even voted. However, by the time of our libel trial in 2007 he claimed in both statements and the witness box to be a Labour Party member and dedicated activist during the 2006 local elections. Moving truths, moving truths.

There had already been outrage after Malik sent out thousands of Eid cards with a picture of the al Aqsa mosque on the front, with the words: "From Shahid Malik your next MP (inshallah)" ... along with pictures of Malik at Yasser Arafat's funeral and praying at his grave.

That wasn't something he discussed much when turning up at working men's clubs and sipping on a soft drink in his 'local' pub pretending to be a good 'ol boy. Funny that.

Malik went so far as to brand Warsi as being "unfit to appear on the ballot paper" in the week Tony Blair finally revealed May as the general election date. On that occasion Malik called her a liar over claims made in her election leaflet. Pot. Kettle. Black.

What the electorate hadn't known at the time was my involvement in this particular spat. Having been apprised of his all-guns-blazing attack I'd phoned him and advised both general and specific toning-down of the content of his press release if he wanted to stay out of the courts himself. It was advice he gladly and wisely took. Ironic indeed.

Malik's election was only slightly tainted at the time by new accusations of skulduggery from an independent General Election candidate, Alan Girvan. He claimed that the MP's sidekick Terry McKay had directly arranged funding for Girvan's bid, in a cynical ploy to try to draw votes away from the BNP and Tories.

Girvan was reasonably well known on the right-wing fringe of local politics and he described how McKay, who he didn't know at the time, arranged funding from "a Manchester businessman" to pay his £500 deposit and personally took him to the Kirklees election office in Holmfirth 15 miles away to register as a candidate.

He claimed McKay helped him with election literature,

some of which Malik's man edited "to give a right wing slant" and which included a dig at Warsi which said: "The Conservative candidate for Dewsbury even made a living helping more people into our country as an immigration lawyer."

Neither McKay nor Malik ever denied the claims when Girvan complained to Rob Vincent, the Kirklees Council chief executive. Girvan claimed to have tape-recorded evidence and emails between him and McKay. Vincent promised to look into the matter, but no action was ever taken. Malik's charmed life continued, for then at least.

When our libel trial came to court, Judge David Eady, not yet famous for his privacy-protection of the rich, powerful and the celebrity-afflicted, would refuse to allow Girvan's testimony of the kind of election 'tactics' The Press was campaigning to highlight and eradicate to be heard by the jury.

But then again Eady wouldn't allow Sayeeda Warsi to give evidence on our behalf, allow the jury to see a police report proving Abdul Hai Munshi was a liar regarding the violent incident in Savile Town with Khizar Iqbal, or the fact be mentioned in court that the Dewsbury Reporter carried the same letter complained of by Malik but that he hadn't pursued them for libel.

And no, they hadn't apologised to him. They'd just rolled over obediently for their bellies tickling.

After the trial, I described what Eady had put us through as being akin to losing the toss in a rugby match and playing uphill both halves, into the wind, with only half a team. And we still didn't lose!

As Baroness Warsi said after the 2005 election dust settled: "I was too black for one half of the community and too female for the other half." It was no bar to personal and political prosperity however. Her passport out of Dewsbury to fame, fortune and a seat at the heart of power lay sparkling ahead of her, down simply to her sex, ethnicity and religion. Although she hadn't quite finished dabbling in Dewsbury's political affairs, yet.

13 - APPEASEMENT

THESE SPIKES OF political activity served in one sense as barometers of the changing socio-political landscape in Dewsbury, a measure of the immigrant community's increasing influence and control over so many facets of life through the 90s and first decade of the 21st century.

The political developments by no means stood in isolation as an indicator of the rise in both confidence and assertiveness of a community that the local authority, police and even health services continually bent over backwards to appease. In trying to gauge the subliminal changes to the entire face of Dewsbury over this period, it was the drip, drip of small, everyday occurrences that best plots the ever widening gulf in community relations.

None of these events made anyone's headlines other than ours, they weren't captured on tv, widely read outside our valley, but in sum total they illustrate how a cultural transformation can take place without apparent design.

The Markazi mosque was a huge construction project funded by Saudi Arabia in 1982 but its location deep in the heart of Savile Town meant that apart from catching the eye from all of the hills that ring Dewsbury, it bore little effect on the everyday lives of people going about their business. That was to change a few years after the 1989 riots and coincidentally in the early days of my tenure as editor-in-chief of the Reporter group of newspapers.

One sunny Thursday morning in June 1994, ironically the weekend of the 5th anniversary of the Savile Town riot, Dewsbury, a town then of probably 52,000 souls, awoke to find 50,000 new inhabitants were arriving, completely unannounced. There were 200 coaches alone descending upon Savile Town.

Buses and minibuses and trains and cars were pouring into town – by foot and magic carpet for all anyone knew – for a four day Ijtema, a religious festival, which doubled our population overnight. No one knows the exact figures but it was just like that. As if by magic, from out of nowhere.

Ijtema is an annual religious festival staged by Tablighi Jamaat and it is the second biggest pilgrimage in the Islamic world after the Hajj. An estimated five million pilgrims attended the 2010 Ijtema at Tongi, Bangladesh, by the river Turag, which rather puts our meagre 50,000 in the shade. But at least in Bangladesh they know to expect them. We didn't.

All of the adjacent fields were suddenly under canvas, massive marquees besides the wide range of smaller, portable accommodations. Local homes were thrown open to friends and families ... within the Muslim community it was a massive event, and actually a massive and successful accomplishment.

What stunned everyone in a semblance of public life at the time – and as editor of the local paper living in the town, I counted myself as such – was how something like this could be managed logistically without a single soul in authority apparently knowing about it.

The police later said they knew all about the event and praised the stewarding of it which 'the community' ran itself, with Superintendent Roger Outing trying to compare it to a football match which would have required a massive police presence.

For this event the police simply went missing for four

days. The truth is, the police didn't have a choice. They were presented with a fait accompli

Afterwards the organisers were dismissive of criticisms, playing the race card for all it was worth, but there were fair complaints. The calls to prayer ringing out from loudspeakers at 4am and then throughout the day bounced loudly around the bowl of hills Savile Town sits in.

Kirklees Council's environmental health officers made a lame play at having a word with the organisers and were roundly ignored.

The self-stewarding led to fun and games for people from Thornhill trying to negotiate the one arterial route into Dewsbury (and back again) because the Muslim community in Savile Town simply sealed the area off as and when it suited them. They put up blockades and turned cars, buses – everyone – around. Go find another way. In a town already rippling with racial tension this was a blatant and thoughtless act of provocation.

There were still quite a number of white residents of Savile Town at that time and they found themselves cut off.

People with hospital appointments could get neither in nor out of the area; a district nurse trying to see a patient was turned away; a woman wearing shorts was abused by 'offended' Muslims and there were numerous complaints from white residents about racist abuse being hurled their way.

For four days the district resounded to the sounds of trumpeted calls to prayer, which while not intended as an audible two-fingered salute at the other residents, were certainly interpreted as one. And then just as quickly as they'd arrived, the pilgrims were gone.

There wasn't a huge public reaction at the time; this story made front page news but there was certainly no xenophobic, let alone Islamophobic overreaction, just fair criticism. People were angry at the behaviour of the people of Savile Town for their thoughtlessness and disregard to their neighbours.

Such venom as there was came from within Savile Town, in a barrage aimed at anyone daring to voice criticism. If the Scarborough rampage was a turning point in terms of Muslim youths getting physical, the 1994 Ijtema probably signalled the maturing of a united and aggressive Islamic front towards authority.

Mainstream resentment of the event itself however was compounded when it emerged that a handful of local (Muslim) GPs had set up their own tents in the neighbourhood and dispensed prescriptions by the barrowload to people from far and wide.

The cost to the local NHS budget was in the region of £10,000 for these opportunist doctors' weekend of overtime, writing prescription after prescription. Revealing this news to the wider public, on the back of the coverage of the Ijtema itself, heralded the first time that the owners of the valley's corner shops and newsagents threatened to boycott a Lockwood-edited publication.

'The community' didn't like the message and was going to display just how much quiet muscle it could flex. The experience provided me with one of the keener insights I've gained into the workings of the Asian/Muslim psyche.

When they woke up and read the paper and didn't like the content, I was hit for the first time with that threatened boycott of all our papers. Because the independent retail trade – the corner shop in effect – is so dominated by the Asian community, here was a perfect stick with which to threaten an off-message editor.

It's crude but potentially effective, and a clear indication of how organised and militant that community can be when it wants. Impressive.

Faced with that prospect and a very nervous Managing Director whose eye understandably was on the bottom line in potential financial damage, I decided to fight fire with fire. If I apologised then a line was drawn in the sand which couldn't be stepped back over.

That was what the police, local authority, health services and every kind of public body you can imagine was already busy doing. Drawing a line, stepping back, drawing a line, stepping back.

So instead I reported the individuals claiming to represent the organisations behind the threat – the Indian Muslim Welfare Society and Pakistan and Kashmir Welfare Association – to the Race Equality chiefs, claiming this was a blatant act of racial prejudice. That reversal of tactics gave them pause for thought. The threat was never carried out, but it was far from the last time it was made.

In a bid to calm tempers the then Chief Executive of Kirklees Council, Rob Hughes, brokered a public meeting in the community centre in the heart of Savile Town one dark midweek evening, which some years hence would be at the centre of the voting row which led Malik and I to court.

In the chair was Sher Azam, the chairman of the Bradford Council of Mosques. Facing me was a packed hall of angry men bearing years-worth of grudges against everyone from me – the current target at the helm of the Dewsbury Reporter – all the way back to the British raj. At least that's how it felt.

I've never considered myself to have a racist bone in my body – though I'm not too keen on the Aussies, especially where a rugby ball is concerned – but my predecessor in the editor's chair at the Dewsbury Reporter, Keith Hustler, had proudly professed politics somewhere to the right of Genghis Khan.

File upon file of Keith's ravings were paraded before me by clearly diligent readers as proof that I was the incubus of this journalistic Satan. I don't think I'd had long enough in the editor's chair to build up my own impressive portfolio of offence. I'm sure one exists now.

I think I was supposed to be overwhelmed that night by the weight of hostility and pent up grievance. That reaction, in both my antagonists' experience with white British authority, and mine in what I've subsequently witnessed, is simply the 'form'. It's a cultural thing, it's how Asian men comport negotiations.

To use the Yorkshire colloquial, it's all wind and piss, nothing more. They shout and gesticulate and demand, and their experience of English authority has been that we nod and soothe and placate and cough up the taxpayers' submission.

So by way of a change, when they'd all vented their spleens about what a wicked Imperialist rag my newspaper was, I stood up and gave them a right bollocking back, with both barrels.

I couldn't and wouldn't answer for my predecessor, but if they thought the public fuss over their religious festival was unacceptable, and I was going to say sorry, then they had another think coming.

Blocking roads on a whim? Dictating who can come and go, where and when? Even a simple letter in the Reporter would have prepared everyone else for the massive influx of people into a town not prepared for it. And given the damage their actions had already inflicted on 'community relations' what were we supposed to write?

What's more, who were we supposed to phone for a comment from their community? Who was willing to take responsibility for the public relations disaster?

There was no one on this occasion, just as there never had been, or wouldn't be where religion was concerned, because the 'community' refused to engage in dialogue. Always had, did then, does now.

Every time a story arose which involved any measure of criticism whatsoever involving the Asian or Muslim communities they preferred to wait until after the fact, and then they ran round shouting "racist, you're racist!" at their critics. This is what I told them that night.

Issues were never, but ever, debated in a civilised fashion because there was never a 'community leader' to speak to until they had something to moan about, at which point they were falling out of the trees to vent their three-pennorth. Every time. And increasingly wheeled out was the blame-and-victim, poor-old-us routine. You're racist, you're racist, with a finger poked in our chest at every turn.

And so I told them plainly: 'Join the process, help promote understanding, join us in breaking down these barriers, let's get a dialogue going'.

I spent quite some time that night in Savile Town trying to explain how the media works. And they listened attentively, respectfully, young and old alike – and it was a healthy mix of people there. By the time we broke up, late that night, I was convinced that there was at least an understanding of where our differences lie. My hand was shaken warmly by men who had entered the room with wrath writ large on their features.

Many of those men have gone on to become important community figures across a wide range of fields, from industry to politics, from their own media to the mosque. Some I consider friendly acquaintances if not quite friends. Others are far from it.

As I was to experience many, many times over the intervening 17 years, that performance was simply part of their culture; to confront, to demand and then to work towards some form of acceptable middle ground.

It's nothing more than the bargaining of the bazaar, that's all. But we Brits don't do that well, and certainly not in local and national government and when dealing with a hot topic like race.

What I had to deal with that night over a heated local

issue was no different from what my advertising and accounts staff had so often to deal with in trying to get payment from so many of our customers from that community – the 'barter' culture. Everything is movable, everything is negotiable, but not everything is ever taken quite so seriously – or with the same commitment – that everything can't change again from one day to the next.

That isn't something that fits well with our rather British way of doing things. And, in the context of bringing two very different cultural ideologies together, it has ended up in rank capitulation from one side, married to a deep and abiding resentment of the fact.

David Cameron talked in 2008 when I asked him about the malign influence in Dewsbury of the BNP, of "listening to the people on the doorstep," completely ignoring the fact that this was the message they'd been shouting at him, and his predecessors in Government, for years.

Ordinary English taxpayers had had enough of systemic patronising of one very specific ethnic minority by politicians and bureaucrats who, when confronted by social, educational, health or cultural differences – and I wouldn't say demands – have responded by throwing either costly initiatives or, failing that, cold hard cash at them.

Is it buying votes or buying a clear conscience? Probably both, but you cannot argue it is immensely patronising, like a distracted parent patting a toddler's head and giving them a sweetie when they've soiled their nappy for the umpteenth time that day, without ever an inclination that the time for potty training might be well overdue.

That attitude merely serves to embolden the beneficiaries because it breeds – it has already bred – a culture of lazy expectation and ultimately a convenient hideaway behind the ever present race card.

The toddler screams, the parent gives.

There isn't a danger of this happening. Rather it is a

statement of absolute, unmitigated fact. And in towns like Dewsbury there is no going back. It's fait accompli.

Where the funding initiatives and the conscience-driven bribes were once volunteered, now they are expected, assisted by a race industry that as been top-loaded to not just assist the process but in so doing conspire against the values of the traditional English aspirational working and middle classes.

That's where the damage runs deepest. An entire (white) bureaucratic liberal class across all sectors of public service has been brainwashed for a generation now into this ethnic favouritism. No? You don't agree?

You've a right to your view, but that's what more and more people feel in my experience. In the words of today's police service, if any individual chooses to ascribe a racial motivation to any kind of incident, whether they are directly involved or not, then racially motivated it is, by definition. Crazy, but it is.

What was politically termed 'positive discrimination', or 'affirmative action' in the idiom of the race industry became bigotry and reverse prejudice. And because it exists in its closest manifestation right in the faces of the working and middle classes of indigenous Britons, that is where it causes most offence and resentment.

The Sun or the Daily Mail regularly lay before us their weekly or daily instance of multi-cultural madness, aimed at raising the ire of white England, but even their worst examples are met mostly with a resigned shrug in towns like Dewsbury where people see it every day.

You work for 20 years in the bank or the building society, to earn your first choice of holidays come Easter when the kids are off school. Then young Mohammed or Hasina, who has been in the company for scarcely a few months, declares that they must be absent for six weeks for religious/family duties "back home" – and the company capitulates. They are granted automatic leave of absence and your plans, your hard-earned entitlements, are torn asunder.

A young Muslim woman is divorced by her husband in the local Sharia court. She informs her manager she won't be back at work for quite some time because she's not allowed to show her face outside the door until she has 'bled' twice.

That was a tale I heard from a manager within a big corporation just recently who had to deal with the girl. She passed the problem onto HR and the situation was blithely rubber stamped. Was it based on cultural or religious fact? I don't know, but it apparently wasn't challenged.

I don't know if that specific circumstance is commonplace within the context of Islamic life or whether it's a complete con, or even if this is one of those apocryphal 'Chinese whispers' incidents that so easily take root. I have no reason to doubt the source of the particular story but if workplace rules are invoked ad hoc, and are singularly prejudicial in favour of one community as seems to be more and more the case, then the outcomes are obvious.

It isn't entirely the fevered excitations of the Daily Mail readership. But neither am I certain that it's a situation brought about entirely by demands from the community, whether unreasonable or otherwise.

What's wrong with employers saying no? Of pointing to employment contracts that were signed in good faith? That's what happened with the veiled teaching assistant Aishah Azmi who demanded the right to wear the full-face niqab in front of young children in Dewsbury.

The establishment for once said no, it resisted and ultimately Azmi lost that particular cultural confrontation.

The last I heard she was reputedly working as a completely unveiled checkout assistant in Argos. I'd love to think that story is true.

But at the time hers was a provocative challenge that

could have opened the floodgates to a form of behaviour from militant young Muslim women which would have driven a massive wedge between communities. You're not telling me that slip of a girl came to that conclusion, trod that path, of her own accord?

But the point is this: what happened when she lost her case? There were no mass protests on the streets, no riots. She (and her religious teachers) had tried it on and lost. End of story.

If only that robust approach had been applied more often. Lots of reasonable, ordinary Muslims who want nothing more than a quiet life, and who don't appreciate these repeated attempts of provocation, breathed a massive sigh of relief when Azmi lost her case.

Too often our appeasement lets them down too and we see the environment of concession and preferential treatment being offered rather than demanded, or at least conceded without the kind of regular tests applied that most of us would expect.

In the early growth years of the immigrant community the British state created an entire industry devoted ostensibly to assuring fairness and equality, but which transmuted into being its mouthpiece for preference.

Now institutional submission to the most whimsical demands of specifically the Muslim community is ingrained in so many quarters. The individual young Muslim goes out into the world armed not so much with terrorist manuals – though there are more than enough of those about – but with a set of hugely inflated 'rights' that have never been tested in law, nor probably passed into law.

And that is accompanied by an all-consuming sense that to merely question the fact of those 'rights' is to be inherently racist. Community cohesion? Where? How?

That night in Savile Town in 1994 however, with Sher Azam in the chair and being a young, newish editor having engaged in a proper debate about live issues, I walked out of the Orchard Street Community Centre with a spring in my step.

I thought we were getting somewhere, that my point had been fairly made, fairly if somewhat reluctantly understood. I was kidding myself of course, at least in the most part.

I came to realise that, over years of similar instances. It was nothing personal to me or to my profession, it was just the way the community works when faced with confrontation.

If there was a beneficial outcome in respect of finding my feet in the editor's chair, it was that we'd got each other's measure, eyeballed each other up close. They wouldn't be trying it on Lockwood for a while – but they did eventually, and at regular intervals. I was just better armed to roll with the punches, throw a few back and not take all their noise too seriously.

Only our race industry does that – but then it's what keeps them in money and influence. It's a simple human equation when you get to the bottom of things.

IT WOULD be glib to simply pass over my assertions of ethnic appeasement without at least pausing to observe a few of the worst excesses of this Chamberlain-esque trait from various public bodies in and around Dewsbury.

I served as the editor-in-chief and latterly acting MD of the Reporter Group from 1993 until 1999, by which time the old guard of white Labour councillors was inexorably being replaced by the new multi-cultural (and multi-party) group of representatives. The fact that some had barely a passable grasp of the spoken language, let alone written, was no bar to a seat on Kirklees Council.

What the district had started seeing by the time I departed for editorships new were the tacitly third-world thuggish tactics of wholesale selling and buying of votes; of mosques dictating who their worshippers should support, of voting fraud and voter intimidation at the polling booth.

Kirklees Council's shameful blanket-covering of this behaviour remains a discredit to successive chief executives whose tenures it happened during, and the numerous police chiefs who came through the town in an approximately two-year revolving door system.

The current incumbent, Chief Superintendent John Robins, is actually in his third year, but then again his command structure has jumped town for Huddersfield, where they aren't battered round the heads with Dewsbury's problems quite so incessantly.

The appeasement came in many forms, shapes and sizes – from craven capitulation to mobs of angered Muslims besieging local police stations, to whitewashing over rank criminal activity in order to keep a lid on simmering community tensions.

Ever was the reminder of the Scarborough in 1989 and the northern summer riots of 2001 at the back of the mind of whichever police chief was on watch.

What was clear to me that what began with almost a quiet, back door nudge towards promoting ethnic minority opportunities – and I certainly would never argue that issues needed addressing there – seemed to become a mad, headlong race among public bodies to see who could throw the most ridiculous, expensive, and quite often completely unnecessary favours at a Muslim community. It was staggering in its brazen condescension at times.

I recall Kirklees Council spending a veritable fortune on having all public signs in areas like Savile Town re-written in the various south-east Asian dialects, Urdu, Punjabi, Gujarati.

Yet any fool driving around Savile Town would have been truly moronic not to notice that about 99% of the private shop and commercial signage was in English! Their choice!

If there was a problem with illiteracy in their community – and there undoubtedly was – then it didn't stop at the door of reading and writing English. It was total. But some cultural diversity professional wasn't going to let that kind of common sense get in the way of gesture politics and budget-pot profligacy. Even the locals laughed and shook their heads at the kow-towing of the English authorities.

In the early months of my editorship, September 1993, we carried a story about a 27-year-old Savile Town man Mr Asad Mahmood, having a good old fashioned rant at Kirklees Council over plans to open a Social Services centre in the heart of the settlement.

Remember that Dewsbury town centre with all its civic facilities was only half a mile away, yet here was the local authority, effectively further insulating the Muslim community by putting more and more (preferential) services on its doorstep.

Those aren't my words – they were Mr Mahmood's and he fairly observed that it was causing, not solving problems. He asked why this funding couldn't have gone to (white) Thornhill Lees which so desperately needed a community centre because locals in Savile Town had been working for years anyway to successfully create their Orchard Street Community Centre which provided many of the service this new Kirklees 'Massarrat Centre' would provide.

"And what on earth does Massarratt mean?" he demanded.

Kirklees Social Services manager Brian Mettrick insisted this idea had been done "with care" and explained patronisingly to Mr Mahmood that Massarratt is the Urdu word for 'Equality'.

Of all the things this stunt might have represented, 'equality' was a long way down the list. Asad Mahmood saw clearly what it was, but common sense voices like his are rarely heeded. An industry depends on these projects.

RACE ATTACKS – either white on Asian, or the reverse – were still not common currency by the time I departed Dewsbury in 1999 to become the editor of a group of newspapers in Gloucestershire (and boy didn't Mrs Lockwood, hailing from North Wales via London welcome that shift!) Unfortunately for her in both the short and medium term, in what rapidly became an enduring fashion, I returned to the family home at weekends and the job in Gloucestershire, in the heart of the beautiful Cotswolds, never worked out.

I won't say I'd been lured there under false pretences, but it wasn't far off. We parted company after a string of technical catastrophes that I'd foreseen and my new MD wouldn't heed; he got the heave-ho and his replacement and I swiftly recognised that there wasn't room for both our egos in the business.

The turn of the century heralded a quantum change in the newspaper publishing business with the advent of widespread internet use, email, the first 'high-speed' ISDN file transmission and ultimately broadband. But for the advent of those technologies, I would never have started my own publishing business a couple of years later.

Over the next two years I worked variously as an editorial consultant in London and Leeds, and ran another publishing group based in Lancaster. For the first time in years I was off the public radar – certainly as far as Dewsbury was concerned – but I was still witnessing the turmoil in the town where several generations of my family had been born and raised and still lived.

And possibly because I wasn't still in the journalistic frontline in Dewsbury but retained my contacts, I was suddenly privy to all kinds of surprising information, reaching me either in the depths of Gloucestershire, or the ancestral heart of either London or Lancaster.

One such titbit came from a serving police officer regarding an incident in the mixed community of Ravensthorpe, a mile or so outside Dewsbury on the main road to Huddersfield.

A quiet Sunday afternoon was disturbed by a row between an 'immigrant' (no longer a term applicable to the town's Muslim community, as more and more refugees poured in from the middle east and former Balkan states) and some local Pakistani men.

A lone patrol car turned up, according to my police source, but the two officers suddenly found themselves surrounded by a mob, pounding their car and inviting them to 'step outside'. The officer who described this to me said there was only one other car on duty that Sunday afternoon in the entire Dewsbury Division – covering 170,000 people.

Eventually a traffic patrol car away on the M62 motorway and a desk sergeant from the Batley station responded, the besieged officers were relieved and a couple of their antagonists were taken into custody. That was not the end of the drama however.

Within the hour Huddersfield Road had become a no-pass route, unless you wanted a brick through your car window. The crowd grew, stories were told, exaggerated, and the mob went on the move – straight along the main road into town where the first major public building happened to be the police station, at that point still a fully operational divisional HQ.

A conservative estimate put 100 people in the crowd baying outside the station for the release of their friends, while raining their hostilities on any drivers attempting to run their gauntlet.

From this delegation there emerged individuals who

would later become the most celebrated of Dewsbury's anonymous celebrities – the so-called 'Community Leaders' with the admirable gift of being able to control a mob but no visible trappings of public authority.

The Muslim community is unique in my experience in this regard. Even when it has elected councillors, it still finds completely unaccountable 'community leaders' to offer themselves as mediators at times of conflict. On this occasion, after conversations between the self-appointed spokesmen and whichever senior police officer could be roused at short notice, the mob dispersed – taking their colleagues with them.

That happened on a Sunday afternoon. I got the detailed account from a Dewsbury police officer while sitting at my desk in Gloucestershire on Monday morning before my first coffee. I immediately tipped off my successor and former deputy editor at the Dewsbury Reporter, John Wilson, thinking it was a decent news story that readers would want to know the background to.

John's a lovely bloke still, a marvellous family man. I always thought we made a good editorial management team – me the laddish council estate boy done good, he the tee-total Methodist lay preacher who wouldn't say boo to a goose, a man with a more considered take on life.

In the space of just a few weeks it soon became clear that the change in editorial policy between my departure and John's appointment couldn't have been more stark.

I picked up the Reporter upon arriving back home from the Cotswolds that following Friday evening and finally found what we term a 'down page' story. As I recall the headline ran something like 'Police And Community Leaders Hail Spirit of Co-operation'.

I don't need to say more really, do I?

Bugger all had happened, it seemed. It was all an unfortunate misunderstanding. Except that it wasn't.

'High spirits' or 'apparent misunderstandings' and similar blandishments were blithely used as a sweeping brush of criminal appeasement. The cops were being bullied. And they were backing down.

I spoke to one or two other contacts. My original informant hadn't been imagining things. Except now the local paper, which I prided myself on turning into a pretty serious news vehicle, was complicit in pretending that all was well in the multi-cultural Dewsbury world.

Suddenly the handcuffs were on the other wrists. The journalists had gone native, hand in hand with the appeasing bureaucrats.

I did take the time to speak to John about it, admittedly with some incredulity, perhaps vainly imagining that my experience, and what I thought we had both stood for when we ran the paper together, counted for something.

"We don't do that kind of journalism any longer, Danny," he demurred.

Forget my personal and professional disappointment at the time. John remains a good man and he was charting his own path which is every editor's prerogative. His may well have ultimately have been the more productive of the two paths – who am I to say?

We were and are, after all, two very different characters. It was probably naïve of me to think that I had somehow vicariously passed on my genetic editorial 'balls'. It was incredibly vain of me to presume that he should adopt my own perhaps confrontational model of editing.

But 18 months later when I decided the time was right to launch my own newspaper in Dewsbury against my former pride and joy of a newspaper, against John Wilson, all my old employees, and their huge publishing conglomerate, I took him out for a fish and chip lunch in Dewsbury.

I wanted to explain that it wasn't personal, but that the area really needed a new voice to speak up for the punters, and I was going to launch The Press.

You'd have thought I'd told him I was sleeping with his wife. In hindsight, he'd probably have preferred that I was.

14 - IN THE NEWS

I MENTIONED at the beginning of this story how an innocent young student from my son's school, Ahmed Hassan, was stabbed and killed in a random act of race-motivated violence by a couple of white drug addicts on Dewsbury Railway Station in 2008, a horrifically needless waste of a promising young life.

At the risk of repeating myself, no newspaper I have ever edited has consciously shown any favour whatsoever in standing up for the rights of crime's victims or condemning its perpetrators. Colour, religion, has never come into it.

If my frustration at the concealment of crime and the excuses for it appear to focus on one specific community, then it's only out of a sense of either 'fairness', or in the wider context of the issues and problems that attitude creates.

Cultural traits, levels of social deprivation, lack of employment opportunity ... all these factors may have some mitigating explanation for anti-social or criminal behaviour. But not wholesale whitewashing of it. When criminality and a sense of being beyond the law is allowed to take root and grow virtually unchallenged, then the question has to be asked – is it about police resource, or police will?

It would be lazy and unfair to suggest that police officers impose one set of laws for one community and one for another; no tax disc is no tax disc, uninsured is uninsured.

Speeding is speeding etc etc. There are regular arrests, prosecutions and sentences passed down, encapsulating the full range of drug, violence, sexual and fraud-related crimes. But such is the level of criminal behaviour, the police would have to walk around with blindfolds on not to occasionally fall over criminals at work.

If you're a young detective wanting to make your way in the world, and you don't mind stepping on a few toes, then Dewsbury's the place for you!

Because – and not to make light of it – we have criminals with a level of stupidity that is simply breathtaking at times. You wouldn't believe some of the 'defences' I've heard in my days covering the local magistrates court and the brazen idiocy of some of the criminal ventures undertaken within the Asian community has been simply gobsmacking.

Surely they didn't think they could get away with THAT?

Yes Mr Trading Standards man, of course those are bona fide Ralph Lauren jeans stuck in a grubby shop window in the centre of town, in front of every passing copper, for twenty-quid.

There's hardly a week goes by when a young Asian man doesn't drive into the Jet petrol station just outside town on Leeds Road, gawp into the bank of CCTV cameras, fill up his motor and do a runner. You'd think the huge poster at the garage entrance asking: "Do you recognise this man?" featuring the image of a similar chancer, might be a clue that the cameras are switched on. But still they do it.

One shamed dad hauled his son down there to confess his crime not long ago, after The Press splashed the picture in the paper – as we occasionally do.

Much of the everyday crime in our area effectively polices or solves itself through the stupidity or obviousness of the act, but there are too many incidences and, more worryingly, categories of crime which people are left with the impression of going unpoliced.

This is undoubtedly a far wider geographical malaise than Dewsbury alone experiences, but our circumstances mean the interpretation is understandably different from other people's. As I write this in the middle of 2011 we are only just discovering how police forces across the country have been suppressing the true levels of crime.

Crimes, we learn, are not generally reported or made public unless the force determines that such publicity might assist in solving the crime, or it is of such significance that they can't ignore it. More and more Chief Constables are admitting to this type of institutional cover up, so it cannot be a specific problem of ours.

By way of backing that up I've argued for years in print that police priorities are ever more focussed on creating an illusion about the levels of crimes, than about either prevention or solution.

When it's a garden shed that's been broken into, car stereos nicked, or shoplifting in Asda, that's barely an issue. When it involves violent, inter-racial crime, what might be bog standard policy takes on a more sinister air of conspiracy, especially in a town where such tensions are already overstretched.

And given that no senior officer will ever acknowledge the situation as an issue anyway, it compounds the public perception of reverse prejudice. Where there's neither a tacit admission of the policy, let alone debate about its rights and wrongs, then people's imaginations will understandably jump to the worst conclusions.

A CID officer might look at the bare facts of a four-on-one street attack with no witnesses (and no dead body) and judge that there isn't a cat in hell's chance of apprehending the miscreants.

He's busy, the department's over-stretched, the Chief Constable has a hard-on this year for eradicating fly-tipping or parking on double yellows etc (yes, a brazen exaggeration but you get the point) and the assault case is filed as 'active' without being actively pursued.

Common sense policing, yes? I say no. And here's why.

For the victim's family, where there's a racial factor involved – which means usually, in our district – it smacks of a cover up. You can understand why.

The questions present themselves to the victimised families: Is it a police reluctance to be seen as 'picking' on ethnic communities? They wouldn't fob it off if it was the other way round, would they? (I suspect they probably would actually, because it's more about resource/outcome than preferential treatment).

Is street-level heroin dealing tolerated because the localised social inconvenience it causes is judged a tolerable price worth paying? Are the cops laying off the Asian dealers because they don't want to upset them? Or because they simply haven't the manpower to cope? Or is it a bit of both?

No senior police officer would or could acknowledge the actuality of any of those possibilities. It would be his shortcut to an early semi-retirement at the force training college in Wakefield. We see plenty of those. And so the predictable outcome is that people reach their own conclusions, and none of those are productive for anyone.

Neither is the situation assisted by the occasional stupidity of a supposedly intelligent political collective like Kirklees Council, especially in deferring to its wildly left-wing officer-class.

However well meaning in concept, some of their policies have too often had negative impacts in practice, from something as simple as driving wedges between Muslim and white communities with their ridiculous diktats, to lumping congregations of young male Shia Muslim asylum seekers from countries like Iraq, slap bang in the middle of a settled Pakistani Sunni community.

Light the blue touch paper and stand well back! The multi-racial violence in Dewsbury is by no means confined to Asian-on-white-on-Asian. And when some of the asylum seekers of recent years kick off, they have no intention of taking prisoners.

THE BEST way I can conceive of illustrating these types of incidents, in a narrative sense, is to select excerpts of news stories from the pages of The Press in the weeks, months and years after I founded it in 2002.

The very first edition was published on March 9th and my editorial collaborator was the editor after I stepped back from the business in 2007, Martin Shaw. Martin was a locally born and bred journalist who cut his teeth in the Reporter group like myself, who also worked at the Yorkshire Evening Post in Leeds, and who had latterly run his own freelance business.

When Martin heard that I intended setting up my own 'small' independent paper against the might of the company that then owned The Reporter, he literally came knocking on my door and said he wanted to buy in.

He shared my vision of publishing a 'news' paper which didn't shy away from big issues, which left (for the largest part) the soft-news cheque presentations and community chit-chat to The Reporter titles.

We in the meantime were going to try to make our name by going for the jugular vein of the news stories that we felt were on the angry lips of most local people.

Martin was, is, one of the best news reporters I have worked with. In his simpler and calmer approach to being an impartial newsman he trumps me as a reporter.

I think he'd doff his own cap in turn to my vision in turning words and pictures into award-winning journalism, my treatment of the bigger stories and issues – more the feature writer than the straight news reporter I suppose you'd say – and my experience and confidence as an editor in flipping a finger at the gathered forces of authority.

Those authorities of ranked politicians and lawyers and police superintendents can be pretty daunting when the only thing backing you up is a pretty thin cheque book and no safety net.

What did I have going for me in trying to buck these odds? Well in launching The Press at the age of 42 I'd had 23 years of journalism across a wide spectrum of the UK media – from the Reporter to the Yorkshire Post, doing odd sports subbing shifts on the Daily Telegraph, running a magazine in California, and working as a sub editor on a daily newspaper in Australia.

I'd been an award-winning weekly newspaper editor, a director of the UK Guild of Editors, and had worked as a consultant on newspapers and magazines up and down the country. I thought, at least, that I knew what I was doing with a paper.

At 42 I'd not long hung up my rugby boots, so I was still 'full of it' energy-wise. And yet I wasn't quite old or cynical enough to fully comprehend – or care – about the enormity of the odds stacked against anyone stepping into the arena of the newspaper publishing business. Plus I am a Sagittarius. Apparently we often go off half-cock.

I'm not sure if Mrs Lockwood shared my enthusiasm for tilting at Dewsbury's windmills like Don Quixote, but I'd had my fill of manipulative employers' empty promises. I fancied my chances.

Well, they do say that God loves a trier...

THE BIGGEST crime that Dewsbury witnessed in the early part of the 21st century was the biggest single crime the world has witnessed on its tvs. In the early afternoon of

September 11th, 2001, I was making a cup-a-soup and a sandwich in the kitchen of the Lockwood family house, a modest stone and brick built semi in Bywell Road, a nice, middle class area just off the Leeds and Wakefield-bound arterial roads out of Dewsbury.

I was at home because a few months previously I had resigned my job as editor of the Lancaster Guardian and a group of motorcycling magazines, which had involved daily 180-mile round-trip drives. The 'job' had been done – we'd turned around a declining circulation and made the paper multi-award winning in the space of 18 months – and I had been busy setting up my own editorial training and consultancy business.

The problem that arose was a simple one. The company I was planning on delivering most of my training courses to was the one I'd just left. They'd seemed fine and dandy with the concept, given the many years' service they'd had from me – so of course they promptly axed my purported services the day I left the company. This was the company that also owned the Dewsbury Reporter, which lent a sizeable added incentive to my shoving two fingers back up at them.

I was delivering some training courses, doing some associate editing for Sport First, a London-based national sports newspaper of the time, but I was needing a plan B and was contemplating using the Apple Macs I'd bought to train journalists on to do something rather more radical – set up my own newspaper, here in Dewsbury, in opposition to the corporate group I'd recently departed.

I'd written the opposition's three-year and five-year business plans for long enough, done all their SWOT analyses for the past eight years. If I couldn't do it, no one could, I reasoned. The biggest problem was convincing my wife Glynis that it was a good – a workable – idea.

We had a small tv on the top of the fridge and I switched it on as I munched on my usual ham and tomato sandwich.

The scene was of breaking news, and what looked like one of the Twin Towers on the south end of New York's Manhattan island, smouldering as if something had ploughed into it, or exploded from within.

Literally, as I took in the scrolling newswire informing us that a plane appeared to have collided with the World Trade Centre, in the background a passenger jet arced around and in a balletic and silent slow motion that defied belief, disintegrated into the other tower.

That was my 'where were you...' moment.

The day the world changed.

The suddenly militant coming of age of al Qaeda and the hunt for Osama bin Laden characterised a violent step change in the until-then undeclared war between Islam and the west. But I can't honestly say that I noticed a sudden increase in the militancy of Dewsbury's Muslims specifically from that point onwards.

In hindsight you'd say it had been a creeping influence over a number of years but possibly only a reflection of the growing numerical influence of the community. Of course the visible difference would increase, the number of shops, mosques everything that would obviously represent a swing in the balance of two identifiably separate cultures.

But there were no pronouncements as such, no declarations of hostile intent from within the Markazi walls, no rallies in support of bin Laden and al Qaeda.

But neither was there any noticeable condemnation, except from the individuals you would expect it of – politicians from the Muslim community, people generally with a vested interest in taking such a public stance. From 'the community' there was very little indeed.

The extremist swing on our doorstep would become clearer over coming years, culminating in July 7th 2005 in London, giving proof that Dewsbury harboured more than its share of disaffected young Muslims.

It became clear too that the Markazi mosque was a common, if visibly 'benign' factor featuring in the backgrounds of many of the Islamic foot soldiers of the 21st century. On a day to day basis the silent expression of radicalism certainly became more pronounced – the volume of women being clad in head-to-toe-black, just the letterbox slit of their 'Zorro' outfits allowing them a minimalist window on the world.

The niqab became the most visible outward expression of physical separation. What I recalled as being rarely seen before September 11th in Dewsbury became a 'fashion' must for Muslim women in the months and years that followed.

The Sun made the point most starkly with a picture essay in November 2006, printing a photograph of happy, modern young Muslims in western dress, in front of designer shops, and another of veil-wearing, black clad women in a concrete precinct.

One group was in Lahore, Pakistan, the other in Dewsbury. No prizes for guessing which was which.

On one simple printed page, it appeared to give the lie to false pronouncements of the veil as a required symbol of female Muslim piety. It was, and remains for most people, the biggest provocation, insult, and barrier to any possibility of two communities ever making solid contact, let alone unthinkably becoming one.

For the most part, the drip, drip influence of the Islamic way of life manifested itself in small ways within everyday Dewsbury life.

The invasion of Afghanistan and Iraq by the USA with Britain as the most willing of lapdogs cannot have helped matters in the mosques, but even they went unremarked upon at large for the most part.

Public pronouncements of any kind were rare. Shops and businesses and buildings were quietly bought up and changed into mosques and madressahs without fuss – or consultation either. The sharia court didn't have a public opening, obviously. The lifestyle revolution has been largely silent, mostly bloodless, and virtually complete.

And where madcap public policies raised wider blood pressure, it was generally 'us' to blame – or at least the representatives of our systems and structures. The voices of common sense? Quite often 'them'.

Indeed at times of national or global outrage where there has been voluble local protest it has come from the race industry's henchmen, the Socialist Worker's Party offshoots within Kirklees's 'Unite Against Fascism' group. They were the ones trying to organise protest marches on our streets, to militarise the Muslim community – quite often with laughable outcomes as sensible Muslim politicians like Khizar Iqbal acted to defuse any potential confrontation.

In the months after September 11th 2001, my plans to launch The Press firmed up. I got a telephone call around Christmas asking if I was interested in throwing my hat in the ring for a senior job on the sports desk at the Daily Telegraph, but I was too far down the line with my plans by then. We launched on March 9th, 2002, a small but merry band, based in an old mill just outside the town centre.

The following excerpts from the pages of the newspaper illustrate the various strands of political, bureaucratic, law enforcement, cultural and criminal issues that have typified life in our patch.

March 16th, 2002

A couple are sentenced to 18 months in jail after their 15-month old son dies from a massive drugs overdose. Born of addict parents already with a heroin addiction, the child, despite being known to Kirklees Social Services, was left with the couple and died after swallowing prescription tablets strewn about the house. Kirklees Council refused to comment on the case.

The Press carries the story of 'Mary' a 52-year-old local woman whose son started stealing from her to buy drugs when he was just 15, and later turned to blackmail after he was beaten up by his dealers and left with a broken cheekbone. She goes to the Turning Point help group in Ravensthorpe where other visitors have nicknamed her 'Posh' because of her middle class roots.

"He knew that I wouldn't want that to happen again. It's like being held over a barrel. I am prepared to admit I have been a fool but there was just nothing I could do about it. I have handed over everything from £10 to £70 most days and I know I have funded my son's habit," she told The Press.

Eventually she sold the family home and moved out, leaving her son homeless – but via phone contact he still pesters her constantly for money. "Sometimes you just think it would be so much better if they were dead. There's not enough help out there and that seems to be the only solution. It's a terrible thing to wish your son dead but that is what heroin does to you."

Judith Wodecki, a team leader at the local Lifeline drugs charity says they are seeing 800 clients and are past their capacity. She says they are starting to see heroin users as young as 12. Meanwhile the police are claiming to be succeeding in their battle against the dealers, within sight of their target of arresting 106 'street dealers' in the Dewsbury Division.

March 23rd, 2002:

Highlighting the case of the single elderly Asian man who has a three-bedroomed council house. He comes around every week to put the wheelie bin out and give an appearance of the house being inhabited – he even brings rubbish to put in the bin.

Across the road are a couple with two growing boys in a

two-bedroom house who applied for the other property but were told by Council staff they didn't qualify under the stringent points system.

"We know what's going on. This man will pretend to live there – we know where he and his family actually live, in a nearby road – until they can buy the house from the council under the right-to-buy system at a knockdown price. Then they'll sell it and cash in." This proves to be a common state of affairs across the district over the years.

April 13th 2002:
An Asian businessman is the victim of gun crime, previously unheard of in this area. He was leaving work on the fringes of Savile Town with £22,600 in cash when two masked Asian men robbed him at gunpoint, firing a shot within a foot of his head – to scare him – and making off with the money. He explained the large amount of cash as being receipts from the bed manufacturing company he was involved in, explaining that Muslim customers prefer to trade in cash ... no arrests were made.

April 20th 2002:
A Polish lorry driver is shot in the leg after making a delivery to a motor spares company in Ravensthorpe owned by Amjad Mahmood, who found the driver unconscious and lying in a pool of blood. Three Asian youths were seen running from the scene. No arrests were ever made, no explanation for the motiveless crime made public.

April 27th 2002
Dewsbury Police report that street robberies have risen by 55% over three years, and car crime by 20% in 12 months, admitting the increase is down to drug addicts, but saying there is no reason for alarm as it only mirrors the upward trend across West Yorkshire and nationwide. Children and

their mobile phones, plus elderly women carrying handbags, were seen as most likely victims.

May 9th, 2002:
Ten-year-old Tiffany Nicholson is sexually assaulted in her school playground in Ravensthorpe when she arrives at 8.30am. An Asian man tried to kiss Tiffany and rub himself against her. No arrests were made.

May 11th, 2002
Community pharmacist Bob Dunkley voices exasperation at GPs signing methadone prescriptions for addicts willy-nilly, fuelling the trade in them swapping their supposed 'treatment' for heroin. "Even patients who are already on treatment programmes are being thwarted by GPs handing out drugs. It takes a totally different mindset to deal with an addict from any other kind of patient.

"I'm not blaming GPs because it can be extremely intimidating to have a heroin addict in your surgery demanding help. They come in with all manner of excuses to explain why they need more methadone and it would take a brave doctor to tell them to get lost."

June 15th, 2002
Probation officers join the demand for more Government help after it is revealed that of 48 drug treatment orders handed out in the district, 20 have been revoked and the offenders jailed. Local figures showed addicts are spending an average of £141 a week on heroin.

July 6th, 2002:
Dianne Bentham, 38, of Ravensthorpe, demands action after three Asian boys taunted her 12-year-old daughter Laura and friend Sarah Labourn, before stoning them. Laura lost a tooth and had three others broken, leaving her

needing dentures at 12. But despite police assuring the family they were treating it as a race-hate crime, and the girls being able to identify their attackers, two weeks later no charges had been made.

By August 10th, no one had still been charged and police refused to comment as "inquiries are ongoing." In mid-October Mrs Bentham described how the boy involved had made threats against both she and her family.

"We just want justice. He is laughing at the law and because he is a juvenile he thinks they can't touch him. He has been down to our house with a gang and we have had him shouting at us over the fence and he has called me a white bitch when he has seen me at the school gates."

She said they had had no contact from the police or the CPS who were supposed to be 'considering' the case. But senior officers Chief Inspector David Lunn and Inspector Keith Hallas had both moved on and a new community Inspector, Joanne Floyd, hadn't taken up her post yet.

July 21st, 2002:

The Labour-led members of the Dewsbury Area Committee vote to donate £1,000 to Ravensthorpe Community Centre in order for them to celebrate Pakistan Independence Day.

Coun Keith Oldroyd (Lib Dem, Dewsbury West) said: "This actually targets and favours one section of the community and it is divisive and if they keep on doing this there will be a backlash of feeling and resentment towards minority groups."

The grant was part of a £30,000 public budget the Labour councillors held sway over. Also among their plans were a grant of £8,776 to the Bismillah Project, a social club for Asian men in Savile Town, and £8,800 for a Good Health programme for Asian women in Savile Town. This was to allow women to "break away from the kitchen, encourage them to take exercise and to combat stress".

Coun Oldroyd pointed out that the Bismillah Project only had 12 members and added: "I know a lot of white married women who feel isolated in their homes, who don't go out and don't have many friends and maybe they could take advantage of this."

Labour councillor for the same ward, Mohammed Razaq accused Oldroyd of playing the race card, saying his attitude was aimed at winning votes from the white community. Coun Oldroyd claimed to be speaking on behalf of his fellow Lib Dem ward councillor Karam Hussain but maybe spoke too soon. Hussain, the local Lib Dem fixer, would shortly stage manage Oldroyd's de-selection and welcome his successor, the duly elected Coun Naz Hussain. No relation, apparently.

October 19th, 2002:
Safeway supermarket bosses apologise after an in-store promotion for halal foods goes wrong – they refused to allow white customers to participate! Forklift truck driver Andrew Sykes, 37, saw the staff member giving out free samples to Asian customers, so he asked for some and was told 'No, it's for Asians only'.

"There was an Asian bloke there and he didn't even ask for any. This woman stopped him to give him some," he said. Mr Sykes walked out in protest. "It is just racist and they wouldn't be able to get away with it the other way round." A Safeway spokesman said: "This was a misunderstanding and we apologise for any embarrassment caused."

Subsequently Safeway had a bigger ongoing problem with some of their other promotions which proved extremely popular with the Asian community – and particularly those in the convenience store business.

After shelves were emptied within minutes of store openings, the Safeway management started to impose limits on how many special offers customers could have. Quite often these proved even cheaper than cash and carry wholesalers.

In terms of local race relations this proved even more disastrous, as it got to the point where entire extended Asian families were turning up and forming long, if orderly queues.

Each son, daughter, wife, aunt, uncle etc etc would take their quota and quite often the father would stand at the till paying for each transaction as the younger family members loaded up trolley after trolley and went merrily on their way, to the obvious fury of white shoppers 'playing by the rules' – and the shrugged shoulders of the Safeway staff.

October 12th, 2002:

Batley businessman Shahid Iqbal Aziz, 28, is jailed for eight years for raping two women after posing as a taxi driver, but Dewsbury District Hospital nurse June Smith claims she had reported Aziz to the police the year before after seeing him cruising round Dewsbury town centre on a Saturday night.

She stopped two teenage girls getting into his car because he had no taxi plates on, but says when she rang police they refused to take her seriously, and wouldn't even take her details. Later when Aziz was charged and she again volunteered information, she was again fobbed off.

"The officer I spoke to said to leave it with him and that he would deal with it but he wouldn't take my name and address. How can they do anything without my name and address?" No senior officers from the Dewsbury Division were available for comment.

On a previous occasion before the launch of The Press, when the Dewsbury Reporter carried a police warning about girls getting into cars they thought were private hire vehicles, a mob of angry Asian taxi drivers laid seize to the newspaper building, which had to be locked down and the police summoned.

October 26th, 2002
The Press passes on information to the police about a 'Mr Big' drugs dealer operating out of a Batley social club. Witnesses tell stories of the man marching gang-handed into pubs to deal with 'bad debtors', about him selling drugs in the car park behind the police station, and even reports that he was considered 'untouchable' because he was a police informer.

One such source of the story however was decidedly questionable – because we had information that he was involved in drugs activity himself and he was trying to 'shop' a rival.

November 2nd, 2002
Kaleem Akhtar, 25, of Lemans Drive, Staincliffe, is charged with possessing a class A drug with intent to supply in the same week that The Press exposes the nearby 'Drugs Den' activities of Yunis Shaikh. Meanwhile a Coroner's court reveals that heroin and crack addict Asa Scott Layzell died from blood poisoning after injecting himself with a dirty needle, at his home in Chapel Fold, also in Staincliffe. He was found by his mother, who was left to bring up her grandson. Layzell stole to feed his habit and had only recently been released from prison.

November 30th, 2002:
Echoes of the Shahid Iqbal Aziz story earlier in the month return when 13-year-old Sinead Brearley and her friend 15-year-old Jordan Quinn were walking home at 10pm and an Asian man aged about 35 pulled up and asked if they were wanting a taxi. He drove them up a lane near Crow Nest

Park and locked the doors before pulling out a knife. He slashed Sinead's jeans from ankle to thigh. She fought back and suffered cuts and scratches to her face before he pushed her out of the car and made off. Jordan managed to get the window down and climb out, screaming for help, while Sinead fought off the man. No arrest was made.

February 28, 2003:
Park Road Junior and Infants School is criticised for 'policing' books on their shelves for any reference to pigs. As one grandmother said: "I can't imagine Muslim parents have complained about this. More likely it's some education official's interference that will just brew up more trouble between communities ... it's just political correctness gone mad."

In the event Barbara Harris, headteacher at Park Road which has 250 pupils, 60% of them practising Muslims, said the ban had been in place for years, but only on general-use books. The story of the Three Little Pigs was still available in the library.

March 7th, 2003:
'Dob in a Dealer' scheme is launched by police, but as drugs campaigner Jackie Frost says, "this will target addicts in the community, but not do a thing about the big dealers."

Local GP Eamon O'Daly reveals he is looking for "a French-speaking Arab with a smattering of Moldovan. I'll pay in flying carpets, elephants' tusks or whatever the heck they want," after he has two Iraqis, a Moldovan and a man from the Ivory Coast attached to his surgery.

March 21st, 2003:
The ARK Project is launched – Anti-Racism Kirklees – fronted by Khalid Hussain, chief exec of the Kirklees Racial

Equality Council, aimed at 'educating' youths on white council estates that could be breeding grounds for BNP recruits.

"We are determined to help people understand the need to live in a tolerant and multi-cultural community," he said. It is aimed exclusively at white young people with a view to altering their perception/behaviour. There is presumably no similar culture within young Asian society.

June 13th, 2003:

The story of Roger O'Doherty, professional council bureaucrat and Irishman with a grudge. He holds the chequebook at Pathfinder, a regeneration body for some of the town's worst-off communities, and threatens to pull the plug on £10,000 funding for the town's main annual summer gala unless Asian people become involved in the organisation.

No Asian people attended the organising meeting and O'Doherty wasn't happy because it wasn't 'multi-cultural'. Many of the planned activities were rejected by O'Doherty for not being appropriate – including a beer tent, pony rides, burger bars and a hot dog stand.

As volunteer Allan Haigh explained: "When he said the beer tent was not multi-cultural it was just beyond a joke." People began to walk out and Mr Haigh, a member of the Friends of Crow Nest Park group, added: "It wasn't anyone's fault there were no Asians attending. Mavis Secker (group chairman) even went into the park to ask some Asian lads if they wanted to join the meeting but they didn't want to come in. You can't drag people off the streets." Mr Haigh explained how Pathfinder even tried to hijack the Christmas grotto with an "Uncle Eid" character – but Santa was popular with Muslim families anyway!

Pathfinder had arranged a 'Mid-Winter festival' – where all the free food was Asian. "If it was supposed to be multi-cultural where was the English food?" he added. "Pathfinder is a publicly funded body that is causing racial tension which was not there to start with."

O'Doherty defended himself saying he had given the gala organisers a choice – to go it alone, accept a small grant, or make it a "community cohesion event" and get the £10,000, explaining that was what was required following the Bradford and Oldham riots. "It is not about 'giving it all to the Asians' which was a phrase used at the meeting, it is about building trust and respect'."

Of the beer tent he said: "If I hear people from Pakistan saying they would be happy to attend an event where beer is served, whether they partake or not, then there would not be a problem. It was my view that a beer tent would not be positive."

IN THE same week Coun Khizar Iqbal calls for the Black and Asian Police Forum to be disbanded, labelling it "racially divisive".

"If local white people approached the police for a white-only police forum they would be turned down flat."

At full council he launched an all out attack on Political Correctness, on the Commission for Racial Equality, and the politics of perception over fact. He also said one crucial thing: that he was able to say it because he was Asian.

"It isn't good enough that I can criticise race and community policies just because I am Asian. We should all be able to speak up on issues that concern us."

July 20th, 2003:

The first tentative public steps are taken into the local political arena by a young immigration solicitor and member of the left-wing Rowntree Trust, Mrs Sayeeda Hussain-Warsi.

After reading of O'Doherty's stance on the town gala, she

wrote in The Press: "It is an insult to me when Kirklees feel that they have to have token Asian people on committees so that they can tick the relevant boxes on national policy forms. If we want to be involved in an event, we will go through choice. And if we are not there it does not mean that we do not support the event.

"When funding for fun is linked to perverse political correctness it leads to resentment. Those who preach this should take responsibility for the ever rising racial misunderstanding and tension. But don't express your views in my name. I will be attending the gala, hot dogs or no hot dogs!"

On the same letters page a Sarfaraz Siddiq wrote: "As an Asian Muslim, who has lived in Dewsbury for most of my life, I find Mr O'Doherty deeply ignorant to the Dewsbury environment and quite alien to the majority of Asians of the area." He added: "Such gaffes as demonstrated by Mr O'Doherty have a detrimental impact on community cohesion and only serve to give incentives and propaganda material to the likes of the BNP.

"I would like to echo what was said by Coun Khizar Iqbal last week: the Asian community does not need preferential/differential treatment, we have been going smoothly as a multi-cultural society through the years, we don't need the status quo to be corrupted by puritans such as Mr O'Doherty."

July 4th, 2003:

Sayeeda Hussain-Warsi steps firmly into the limelight with what is to prove her audition for mainstream politics. Backing up the frustrations aired previously by Conservative councillor Khizar Iqbal, she also publicises a charity for Asian women she has set up in Pakistan, the Savayra Foundation, and an upcoming fund-raiser at the town hall which is due to be addressed by the ill-fated former Pakistan Prime Minister Benazir Bhutto, who would later be assassinated during her forthcoming campaign to return to office.

July 11th, 2003:
Nazi and NF graffiti is daubed on the homes of Asian people on the Staincliffe estate between Dewsbury and Batley. Councillor Paul Battye says: "This is the kind of thing you expect when you have extremist parties involved in local politics." This was in the week that the BNP were fighting – and would win – a by-election seat in neighbouring Heckmondwike.

Daniel Haigh, 16, is set upon by three Asian youths in Heckmondwike town centre. Police decided there was "no immediacy to attend" and advised the family to take their son to hospital. A week later the police still hadn't seen the boy and apologised to the family if their service hadn't met expectations.

July 18th 2003:
Two fire bombs are thrown into the Hot Spot Snooker Centre on Bradford Road, the main arterial/commercial highway between Dewsbury and Batley, but the petrol-filled bottles fail to explode. The two suspects were men wearing hooded tops.

Det Insp Bob Davies said afterwards: "We are still trying to establish a motive for the attack." Club manager Zafar Iqbal added: "Somebody shouted when I was in the office. I shot out and saw a fire on the floor and started stamping it out. I kicked the other bottle out but that made it worse. It could have been really dangerous. These people need to be caught." Some years later the club, well known for the criminal activity it harboured, would be raided, arrests made and drugs and cash recovered.

August 8th 2003:
Two men are shot at in a drive-by incident outside a takeaway in Westtown, near Dewsbury town centre. The next day rival gangs have a street battle with knives and machetes in Warren Street, Savile Town. A shot is fired at close range and five people were later arrested for possessing offensive weapons and wounding. Tory councillor Imtiaz Ameen said: "This is not the first warning we have had and if there is one problem the community has in Savile Town it is drugs."

Four cars of men from Bradford had reportedly arrived in town after a deal that went bad. A local dealer was beaten in the car park at the town's Asda supermarket.

Residents knew the gang would be back and alerted the police. One of the Savile Town Asian men claimed he was told by an officer that it was "a personal matter" and "you finish your business then we'll come along to clean up".

The running battle through the streets went on for 45 minutes and police did not arrive on the scene until a man reputed as one of the bigger local dealers collapsed bleeding in Mill Street, Savile Town. Supt John Cocliff said he was aware of the earlier beating incident at the Asda but denied any prior knowledge of the later clash.

August 15th, 2003
Coun Gulfam Asif says the fights on the streets of Savile Town were about young people sick of the crime and the drug dealing and fighting back against the criminals. "I am not defending what they did but how would you feel if these gangs were coming into your home or your street to sell drugs, to steal or to rob? You report it to the police but it still goes on. Are you being a vigilante if you are just defending where you live?" His views are widely ridiculed.

Coun Khizar Iqbal said police pay too much attention to

self-appointed 'community leaders'.

"The police seem more interested in sitting down with these community mediators over tea and biscuits rather than policing the area as they should. If criminal gangs are coming in from outside they need to be stopped.

"There is no need for the police, every time there is an incident in Savile Town, to sit around a table and ask these community mediators how they should react. This attack in Savile Town was about criminal activity and was not racially motivated so the police do not need community mediators."

August 15th, 2003:

Chief Supt John Cocliff calls for the community to help fight the drug dealing, shootings and knife fights.

Meanwhile two girls beaten up by Asian youths in the town centre, manage to get the car registration and a full description but claim the police do not want to know.

Michelle Wigglesworth, 27, and Samantha Ball, 32 were walking home in the town centre at 10.35pm on July 27. A sexist remark was called out by one of the gang, Samantha replied and subsequently she was pushed to the ground. Michelle was punched in the face and kicked twice in the head, leaving her with a broken nose and ripped gums – the three men escaped in a silver Honda Accord.

Police told them they had traced the car owner but he said he was out of the country and had lent the car to his friends. Despite the girls seeing the attacker in his car the week after, the police said they could do nothing.

In the same week a police officer held up a cortege of hundreds of people at ex-rugby player and popular local landlord Dennis Trotter's funeral because he had noticed a yellow bolt which made an O look like a C on one of the mourners' number plates.

August 22nd 2003:

Muslim graffiti and attacks have been carried out for years on the Rock House Bowling Club in Batley Carr – a club of mostly elderly white men and women in a predominantly Asian area. This time the star and crescent of the Pakistan flag are carved into the bowling green.

September 19th 2003:

A young Muslim family who moved 'up the hill' from Savile Town into Thornhill suffer racist abuse and have pigs heads dumped in their garden – the fourth attack in six months. White neighbours are disgusted with it. One neighbour says: "They are a quiet family who keep themselves to themselves. Why do these idiots have to go looking for trouble?" The police relaunch a Hate Crime hotline.

September 26th 2003

Some £400,000 of funding is granted to tackle race hate in white teens susceptible to recruitment by far-right parties, announces Khalid Hussain, chief of Kirklees Race Equality Council. There is no provision for addressing race hate attitudes in young Asian men.

October 10th 2003

A boy of 14 and his friend, eating lunchtime fish and chips in Dewsbury town centre, are attacked by a gang of Asian youths. One boy was punched, the other was sprayed with an aerosol which was then set alight – he suffered flash burns to his hands and face. When nearby shop staff went to the boy's assistance and called police they were told Dewsbury town centre had "no available officers".

October 17th, 2003

A new drug workshop 'Save a Friend' is launched after a dramatic increase in the number of drugs deaths. Lee

Massey is run down by an Iraqi Kurd illegal immigrant, whose gang also stab Danny Lee and his stepfather Darren – see next chapter.

January 30th, 2004:

Complaints come from the Asian community about organised gangs of asylum seeker beggars going door to door. Arif Shaikh, 30, of Savile Town, said his wife Yasmin, 23, was at home with their two children when a woman actually walked into their house.

"My wife was able to get her out of the house but I am worried about what could have happened. Asian women are often more vulnerable and my wife was really shaken up."

Coun Khizar Iqbal revealed the beggars were seen getting out of vans with pushchairs and children and carrying notes saying they are from Bosnia and hungry. "Even though they say they are starving if you offer them food they will refuse it and ask for money instead."

Insp Joanne Floyd said the issue had been raised at the North Kirklees Ethnic Minority Police Forum. Police had looked into the problem but found no evidence.

March 5th, 2004:

A father of two, aged 37, is jumped by gang of Asian men who pulled up alongside him in a car in Manor Way, Staincliffe, and beaten with a baseball bat. The police confirmed that it was an unprovoked race attack. No arrests were made.

Howden Clough junior football club in Batley is in the news with its £700,000 fund-raising effort for a brand new 3G soccer pitch. But after successfully applying for government funding the bid was challenged by the Inter Batley FC, an Asian team playing in the Spen Valley League, which said that ethnic minority groups had not been consulted in breach of Campaign for Racial Equality guidelines – despite the fact that Howden Clough High School is 70% Asian.

The Football Foundation was told by a judicial review it had to review its guidelines before the scheme went ahead. Typically, no one from the Inter Batley football team would not reply to The Press when asked to comment.

March 19th, 2004

Supt John Cocliff suddenly disappears from the Dewsbury division and is replaced by Supt Barry South who in turn is replaced by Supt Marc Callaghan after just six weeks. His message is: "It is time for people to fight back and say 'no, not in my neighbourhood'." The fact is, Callaghan is babysitting while South plans the merging of the Dewsbury and Huddersfield forces.

June 11th 2004:

Kirklees District Drugs Team celebrates its first anniversary by shouting about its success – 392 people arrested on drugs offences, 341 on suspicion of supplying class A drugs, with £697,000 recovered and £523,000 of goods seized. Was this evidence of the scale of the problem, a signal of the battle being won, or the team's ability to 'farm' the wealth of local dealers? The Drugs Team would eventually be disbanded.

July 16th, 2004:

Old age pensioners at the top of Manor Way in Staincliffe tell how they are sick and tired of abuse from drug dealing young Asians, with no help from the police.

One woman regularly watched a dealer weighing out drugs in his car, and occasionally had her garden used for stashing transactions.

When enterprising neighbours saw a dealer hiding a stash in a wall they went and recovered it themselves and called the police – and were asked to bring the drugs to the station.

"I was told by the officer I could have made £400 selling the stuff on the streets," said one woman. Tony Gott was sick and tired of phoning the police and also his Lib Dem councillor Paul Battye, but nothing was ever done.

"On one occasion one dealer was at it in his car," said Tony. "I called the police and they said they would send someone up. Sure enough a patrol car drove up the road, turned around and drove off! The dealer was still here. They just don't want to know, it's as simple as that. We can see the packets changing hands.

"The caretakers at both local schools are picking up needles left right and centre. The bushes at the back of the bungalows are full of them. It has been going on for quite a while. We have been reporting it and reporting it."

Councillor Battye refused to get involved in the matter as he said he had "a family to think of".

September 17th, 2004:

Forty taxi drivers besiege Dewsbury Police Station after cabbies' boss Mohammed Raja is arrested in a row over a parking space. The taxi drivers also brought Batley's 'golden mile' pub and club promenade to a halt with a slow-moving convoy to the station where they demand Raja be released.

October 1st, 2004:

Dean and Amanda Foley go public about a complaint they made to police three months previously regarding an attack on their 11-year-old daughter Saffron by an Asian woman. They gave the police the woman's name and address and that of other witnesses yet nothing was done.

But when their 15-year-old daughter Cheri was involved in a shouting row with an Asian girl after the two friends fell out, the family were knocked up within an hour by police over allegations of racial abuse. "The police have got their priorities all wrong," said Mrs Foley of Ravensthorpe.

"They have refused to investigate a serious attack by a woman on a young girl, in front of so many witnesses, yet they can be around within the hour when two girls fall out and have an argument, like they do."

Saffron had been attacked by the woman and punched repeatedly after two groups of children had been making fun of each other. Another woman had pulled her off the girl. A police spokesman said "if the complainant wishes to discuss any of the matters further we will be happy to speak to her."

February 18th, 2005:
An 18-year-old white man ends up in intensive care after a mass brawl in Birstall town centre between the white occupants of a taxi and the staff of an Asian private hire firm. Following the incident 80 taxi drivers converged on Dewsbury Police Station.

April 22nd, 2005:
Mohammed Yaqoob, 23, "a high living gangster" who ran a heroin factory from a two-up, two-down house in Mirfield is jailed for 12 years. He was unemployed, had learning difficulties and lived with his mum and dad in Sackville Street, Ravensthorpe – where I was born – but still managed to drive a Ferrari.

He had laundered hundreds of thousands of pounds in London and was in the process of trying to double production when police seized him. He had been in the process of taking £150,000 to an address in Harrow. On his laptop police found pictures of him sitting in piles of cash.

Defending barrister Mr Bill Evans said Yaqoob came from a hard-working middle class family but hadn't shone like his brothers and sisters. They certainly 'shone'.

One of them, a notorious local character known as Mr Sparkles (after his car wash) was jailed in September 2009 for money laundering and fraud, a charge he had shared with another brother who also happened to be an assistant governor at Armley Jail in Leeds. The brother was cleared.

Previously 'Mr Sparkles' had been a regular in the news after he bought a handsome detached home in Mirfield for £295,000, tore it down and erected a nine bedroomed £1m monstrosity – without planning permission. Planning officers ordered it demolished, but after a public inquiry – when several neighbours who had objected decided to withdraw their complaints – it was allowed to stand.

Fraud Squad investigators may have been intrigued by Sparkles telling the town's magistrates that his earnings were less than £20,000 per annum when he was earlier prosecuted for fly tipping.

July 1st 2005:

Elderly women are reported as selling over-prescribed drugs like Valium, Temazapam and Diazepam to Methadone patients. Bob Dunkley noticed the number of attempted break-ins on his pharmacy were down and asked one of his many friendly addicts where they were getting their benzos from – and he replied "little old ladies".

August 5th, 2005

Rafiq Siddique, 38, who runs Trade Price Beds in Dewsbury tells how he and three friends were abducted by secret servicemen in Dubai and tortured in a 10-day ordeal. His business partner Alam Ghafoor, plus Faisal Raja and Zaya Dad feared for their lives after being handcuffed and dragged from their hotel. Siddique said they were questioned over the July 7 bombings and new MP Shahid Malik called for an investigation and apology for the men.

But...December 1st 2006

Naz Ashiq, Billy Jones, and Balal Ali Khan, all of the Trade Price Beds company in Dewsbury, are arrested in Brazil at a hotel in Foz go Iguaca, a city near the border with Argentina and Paraguay. They were found with more than £50,000 in Brazilian currency and a kilogram of pure cocaine. Police also arrested five Paraguayan men.

Back in Dewsbury, co-director Shaf Siddique said they were all innocent men, who were importing pine beds from Brazil. Shaf said: "Naz is a genuine, honest man. He is well liked in Dewsbury. He doesn't have a criminal record, not so much as a parking ticket."

Shaf had previously featured in The Press when he was beaten up in a "motiveless attack". However in a follow-up raid on the premises of Trade Price Beds and associated financial services businesses in town, police seized £35,000 in cash. Eighteen months later Shaf Siddique was still trying unsuccessfully to get his £35,000 back.

August 12th, 2005:

A letter in The Press from Aafaq Butt after the July 7th bombings says: "My message to Muslims in this country is simple, please respect the fact that this is not an Islamic country, never has been and never will be..."

September 23rd 2005:

Shaun Conway, 22, is attacked by a group of Asian youths near Thornhill High School. He confronted them after they shouted racial abuse at him. He ended up with a broken leg, as his attackers filmed the incident on their mobile phones.

Conway said detectives who visited him said that if he made a formal complaint he too could be prosecuted, persuading him to let the matter drop.

September 30th, 2005:
Lee Pygott, 31, suffers horrific facial injuries in an assault. He was pushing his bike along High Street towards Dewsbury when he was attacked by three Asian men. Three hours earlier a 24-year-old man had also been beaten by a gang fitting the same description. No arrests were made.

October 14th 2005:
Diane Oldroyd 35, and her four children are evicted from their house in Dewsbury Moor after a year of racist threats, obscene behaviour and threats of violence towards neighbours.

November 25th, 2005:
A gang of 15-20 white men and women break into a flat in Thornhill and beat up two Asian men who had gone there with white girls.

December 23rd, 2005:
Taxi driver Khalid Akbar, 33, is shot twice in the legs by other Asian men in a targeted attack, say police – but they don't know the motive. No arrests were made.

January 6th, 2006:
A shotgun is fired twice at a block of flats where Iraqi Kurds live after a number of clashes with local Pakistani youths. One local resident said: "Some Asian friends told me the trouble was over Iraqi lads making passes at Pakistani girls and women.

"It's nothing new round here, though it's quietened down after the Lee Massey case (see separate chapter) when some of the troublemakers were dispersed.

"But that all blew up in the first place out of these young Iraqi blokes having a go at white girls. Whereas the white community had to put up with it, the Pakistani and Asian men won't stand for it and I think that's what you're seeing here."

Kirklees Council is one of the most pro-active local authorities in the country in bidding to 'house' asylum seekers (and thus attract Government funding).

Unfortunately its policy of placing the young men in existing Muslim communities has occasionally explosive repercussions. Literally.

January 20th, 2006:

Colourful Dewsbury businessman Azam 'Mr Sparkles' Yaqoob is arrested for kidnap by Greater Manchester police over an incident concerning an Asian man from Rochdale in summer 2005.

Yaqoob said he had lent the man "a substantial amount of money" to import Chinese commodities, a business deal which apparently went wrong, but denied the sum was the £50,000 a police source had suggested. The man eventually dropped his complaint and no charges were brought.

January 27th, 2006

Mick Merritt, 55, of Headfield View in Thornhill Lees, on the border of Savile Town, answers a knock at the door and is savagely beaten by three Asian men, dressed in black. They did not speak and just left him crumpled on his doorstep. No arrests were made.

March 10th, 2006:

Anjam Yaqoob, 25, of Ravensthorpe fails in his bid to get his 12 year prison sentence cut. Barrister James Pickup QC said "all of his many (eight) brothers and sisters were either doctors or lawyers" although brother Azam "Mr Sparkles" has no such profession. Appeal Court judges said he didn't get "a day too long".

April 7th, 2006:
Kirklees planners announce a project of 28 five-bedroom houses in Savile Town which they describe thus: 'The houses are designed to suit the needs of the local Muslim community in Savile Town who are considered to be the most likely purchasers. They are large family houses with four parking spaces each.'

Councillor Khizar Iqbal said he was "insulted" by the remarks. "This is almost a racist comment. Imagine if we had said this was a development for the indigenous white community? The council would have been jumping up and down all over it."

June 2nd, 2006:
Father of two Amjid Rehman, 40, found his new council house daubed with racist grafitti on the mainly-white School Lane estate in Dewsbury Moor. Mr Rehman said he would not be deterred. However, in an echo of similar reported incidents over a number of years, neighbours complained that Mr Rehman despite having the tenancy of the house, didn't appear to have moved in or used it in the coming months.

June 9th, 2006:
Terrorist police swoop on Savile Town after arresting a 16-year-old schoolboy Hammaad Munshi, grandson of senior Islamic cleric Yakub Munshi, who runs the Shariah court, and nephew of failed Labour council candidate Abdul Hai Munshi.

Meanwhile a 16-year-old boy, wearing his school uniform for St John Fisher RC High School, is on his way to sit a GCSE exam when he is punched by a youth holding a bunch of keys and 'happy slapped' by a gang of seven Asian youths in the middle of Dewsbury at lunchtime.

When the boy managed to crawl into a coffee shop one of his attackers popped his head round the door and said "Sorry mate, can we give you a lift to school?" Despite numerous witnesses and the incident happening yards from the divisional police HQ, no arrests were made.

July 28th, 2006:
Pakistani and Iraqi Kurd gangs are involved in running street battles in Savile Town with baseball bats and metal bars on the night of Sunday July 23rd. One Kurd underwent brain surgery in Leeds, after 12 police cars and riot officers brought the situation under control. Only two men were arrested.

The asylum seekers were living in Savile Manor, a building used as a hostel by Kirklees Council. Four more men were arrested after more clashes on the next night, Monday, and the violence spread to Ravensthorpe on the Wednesday night when a gang of Pakistanis surrounded a car with three Iraqis inside.

Police said there were unconfirmed reports of shots being fired. Two of the Iraqis escaped but the third, Sirkot Mahmoud, 22, was hit by an iron bar before he fled to his home.

August 11th, 2006:
A group of young white men and women complain about police treatment of an incident where they claim to have been attacked by staff in a curry restaurant following a disagreement about their meal.

When they flagged down an ambulance for assistance, and one of their group became over-excited in his complaints to attending police, he was arrested. The officers refused to go into the restaurant to question their attackers. The man, who needed stitches in his wounds, was held in a cell for 12 hours before being charged with common assault. A young woman suffered a broken nose and swollen face. Five months later, despite repeated requests for an investigation, the police had taken no action over the attacks.

A police spokesman said: "We accept that there have been some communications issues." One of the men said: "The police had just decided we were a bunch of drunken whites, carrying on in a curry house. It couldn't be further from the truth."

October 13th, 2006:

Chief Supt Barry South apologises after yet another racial attack is ignored by Dewsbury police. Jane Birchill asks if someone has to be killed before police act, after a gang of a dozen Asian youths attacked her son Thomas, 17, who was beaten to a bloody pulp.

It followed a case three weeks earlier when police declined to attend a reported incident of three schoolboys being attacked. Mrs Birchill described how a woman had saved her son from serious injury. When the police were called they asked if a weapon had been used, before saying it wasn't an emergency and they would visit the next day. Five days later they still hadn't been to see the mother or victim.

Mrs Birchill said: "We live in a mixed area. The Asian lads round here play football and cricket with Tom. They get on fine. As my (older) son was putting on one shoe to go looking for the gang I was pulling off the other one stopping him.

"An Asian neighbour who's a taxi driver and whose kids come in our house asked why I'd stopped him. He said if it was his child he'd go after them too.

"It's our own police making us prejudiced and racist, not the people we live with."

Despite accepting the police had not provided the service

people had a right to expect, Chief Supt South refuted the accusation that the matters were not taken seriously.

November 17th 2006:

A gang of more than a dozen young Asian men are accused of systematically beating up white youths. After 17-year-olds Thomas Abbott and Luke Elliston were both attacked without any meaningful response from the police, Supt Barry South admitted that officers had "failed the family".

March 30th, 2007:

Non-teaching assistant Aishah Azmi loses her appeal against Kirklees Council's decision to sack her for refusing to remove her full face niqab garment when helping children at Headfield Junior School.

Azmi's father was subsequently revealed as being the head teacher at the fundamentalist school linked to the Markazi mosque, Mohammed Mulk, of the Jaamia Talimul Islam. Ofsted had critcised the school the year before for its "over-emphasis on religion".

Mulk had told the Times Educational Supplement: "Parents send their sons here for an Islamic education. They don't want their sons to take exams."

Ironically Kirklees Council was sued by Azmi via the council taxpayer-funded Kirklees Law Centre.

May 5th, 2007:

It is revealed that a Sharia Court sits every other weekend at the Islamic Institute of Gt Britain in Thornhill Lees – the former White Hart Inn.

In its defence Conservative shadow cabinet member Sayeeda Warsi said: "Sharia law is often misunderstood and what is important is that we have a grown up debate. When people talk about Sharia law they think of punishments like hands being chopped off or men being allowed to have four wives but Sharia law is more complex than that. I live my life according to Sharia principles."

Warsi added: "As a lawyer I have seen the heartache of Muslim women divorced under British law but who remain tied to the man because they are not divorced under Islamic law."

Despite publicly proclaiming the virtues of arranged marriages to Pakistani relatives and the bliss of her own such circumstances, Warsi and her new beau would subsequently have low-key Sharia divorces – after she became Baroness Warsi of Dewsbury.

May 25th, 2007:
Fighting erupts between 40 Hungarian and Pakistani men in Ravensthorpe, after the eastern Europeans are alleged to have "touched' an Asian girl.

Police recovered weapons at the scene and two men were treated in hospital. Shopkeeper Vinny Burman reported how grown Hungarian men were chasing Pakistani youths down Spen Valley Road brandishing machetes and knives.

Insp Jon Carter said: "We are working closely with the Ravensthorpe community to discover what happened." The police don't disclose details of arrests, if any are made.

July 6th, 2007:
A gang of Asian youths known locally as the 'Ravy Terror Squad' comes to prominence after a series of attacks on isolated white people on the Spen Valley Greenway, a converted railway cutting turned walkway and cycle path, running between Ravensthorpe and Dewsbury Moor.

In May of 2008 members of this gang would be involved in the brutal murder of one of their own community, 17-year-old Amar Aslam, in 'the Wildflower Garden' at the town's Crow Nest Park. Amar, a loner with learning difficulties, was kicked and beaten beyond recognition.

Initially police indicated that it was a racially motivated attack on the quiet-spoken Asian youth, prompting the mass descent of the national media, but this transpired to not be the case. The national media quickly lost interest and moved on.

September 28th, 2007:
Two men aged 37 and 41 are beaten up by a gang of 30 – members of the Ravy Terror Squad, who ambush them after hiding in trees. This is a week after a 15-year-old was stopped and beaten by the same gang.

Insp Jon Carter repeats a previous mantra he has used about the perpetrators: "This is not a gang as such, more a peer group which has got involved in crime and anti-social behaviour. They hang out together and one or two have become misguided and unlawful."

A Kirklees councillor, the BNP's David Exley, says he is still waiting for a response from Insp Carter nearly a month after complaining about the police's failure to investigate the racist abuse of two white women.

Meanwhile driving instructor Paul Berry, 41, was called "white scum" by two carloads of Asian men who tried to drive him off the road. He got the registration of the car and the mobile phone number of the main aggressor after the man phoned him to abuse him – the aggressor had got Mr Berry's phone details from the sign on his L-driver car.

Five months later, the police asked him to do an identification parade via a DVD – and then only after the newspaper reported the delays in the case being investigated.

December 7th, 2007:
Dewsbury District Hospital suggests that nurses could turn Muslim patients' beds towards Mecca and that female

Muslim patients could be treated only by female doctors.

Councillor Khizar Iqbal remarked: "It appears that political correctness has again reared its ugly head. It is not the Muslim community that is asking for these changes. It is probably some do-gooder who thinks they are doing the right thing, but they are doing more harm than good."

Head of Nursing Tracey McErlain-Burns denied the claims but accepted it might be necessary for a caring nurse to "adjust the position of the bed".

December 21st 2007:

Ahmed Hassan, a 17-year-old pupil of Heckmondwike Grammar School is stabbed in the back and killed at Dewsbury Railway Station while preparing to go on a shopping trip with friends to Manchester. Michael Brook, 18, and a 17-year-old youth were later charged with murder.

January 11th, 2008:

Mayor of Mirfield Bob Bennett apologises and resigns after someone leaked a private email which made derogatory comments after a Muslim group asked to address the Town Council.

Mr Bennett wrote: "I am aware Islamic organisations are keen to promote a view that they are peaceful, forward thinking individuals who wish to integrate into the British way of life.

"The policy of clothing the feminine population of Dewsbury in black sack-like clothing from head to toe, the occasional trip out to cause mayhem with explosives and the proposal that all those of homosexual persuasion should be killed by shooting or other means is adequate and practical testimony to the level of progress made in this direction. I for one am not prepared to spend the time on something that can be dealt with elsewhere. We have enough non-religious problems to address in Mirfield at this time without adding a religious dimension to our discussions."

February 29th, 2008:
Police investigating the disappearance of schoolgirl Shannon Matthews say the crucifixion of a man on the estate is not related to their search.

The man, 43, was found nailed to a makeshift wooden cross. He had been in his flat in School Lane when he was reportedly attacked. The police said "he was not believed to have been seriously injured."

March 28th, 2008:
In the early hours of Tuesday March 26 there are a series of tit-for-tat firebombings, on the Nawroz restaurant used by Iraqi men as a social club, on a BMW car, then at Highgate Beds – owned by Sunday Times rich-lister Mohammed Ayub – and also on a house and on two cars owned by Pakistani men. Three adults and a baby had to be rescued after an arson attack on a house in Dewsbury Moor the same night. None of this attracts media attention outside the pages of The Press.

May 30th, 2008:
Outgoing Kirklees Mayor Jean Calvert describes how her year in office was spoiled by incidents at public occasions when Muslim men refused to be photographed with her. One event at Dewsbury town hall was the North Kirklees Sunni Muslim Council of Mosques. The men were happy to have the Mayor along to validate their jamboree, but firmly told her "we don't have photos taken with women".

She hit back when her replacement as Mayor, Dewsbury West councillor Karam Hussain, chose his daughter-in-law as his mayoress. By tradition the outgoing Mayor's consort places the chain of office on the successor's neck, but Hussain refused to allow Nasreen Akhtar to be touched by a man, and asked that the ex-Mayor herself do the job. Mrs Calvert refused on principle.

Of the photo incident, Hussain said: "This kind of talk is not appropriate. It is past history."

June 30th, 2008:
Top Break Snooker Club in Batley is raided six years after The Press told police officers it was a drugs den. Police seize £40,000 of cannabis, two stun guns and £8,000 in cash. Four arrests are made.

September 26th, 2008:
Retired builder Tony Gott speaks out once again after years of drug activity in the cul-de-sac at the end of Manor Way in Staincliffe. He's called a "fat, white bastard" and showered with bricks by Asian youths. Police say they are stepping up patrols.

April 10th 2009:
Rashid Farid, 35, an accountant who ran Lifestyle Mortgages is revealed as having organised a mortgage and money laundering fraud that netted £800,000. He used the internet to find mortgage-free homes then changed Land Registry deeds before obtaining mortgages or re-mortgages.

The money was moved into various accounts before being transferred to Pakistan. Rashid, a business neighbour and 'friend' of us at The Press, got 11 years and his brother and father were locked up for four and two years respectively.

15 – LEE MASSEY

THREE TIMES in the late autumn of 2003, senior medical consultants asked Lisa Massey if they could switch off her husband's life-support machine. Scans showed no brain activity, at any level. Iced water, sprayed into his ear, drew no response. His eyes were bottomed out in a lifeless pool.

If there was anything left usefully alive of Lee Massey, no medical expert practising their clinical arts at Leeds General Infirmary could detect it. But his healthy organs could be used to save others ... after all he was in excellent shape. His dead brain apart of course.

At the age of 29, Lee was an incredibly fit young man, a talented rugby league player, hence his body surviving as long as it had, given that a car had been aimed deliberately, directly at him, accelerating all the time, throwing him 15 feet into the air, shattering his bones. He landed on his head.

The first ambulance that arrived stopped 100 yards away from his lifeless body at the top of North Road in Ravensthorpe and refused to approach the crime scene on health and safety grounds.

They were waiting for police to arrive, even though Lee lay dying in the middle of the road, while two of his pals were trying to staunch the blood flowing from stab wounds they'd had inflicted while innocently entering the back door of the Royal Hotel in Ravensthorpe. Witnesses and friends of the injured men pleaded with the paramedics. Nothing doing. Rules and regulations.

The frightened ambulance staff need not have worried as it transpired. The gang of up to 20 illegal Iraqi Kurds who had ambushed Lee Massey, Danny Lee and his stepfather Darren Lee, plus their friends out for a friendly Sunday afternoon drink and karaoke session, had already fled the scene. It would be months before police rounded them up, and particularly the man who used a car as a missile to aim at Lee Massey.

It was a case that would end up with me, a journalist, in the dock at Leeds Crown Court. For a while it looked like I was the only one who would go to jail over the whole despicable exercise in judicial arse-covering.

Lisa Massey, Lee's then-wife, admits there were times she wavered over the requests to mercifully shut Lee down and help save a number of other lives with his valuable body parts.

Her uncle – my next door neighbour and best friend Keith Ward, an eminent member of the clinical teaching faculty at Huddersfield University – intimated privately to me that he couldn't envisage any way back from Lee's coma.

He was as brain dead as Keith had ever witnessed in his many years working on wards and in theatre, before he took to the classroom .

Keith wasn't just a lecturer in clinical studies. When I'd met him 17 years before he had been the charge nurse on the ward at Dewsbury Hospital where my dad was trying to come to terms with his terminal cancer.

Jimmy Lockwood wouldn't hear wisdom from anyone's lips, consultant, doctor or whatever. But when Keith Ward told Jim that was that, he nodded his head and started coming to terms with the terminal reality of his condition.

We buried Jim on what would have been his 53rd birthday. He never saw any of his grandkids, or his son become the editor of the local paper.

Keith shook his head as we had a bottle of beer each over our garden wall in Dewsbury that evening discussing Lee Massey. He was a lost cause to all intents and purposes, at least judging by Keith's long experience.

But three times Keith's niece Lisa and Lee's mum Margaret refused the doctors' requests to pull the plug and donate his organs. Lisa even brought in a faith healer to pray over her husband's badly broken body.

Blind faith? The power of prayer? Whatever it was, six months later Lee Massey walked in unaided to Leeds General Infirmary to greet the doctors who had wanted to end his life.

I see Lee still on occasion, driving his transit van around the district or walking his daughter Jessica to school, his big rottweiler on its lead. I put a free advert in the paper for his new business venture cleaning wheelie bins just last week.

Lee has been left with a limp and brain damage – his speech is impaired, though he still makes eminent and occasionally brutal sense – and though he's divorced from Lisa now and he'll never play rugby again, he's alive.

That wasn't just a miracle, it was the only good news to emerge from one of the most shameful episodes in the history of the Dewsbury division of the West Yorkshire Police Force.

I RECEIVED a call that the main Huddersfield Road through Ravensthorpe had been sealed off on the Sunday evening of October 24th 2003, after I got home from work, producing my rugby league newspaper League Weekly. It was too late to head back out and too dark for any useful photographs. We'd find out what was happening on the Monday morning.

My colleague, news editor Martin Shaw, phoned the police newsline on the Monday morning to hear details of what they briefly described as "a minor incident" between two groups of young men outside a Dewsbury public house which had left two requiring hospital treatment.

And that was that. As big a blanket thrown over any potential negative publicity, any multi-racial violent incident as you could ever wish to see. But the local tom-toms had already been beating, word having it that Lee, a very well known and 'colourful' character, was either at death's door or, if things could be any more distressing for his family, already dead.

At that time the Divisional police HQ was still in Dewsbury, but as they were becoming increasingly practised in, the local officers were all hiding under their desks and shoving all inquiries in the general direction of the Regional Crime Squad. 'This one's not on our shift, beyond our pay scale, sorry!'

This is as accurate a description as I can contrive of what happened on the fateful day, though the catalogue of incidents leading up to it reflect grievously upon policing attitudes in the town.

Lee and a group of pals had been on a typical Sunday lunchtime pub crawl round Ravensthorpe, as previously described another former mill community packed with old terraced houses stretched alongside the river Calder a mile or so to the west of Dewsbury.

It is not so much a community as an ethnic web of 5,000 souls leading incredibly disparate existences, with a dominant Muslim population that had been managing to co-exist reasonably well alongside established white neighbours. What happened that Sunday would quite incredibly unite British Muslim and white alike against a new common foe – the Iraqi Kurds.

Many of the terraced back-to-backs that were my first

home in Sackville Street – about 300 yards from where Lee was attacked – have now been replaced by more suitable social housing. That was one of the benefits that the 1990s Single Regeneration Budget brought.

Living harmoniously beside us in the 50s and 60s were the Poles who had escaped Hitler's mad rush through Europe. Like Savile Town, Westtown and Scout Hill, as white families moved out of Ravensthorpe it became a largely Pakistani community by stealth.

Apart from the pubs that line Huddersfield Road – Ravensthorpe straddles the main arterial route between Dewsbury and the Council headquarters up the valley – the vast majority of the businesses on the busy road are Asian, and it is now a gaudy, neon-blighted succession of curry houses, taxi firms, utilitarian open-all-hours shops, retailers of Muslim clothing, jewellery, mobile phones. And drug dealers. Lots of those.

The occasional tensions and the violence have simmered underneath the surface with occasional explosive ruptures but like Savile Town, the police apply a very hands-off approach. Street law prevails.

Then came the next wave of migrants – this time the Iraqi Kurds, dissolute young itinerant men, 'refugees' of Saddam Hussein's regime, apparently hungry for nothing except trouble. That was Dewsbury's experience at least.

Whether because they were Muslim like the predominantly settled migrant population, or because there was simply the housing capacity, Kirklees Council vigorously applied itself to taking more and more refugees, complete with the accompanying Government handouts.

It was a financially lucrative exercise for the (small 'l') liberal council in Huddersfield and they fondly imagined it ticked lots more of their left-wing socially engineered multicultural boxes.

They literally poured these dissolute, non-English

speaking young men into Ravensthorpe and Savile Town and other heavily ethnic, but socially deprived areas like Westtown, which found themselves still acting as migrant staging posts 150 years after the Irish first came to town.

But it was to prove a firework so combustible that Kirklees Council's Politically Correct social engineers didn't even need to light the blue touch paper. The Kurds were fiery enough to explode into the local consciousness without anyone else's help.

Much of the public violence witnessed in Dewsbury in the second half of the 21st century's first decade was Muslim on Muslim – Iraqi on Pakistani and vice versa.

Still, having built the bonfire Kirklees made sure they stood well back both before and after the chain of events unfolded which would leave Lee Massey at death's door.

They are probably puzzled why Muslims don't simply get along famously together and walk hand in hand to mosque. The morons probably don't watch the news or read the papers. Sunni-Shia seems to trump Muslim-Christian every time in the hate and violence game, wherever you look in the world at large.

Maybe it's because they have a tendency to fight back.

AS ANGELS GO, Lee Massey would be considered a bit of a devil by even those nearest and dearest to him. He was a charmer with an eye for the ladies, despite being married to Lisa, with whom he had a four-year-old (at the time) daughter Jessica. Theirs was a turbulent relationship, to say the least. He worked as a driver and was a talented rugby league player – but that devilry lay at the heart of the reasons Lee never made it as a professional. He was too fiery, too unpredictable.

Only of middling build, he was deceptively strong, immensely fit, but that competitive nature and a tempestuous fire – especially when playing alongside his older brother Dave – made for entertaining viewing, especially if you liked your rugby of the combative type.

I played for quite some time for the same rugby club as Lee and Dave, Dewsbury Celtic, one of the north of England's most famous amateur rugby league clubs, Irish Catholic-based as its name suggests. I was the senior player in matches Lee participated in once or twice. Controlling Lee was like trying to put a muzzle on a cobra.

The best thing the opposition could do with Lee was not upset him, which in Yorkshire League Saturday afternoon rugby league was not an altogether familiar concept.

The rougher and tougher the game got, the more Lee and Dave Massey punched – often literally – above their weight. In those games, you were glad they were on your side, even if you occasionally finished a game playing a couple of men short.

On that fateful Sunday, the lads had been out for a usual Sunday lunchtime wander which generally ended with a karaoke session in the Royal Hotel on Huddersfield Road, near its junction with another 'main' thoroughfare, North Road, which runs at right angles. Waiting in ambush for them was that gang of up to 20 Iraqi Kurds, armed with knives, baseball bats, bricks and table legs.

A concerned member of the public living on a nearby road, having seen the Kurds gathering and sensing something amiss, had already alerted the police. The police didn't respond, unlike the day before, when some members of the same Kurdish gang had been involved in a disturbance in another pub 200 yards along the main road – Rosey's Bar.

On the Saturday evening England's football team had been playing a World Cup qualifying game, and though Lee wasn't present in Rosey's, some of his pals were in there to watch the game – one of them being an Albanian, an immigrant himself ironically.

Albi – no lack of a sense of irony among these lads – and his girlfriend Michelle, a barmaid at the Royal Hotel, had had trouble with the Kurdish gang some weeks before. There had been a catalogue of incidents over the past few months involving sexual overtures towards local girls by this gang of young 'incoming' men. When a couple of them first made sexual comments, then made a grab for Michelle's breasts outside a local takeaway one night, after she'd finished work at the pub, Albi took offence.

When the Kurds persisted with their attentions Albi waded into them throwing punches. They retreated – but swiftly returned with both reinforcements and weapons.

Albi ran for his life. Michelle hid under the counter of the nearby Zam Zam takeaway in North Road and dialled 999. That was around midnight. No one from the police force attended – in fairness these incidents are ten-a-penny – and she eventually made her way safely home.

A young policewoman arrived at Michelle's house at 9am the next day and listened to her story but persuaded her that the matter wasn't worth pursuing. It had all blown over. Albi had got home safe and everyone was in one piece.

But of course it hadn't blown over.

On the Saturday evening in Rosey's some of the Kurds visited the pub, saw Albi and his pals watching the match on tv and called up their friends who rapidly arrived in cars, armed with a variety of weapons and piled out.

A fight ensued, spilling out of the pub, before several police cars attended and broke things up. Strangely enough – or not if you know this town – there were no arrests made.

That was Saturday late afternoon, but it hadn't been the only violence in Ravensthorpe that weekend. On the Friday night a young man walking in Sackville Street near where some of the Kurds lived was jumped upon for no reason by a gang of men he could only roughly describe as Asian, and kicked senseless. By location, behaviour and description, it sounded like the Kurds.

Police did not respond to that attack either and his furious mother spent most of both Saturday and Sunday going between the hospital and police station trying in vain to get someone to take her complaints seriously. The police certainly hadn't by the time I spoke to her a few days later, but then again matters had escalated somewhat.

You don't need to have been Sherlock Holmes or Inspector Morse to have detected that the writing could not have been more clearly on the wall. Not if graffiti king Banksy had been given a weekend in Ravensthorpe and a lifetime's supply of spray cans. Trouble was brewing.

And yet despite the serious nature of the incident on the Saturday night, plus the attack on Friday, and the history of incidents plaguing the area, there wasn't a single community officer or patrol car keeping the remotest of watchful eyes on the streets of Ravensthorpe the following day.

The police didn't even respond to the alarm call from a citizen who could see that mayhem was about to occur. And she wasn't wrong.

Behind the Royal, and the back door that regulars usually used, was a car park with a skip on it, and a back street leading onto North Road, forming a square between that back road and the main Huddersfield Road. It was there that the Kurds lay in wait. When they finally attacked it wasn't Albi they got to – a number of the group were already inside the Royal – but Danny and Darren Lee.

Landlord John 'Butch' Butcher saw the attack and raised the alarm with a shout, at which point Lee and Dave Massey and their pals, despite being unarmed, stormed out of the back door to confront the attacking gang.

At that point the Kurds, although outnumbering the

local lads and with their variety of weapons, gave flight, scattering back towards their homes down and across the other side of North Road. Two of them, with a man called Mohsen Sadiq in the drivers seat, jumped into a blue Honda Civic parked nearby.

Khan revved up, accelerated away along North Road and aimed his vehicle straight at a group of the people who had spilled out of the pub. Fortunately most saw the danger and jumped clear, but Khan and the Honda caught Lee Massey full on and just kept accelerating away, leaving him for dead in the road.

That's what happened, in brief. In the immediate aftermath and hiding behind a bland and – in my opinion criminally culpable – statement, the Dewsbury police simply pulled down the shutters and refused to comment, leaving the investigating to the regional big boys.

Suddenly there were detectives and coppers and patrols all over Ravensthorpe, but of course the horse had well and truly bolted and most of the Kurds had abandoned ship, heading off to stay with 'cousins' and friends across the country.

As Lee battled on, hooked up to his life support machinery, the community of Ravensthorpe, British white and Muslim together, suddenly found a common cause and a united front.

They marched together from Ravensthorpe to Dewsbury town hall to protest against Kirklees Council's policy of housing migrants and illegals and creating such a combustible mix. For the most part they were making a decent fist of living alongside each other; the last thing they needed was another incendiary ingredient being poured into an already unstable mix.

In subsequent days police arrested five men, but no charges were laid at that time.

Jackie Frost of the Turning Point drugs drop-in centre on

the road where the violence erupted, said: "Ravensthorpe is ready to kick off big time and no one can say the warning signs haven't been there.

"There has been trouble with the Iraqis for months. They are going around with knives, machetes, baseball bats and iron bars. Young lads are being beaten up and girls can't walk the streets at night.

"They are being propositioned and offered £40 to go upstairs. They talk about living in the Bronx but that is what living in Ravensthorpe is like and the council have created that.

"We have the homeless, addicts, Africans, Iraqis and Albanians in this area and all this is breeding contempt in the community. This is probably the first time the Pakistani and English communities have been united.

"The dealers rule Ravensthorpe. They threaten and beat up the users and force them to work for them. They go into their homes and 'tax' them as they call it, just taking what they want. There's nothing they can do about it. They can't call the police because what they are doing is wrong."

Jackie, locally born and bred, wasn't a lone outspoken voice. Father-of-seven Javed Iqbal moved to the UK in 1985 and gets on well with his white neighbours.

"We are family people and we don't want bad people round here. The Pakistanis get the blame for what the Iraqis are doing and that is not good ... the Iraqis are ruining this community for all of us. People are coming from outside and ruining our friendships. I have never seen anything like this before," said Mr Iqbal.

I spoke to the pub landlord John Butcher on the Monday. He told me he had been aware of some men hanging about in the car park behind his pub.

"I saw Darren (Lee) coming in the back door, he was just on the wheelchair ramp I have when this bloke came up and, I thought, punched him on the back. But when his hand came back it had a knife in it."

Darren had been stabbed and suffered a punctured lunch. A half inch to one side and he would probably have been killed. His stepson Danny ran to his aid and was struck by a machete on his arm and side. Both men were hospitalised for several days.

Butch said customers then ran from the pub to confront the gang, numbering about 15 men, led by Lee and David Massey. Some of the Kurds ran back down North Road towards Sackville Street and Dearnley Street where they lived, others to parked cars including Moshen Sadiq's Honda Civic.

Over the next few days questions were put repeatedly to the police from The Press on the variety of incidents that pre-dated the attack on Lee but I hadn't received a single answer by the Thursday when we went to print.

After that edition of The Press on the following Friday, our reports on the attack and the events that had preceded it, The Press was reported to Chief Constable of West Yorkshire and Trevor Phillips, head of the Commission for Racial Equality, by the now professional Race Industry bureaucrat and successor to Khalid Hussain, Jamil Akhtar. (Note: Why don't there seem to be any white race industry professionals?)

He remarked in his official complaint: "The police have handled this very well and reassured the community that this was not a matter of race but of young men behaving as young men all too often do."

Oh really? Lee Massey and his rugby mates go around with baseball bats and machetes trying to kill people? I must have been on holiday for that week's edition of the paper...

Akhtar went on: "Not only has the paper (The Press) done all it can to stir up the senses that this incident was racially based but has given information on how to gain access to the Iraqi men involved to anyone wishing to make trouble out of this."

We had published that some of the men were believed to live in the neighbourhood, nothing more. We didn't have any names to print.

He concluded: "This newspaper would be very worrying at the best of times. With the current activity level of the BNP in North Kirklees this newspaper is causing us a great deal of concern. Please do let me know what action you think the police can take regarding this problem."

So that was it. The newspaper was the problem, not the violent criminals intent on mayhem, not the non-existent policing, nor the incompetent social engineers at the unfit-for-purpose Kirklees Council. It was my fault!

There was no response to the demands for the prosecution of either The Press or myself from Chief Constable Colin Cramphorn, from Trevor Phillips, and nor indeed have there been on the numerous occasions that Akhtar, his agitators, and the combined membership of KRAFT (Kirklees Refugees and Friends Together – an immigrant support quango) have reported us for "inciting racial hatred".

Akhtar's written complaints that he referred to over the Lee Massey case were from Shahid Malik's soon-to-be new best friend Terry McKay and his left-wing sidekicks in their anti-fascist brigade.

In January 2004 Mohsen Abdul Rahmen Sadiq, 27, was arrested and charged in regard to the incident on North Road. Sadiq had fled and lived in the Bolton and Preston areas with countrymen.

It transpired that he had been in the UK altogether for four years after reportedly fleeing a massacre in his home town of Haladje. He was arrested on January 15 at a Preston takeaway. He was charged with causing grievous bodily harm with intent.

In quick succession six more men charged with wounding with intent and violent disorder. Bestoon Osman Mohammed of Ravensthorpe was charged with wounding Danny Lee, Bahgat Fayzulla, 26, of Dewsbury Moor, Nizar Maeloud 25 of Pontefract, Dana Ali Mohammed of Huddersfield, Ari Karim 26, of Birmingham, and Saman Ahmed of Dewsbury were all charged with violent disorder.

Eventually on Thursday November 26, 2004, 11 men went on trial at Leeds Crown Court in connection with the attacks outside the Royal public house. One defendant never appeared in court.

In turbulent scenes even before the trial started David Miller, a freelance reporter acting on behalf of The Press, was thrown out of court and verbally abused by a defence barrister while simply trying to collect the names and addresses of the accused – which he was entirely within his rights to do.

When the barrister tried to have the men's details kept secret reporter Miller had to take the stand, and after directions over the phone from his editor – me – the trial judge, Alastair McCallum, sided with us.

After nearly two months of delays, legal arguments and adjournments Judge McCallum threw out the violent disorder charges against four of the defendants including Mohsen Sadiq, who still remained charged with driving a car at Lee Massey.

The remaining accused were eventually all acquitted, one by one, by Judge McCallum with alleged knifeman Bestoon Mohammed even awarded £200 from public funds for his inconvenience.

After landlord John Butcher was ruled to have confused some of his identification parade evidence, one by one the slick, publicly-funded defence barristers, had the charges against their clients knocked over, despite there being barely an arguable doubt whatsoever that they had been present, and armed, during the attacks.

The families of the three men so grievously injured had to sit and watch open-mouthed as the grinning defendants walked away without so much as a breach of the peace or threatening behaviour conviction against their names.

Upon the conclusion of the acquittals and the end of that stage of the trial Lee's mum Margaret Massey and Danny Lee's mother Ady Lee stood up and lambasted the judge in open court, who let them have their say before replying "I know how you must feel".

Margaret and Ady described how the defendants laughed and joked throughout the trial and described one, who claimed to need an interpreter, as sitting reading an English newspaper.

Another young woman, Debbie Lee, 21, had seen the entire incident but was puzzled why she was never called as a witness. One of her friends who also witnessed all of the violence was not even interviewed by investigating police.

At one point Lee Massey, in a wheelchair, attended the trial and wheeled himself to the front of the court so that he could get a good look at Mohsen Sadiq, at which point Judge McCallum ordered the jury out and had Lee and his family removed.

AS A newspaperman and especially when you take the editor's chair, you have something of a choice. You either develop a big brown-puckered kiss to administer to the appropriate backsides where the police and judiciary are concerned, or you strengthen the first two fingers of your hand of choice, and get used to sticking them in the faces of authority.

I've always by nature favoured the latter. However it helps if you have a passing acquaintance with the law, which all qualified journalists (certainly of my old school) are required to have. I've lost one particular courtroom battle where I got a bit too big for my own boots, because as I found to my cost, however much a judge can see through a duplicitous son-of-a-bitch's lies, he will generally side with a smart-mouthed barrister who knows the law, over a self-righteous editor who really, really, should have spent money on a lawyer.

The Mohsen Sadiq case was rather different.

In the fall-out from the Lee Massey case the coverage in The Press particularly was exhaustive. Even when the BNP picketed tv studios in Leeds for effectively being complicit in the police cover-up by suppressing coverage of the incident we covered the story in full.

On the streets of Ravensthorpe in the following weeks we dotted every 'i' and crossed every 't' in the case – which we were explicitly allowed to do, because no one had been arrested, let alone charged. Only when that happens does the concept of a case being 'sub judice' become live. And the police were so slow bringing anyone to justice that everything that could be said and speculated about Lee's case in Dewsbury already had been.

As had become so familiarly frustrating in these cases, and would continue to be so until the day they literally packed their bags and retreated to Huddersfield, the Dewsbury police command simply shut up shop to public inquisition. All the questions we asked about the weekend of violence in Ravensthorpe were stone-walled.

No comment, can't comment, Regional Crime Squad matter now ... Blah-de-blah.

The trial was brought in Leeds Crown Court 10 miles away, but far enough out of our circulation area that a jury could be comfortably found, without needing to draw from our readership. As explained, Sadiq was tried and acquitted along with his countrymen on all of the general affray charges.

I had written to Judge McCallum trying to gain guidance on the legal protocols involved, because Sadiq was on a separate charge of GBH with intent, over his driving of the Honda at Lee. That had not been part of the general attack evidence.

When Judge McCallum discharged everyone and Margaret Massey and Ady Lee kicked off, I once more attempted guidance from the court but never got it – and so reported the families' understandable anger at these laughing criminals walking free with utter contempt for all of us, not least our legal system, but more importantly for Lee Massey.

I saw that as being a separate process to the trial of Sadiq for his attack on Lee, hence my attempt to seek clarification.

The defence legal team however decided that the only person in contempt wasn't the grinning thugs, but me for writing about that concluded part of the case. McCallum stopped the trial, dismissed the jury and summoned me to Leeds Crown Court.

I had to take the stand and explain why I should not be reported to the Attorney General for contempt of court, and not be personally made to pay for the trial being halted, then moved to another court.

My personal experience of judges – mostly – is that they are pompous arseholes, but McCallum was right up there with the best. In my respectful view of course m'lud, if you're reading. I understand that he's a keen golfer. A right shanker, I'll bet.

When a judge puts you in the dock as an editor, you're supposed to come over all contrite, apologetic and respectful, and explain how misguided you realise you were with a full ration of 'ever-so-humble m'lud' backtracking. I do confess that I was as nervous as a newborn kitten.

My problem was that, as far as I understood the law, I

hadn't done anything wrong. So I said so.

Sorry for the inconvenience and all that, but we could not prejudice the trial because due to the geography and our limited circulation, no juror could/would see the reporting, but more than that, because of what had been so extensively reported before any arrest/charges were made, you couldn't get an unbiased juror from Dewsbury anyway.

And besides, the two trials had been separate entities, certainly in respect of evidence given, and we hadn't reported anything that could possibly prejudice Mohsen Sadiq's case. We had focussed specifically on the two women's reaction to the collapsed part of the case.

At least so I believed and explained to the court.

Those blond wigs that judges wear? I thought McCallum's red face was going to blow his through the Crown Court ceiling. This was not the right answer, on any level. The courtroom was a picture of stunned silence.

"And that's my view, with respect, you honour."

McCallum stormed out. I never did hear whether he referred the contempt to the Attorney General or not. I never received a bill for the completely wasteful and unnecessary halting of Sadiq's trial and its switch to Bradford Crown Court either.

However towards the end of February 2005 Mohsen Sadiq received a 12 year jail sentence for the attack on Lee Massey, the jury taking only one hour to find him guilty. Judge McCallum described Sadiq as "callous and wicked" and said he wished he could have given him a longer term.

When told of Lee's injuries Sadiq said indifferently: "That's his problem."

In one statement he said that in his country when people get into a fight they have to be prepared to die.

The judge said he demonstrated "a lack of humanity I have not encountered in the many people who have come before me. I wish I could pass a higher sentence for this crime but I am bound by precedent."

It was revealed that illegal immigrant Sadiq had already had his application for asylum rejected. He appealed against the severity of his jail sentence in October 2005 but it was thrown out of court.

There may be better examples in recent British social history of a more cataclysmic failing of local authority social engineering, plus corporate police dereliction of duty in the face of 'ethnic tensions', but I believe the Lee Massey case will take some beating.

I saw Lee a few months ago walking through Crow Nest Park, close to his daughter Jessica's school and not far from where we played rugby together. He was smiling through his gold teeth, limping along as well as could be expected, and coping admirably with his speech impediment.

He told me he'd received his compensation payout from the Criminal Injuries Board, that it was a "fair whack" and he'd bought a nice place, and things were going along pretty well. He was with a new girl.

His ex-wife Lisa had moved on from their relationship and had a baby with her new chap.

I suspect – no, I know – that whatever the "fair whack" of a payout Lee had received for his injuries, he'd have preferred his old life back. And five minutes alone with Mohsen Sadiq, armed or otherwise.

I know who my money would have been on.

16 – MALIK VERSUS NEWSPOST, LOCKWOOD & SCOTT

IF THE OLD nipsy was twitching like a cat with an itchy nose in front of Judge McCallum at Leeds Crown Court, it was as nothing compared to the prospect of a two week, full-on, jury trial in England's senior libel forum, Court 13 of the Royal Courts of Justice in The Strand, before Judge David Eady, the British judiciary's pre-eminent libel judge of the day.

In November 2007 Eady's reputation as the back-door architect of a British privacy law, and friend of pants-down celebrities everywhere, had not yet been cemented. It wouldn't come as a surprise to me that Eady was no apparent great admirer of the British press, even as minuscule a public organ as The Press.

What a bloody fool I was to get into that battle.

If you've never been in a situation like that, and understandably the vast majority of people never have, then it is quite a surreal experience. There I was coming up to 49-years-of-age, with more miles on the clock than the entire Ferrari Formula 1 team, yet I remained as wet behind the ears as Nellie the elephant at bath time.

I've mentioned some of the elements behind the libel case and will state them again here just to set the scene. Few of them were seriously disputed in the trial.

The only surprise, in hindsight, was that they ever saw the light of day in court. That was down to the vanity and ego of both myself and Malik, mostly.

As described, Jonathan Scott, the political sidekick of ultra-popular Muslim Dewsbury South councillor Khizar Iqbal, was defending a healthy majority in the 2006 local elections. There had been a confrontation between the canvassers and Labour supporter Abdul Hai Munshi two days before the polls in the heart of Savile Town.

After that, Munshi phoned MP Shahid Malik and asked him to put pressure on the police to prosecute Khizar for assault. Malik rang Chief Inspector Keith Hallas and insisted on action. Hallas said he'd look into it and he did.

Unfortunately for Malik and Munshi, CCTV footage revealed Munshi as the instigator and aggressor. Unfortunately for us, our instructing solicitor Stephen Taylor-Heath neglected to introduce the CCTV report as evidence until well into the trial itself and Eady simply threw it out. Munshi's lies in the witness box couldn't be exposed.

Canvassing in the area before the election, Scott and Iqbal were met on so many doorsteps with sympathetic ears but entirely understandable responses that they had promised to vote for their Muslim brother – Labour's Masood Ahmed. Sure, they were angry with Blair and Labour over Iraq, but Masood was one of them! What's to argue about?

Frustrating maybe, but that's how 'the community' works. It certainly didn't come as any kind of surprise to those of us within the Dewsbury and Batley political system. It wasn't even newsworthy.

On the day of voting, various witnesses described the scene outside the Orchard Street polling station in Savile Town variously as 'quiet', a 'mob', a 'carnival atmosphere' or a 'tense and intimidating crowd' all depending on their political affiliation. The truth? Probably both, again depending which side you were on.

Scott stood and watched Labour tellers greet their friends and neighbours on the door of the polling station and breach just about every electoral guideline you could find. He complained to the deputy returning officer, then again. He got nowhere. All of this after an already typically dirty campaigning season with inflammatory literature, lies and counter-lies and slurs and mischief everywhere you turned.

It was just part and parcel of a Dewsbury election from where I sat.

For Scott there then came the 'thousand yard stares', the implicit threats from flash young Pakistani men in their fancy cars, letting the middle-class white bloke in the suit and blue rosette know exactly what they thought of him. "Remember this face," said one young man, the son of a millionaire local businessman. "You'll be seeing it again."

Scott, who was brought up in the white working class neighbourhood of Chickenley, not much more than a mile from where he stood, had had enough. He phoned Chief Insp Hallas and told him of his problems. A full-time police presence was put on the Orchard Street station.

Despite Labour suffering electoral meltdown across the country, in Dewsbury South a massive swing to them and Masood Ahmed left Jonathan Scott out of office and, understandably, bruised by the whole experience. This might have been politics, but not as most British people would understand it.

The problem for all of us, ultimately, was that Shahid Malik was rather too close for Scott's comfort to the action. You would never have got his predecessor, Ann Taylor, so involved in a grubby little local ward campaign. She was smarter than that.

However involved Malik was – and views on that understandably polarised as the issue took on greater gravity – the MP delighted in the result, especially in the face of Labour's dire performances elsewhere. On the ground, he was crowing about the result his campaign in Dewsbury South had delivered.

And equally understandably, Scott was left incredibly disheartened, as a democrat, over what he'd experienced and witnessed at the Savile Town polls.

He wrote his letter decrying the 'death of democracy' and submitted it to both The Press and the Reporter. We used it as was, the Reporter took maybe one line out. I didn't, and still don't, find it as grievous a slur on Malik's character as his London lawyers subsequently played it.

Scott was bemoaning the death of democracy as middle England might see it, but as an editor I was seeing it in the context of the already blighted, less-than-honest political realism on our streets.

Scott's views didn't make front page headlines in The Press even when news editor Martin Shaw followed the letter up the following week with an interview about the treatment he had suffered in Savile Town. It was perhaps understandable, if regrettable (for all concerned), that Scott chose to pin Malik's colours too closely to the flag of what he'd undergone at other individuals' hands.

In general political terms most people would say it was understandable. After all, as the town's MP Malik was the Labour figurehead in and around the election generally, especially in the manner of his presence there, if not in any tangible responsibility.

In any political mudslinging it would be unusual for one party not to spread it far and wide, to include the opposition's leader. Just everyday fare, I thought, especially by the standards of Dewsbury's political knockabout.

When we finally settled the case more than 18 months later I was happy to state that there had never been an intention on the newspaper's part to accuse Malik of any wrongdoing, during Scott's experiences of polling day. He really hadn't done anything wrong, either in my mind as the editor or even as a third party observer, but that in itself was part of the problem – interpretation.

Much of the trial would revolve around the meaning and interpretation of words, not a black and white case of facts. I make no wonder the jury were befuddled, especially after Judge Eady's various rulings meant they were only seeing half of the pieces of a very intricate political and personal jigsaw.

At an early stage of the trial preparation Eady made it clear that not only would we be unable to test Malik's wider character in defending our position, but that no mention could be made of the BNP.

Given that most of Dewsbury's politics revolved around the issues which had promoted the BNP's vote to the highest in the country, and Malik's reputation as the bete noire of the nationalists, this felt like we were being handcuffed before we ever got close to trial.

At the time of publishing Scott's letter and interview and even in the weeks afterwards – apart from one conversation with Malik 10 days after the original letter was printed – it didn't appear to be a problem.

We carried on our cordial editor-MP relationship until he blew up over a letter from Sayeeda Warsi's sister, as detailed earlier. At that I can only surmise that the Labour party's pet lawyers, Bindmans, and their pitbull-in-chief Tamsin Allen, decided the Scott stuff would be best to beat us over the head with.

If you've ever received a solicitor's letter you'll be aware that they don't deal in polite diplomacy. It's blitzkrieg from the off, the clear tactic, their default position, to scare you shitless into rapid submission. They probably even dream in terms of Armageddon. With just a few, rare exceptions, I hate the bastards with an abiding passion.

And me being me, their aggressive tactics bring out the

very worst. There is no jockeying for position, no diplomatic tact involved by way of response – I sent back a letter conveying several dozen varieties of an invitation to 'go stuff yourselves'.

It was a piece of furious prose which didn't help resolve the impasse, obviously, and which would be used against my character when we came to court. What followed was a 12 month pantomime that, in hindsight, was little more than a game for the lawyers.

Our solicitor Stephen Taylor-Heath, and barrister Jonathan Crystal, advised us that these cases never came to court. Well, 99 per cent didn't. They hadn't dealt with a couple of stubborn mules like Malik and I before. And while ever we remained resolutely intransigent, the lawyers could continue feeding our daft ideas and – certainly on our side – milking our rapidly dwindling financial reserves.

Malik was represented on a CFA, a Conditional Fee Arrangement (no-win, no-fee in layman's terms) meaning Bindmans were so confident that they were throwing the kitchen sink at us for no cost to him and would milk us dry at the end.

They didn't think it would end up in front of a judge either. They also must have thought we had a) lots of money, or b) libel insurance. Wrong, and wrong.

I didn't think it would come to court either, but we had to carry on posturing as if it would. I couldn't believe that an aspiring young MP, self-proclaimingly close to Prime Minister-in-waiting Gordon Brown and darling of Labour's National Executive Committee, would want all of his (and Dewsbury's) dirty laundry airing in such a public forum.

But then again I couldn't begin to understand how narrow-minded the laughingly titled 'law' is, or the fact that the legal profession is a barely veiled industrial process of removing vast amounts of cash from fools. That was us.

The case itself? This would not be about the wider issue

of 'Paki Politics' that had infested and degraded Dewsbury, long before Shahid Malik entered the fray. It would be a battle instead of legal semantics. It truly is a marvel that Scott and I emerged through the other side in more or less one piece.

A judge's job, as I came to understand, is to 'manage' the process using his legal knowledge as a sort of intellectual car manual. In that Eady clearly failed because after two weeks the jury was patently split with no hope of reaching a verdict. This motor wasn't going anywhere.

Half of them instantly took to Malik and didn't like the look of me, while some of the others could smell bullshit when it got right up their noses, and some of the rubbish spouted in the witness box on Malik's behalf was as patently credulous as some of the frankly embarrassing evidence given on ours.

I spent half the fortnight either biting my lip in frustration, or cringing.

Bindmans set about deconstructing our defence line by line and they were spectacularly successful. Our flash young Leeds solicitor Stephen Taylor-Heath was and is a personable enough chap, but by the end of proceedings I felt he was so far out of his depth up against Malik's legal team that he ought to have been passing instructions to our barrister Jonathan Crystal from the bottom of the Thames.

It was almost all so very different however – we came within an ace of having to defend ourselves in court. Taylor-Heath worked for the legal firm Fox Hayes of Leeds, later disgraced by the Law Society, broken up and put into administration.

Having extracted over £90,000 in fees from us during the 12 months before trial, Fox Hayes got in touch less than a fortnight before it was due to start, saying that if we didn't find them another £50,000 by close of play that day, we were on our own. Just like that – and then they refused to pick up the phone when we tried to reply.

The three journalist directors of NewsPost, our publishing company, met with Scott and agreed that we simply didn't have that money. Nowhere. We were skint, all our personal credit cards were maxed out. There had been a very spirited public fund-raising effort to help us foot our legal bills and that had been emptied out too.

That was that. So we left a message on Fox Hayes' answer phone – they were probably sat listening – that there was no money left and we'd represent ourselves as best we could.

Cue Fox Hayes to come back and offer to do the trial part on a CFA like Malik/Bindmans. If they won they doubled their fees – which Malik would have to pay. If we lost, at least we wouldn't have their bills for the trial on our backs.

Given that any kind of loss would have bankrupt the lot of us (via Bindmans' costs alone) never mind damages for Malik, it was hardly an issue. Onwards we ploughed.

In the event, and despite our legal efforts being slapped around like an ugly stepchild (Malik later confided to me that Bindmans couldn't believe how poorly our case had been managed) we were assisted in no small part by the former MP himself.

The judge had ruled that we could not mention that Malik had brought his libel writ only against us, even though our competitor newspaper the Dewsbury Reporter had also published Scott's letter.

They hadn't published a subsequent apology, so what was the difference if he wasn't just trying to bully us, the small independent paper, into silence? Not relevant, ruled Eady. So on his first morning in the witness box Malik blurted it out himself. That puzzled the jury for starters.

When I eventually took the witness box there was nearly blood and snot flying between me and his barrister Adam Wolanski. I went off on so many tangents, spreading muck left, right and centre, that even Judge Eady sat back looking aghast. It was like a referee throwing his red and yellow cards into the crowd and going to the bar for a beer.

The poor jurors were clearly wondering what the hell was going on, because I left them in no uncertain mind that in my view at least the entire case was decidedly NOT about Scott's letter, but that I wasn't allowed to mention what had actually prompted this libel action.

I got away with that one, and not half.

I even escaped censure for the trial diary I'd been writing in The Press in which I'd repeatedly and insultingly 'misspelled' Wolanski as Wankowski. Someone must have scanned and emailed it to him from Dewsbury, because the little dandy tosspot threw a wobbler and demanded that it be given to Judge Eady, inviting him to rule on it as a clear case of contempt. The clerk duly took it into chambers.

It's probably my fanciful imagination, but I swear I heard Eady laughing. Either way, there was no legal recrimination against me. Not over that, at least.

I'd managed to throw in a few hand grenades about Malik's character – like his stern words to hardline British Islamists that if they didn't like it here in good old blighty, they should ship out.

That was very popular to the mainstream public, but it didn't paint quite the same picture if you picked up copy of a Muslim-only publication to find a photograph of Shahid Malik protesting outside the White House in Washington, accompanied by a Palestinian flag.

'Paki Politics' in its simplest form – two very different messages for two very different constituencies of voter. Nothing wrong, per se, in either stance, but all too often completely inconsistent. And coming from an ambitious and often controversial would-be minister of state it was always, but always, bound to draw attention and comment.

Neither did Malik help himself by standing in the

witness box and saying that he'd been chatting with one of our defence witnesses, Chief Insp Keith Hallas, at a Remembrance Day service just before the trial started, and that the senior officer had told Malik he'd been 'bullied' into giving evidence.

Our barrister Jonathan Crystal was on that like a rat up a drainpipe. Malik stuck to his guns as the instructing solicitors raced each other out of court to ring Hallas and find out if that was true, because Malik was impugning a decorated officer's integrity and character, and implying deceit. For good measure Malik told the court that he felt Hallas wasn't "assertive" enough in his job.

Keith Hallas was understandably furious in denying anything of the sort although sadly, ultimately, it could be argued that he paid for that episode with his career, because he was a virtual leper back at HQ when proceedings were drawn to a close.

Under advisement and with the jury sent out, Malik told the judge he would like to change his mind, go back in the witness box and apologise for what he'd accused Hallas of. Eady ruled against him, meaning Hallas could take the stand and show the MP to be a liar.

So Wolanski simply got to his feet when the jury was back and told them anyway! Eady sat there like a lemon. My heart just sank through my boots.

Justice? As tv character Jim Royle would say: My arse.

There was more, lots more from Malik, some of it not really seeing the light of day until the MPs' expenses scandal much later. A critical piece of the evidence was our disputed attempts to phone Malik to give him a right of reply. He swore he only had two mobile phone numbers. In his shamed expenses claims, he clearly had three.

It was a small thing in context of the trial, but symptomatic. Further dissembling about where he actually 'lived' played a big part in our attempts to hold him to scrutiny. Again, his subsequent expenses difficulties gave the lie both to his witness statements and his sworn testimony.

It appeared he had flipped second homes in both London and Burnley to maximise his public expenditure claims, which flew in the face of his testimony. You could argue the importance, relative to the case, but it does help paint the picture of what we were having to deal with.

These things probably weren't crucial in deciding a trial outcome that was pretty unreachable due to other factors, but I did, and still, feel that it represents so much that is a problem about dealing with the south-Asian culture – yes even among, in fact specifically among, elected politicians.

Today's truth is THE truth. Yesterday's truth? Well, we've all slept since then, the world has turned. What's your problem?

When the rump of Malik's witnesses came down from Dewsbury to give evidence they all piled aboard a minibus. The court that day had to be delayed because they were stuck in traffic. The key witness we wanted to scrutinise, successful Labour council candidate Masood Ahmed, cried off because his child wasn't well and Eady refused to demand that he attend at a later date. Stymied again.

Eventually on that morning, out in the grand hall of the Royal Courts of Justice, in paraded these clearly impressed men, some of them barely literate in English, finding themselves central players in a very imposing drama.

Many of his witnesses – the Muslim ones, not the white ones – greeted me amicably like an old friend. There were handshakes and hellos. I'd encountered these men many times over the years in one fashion or another.

And then one by one they traipsed up into the witness box and spouted their well rehearsed if occasionally barely believable lines. At certain parts of the testimony I just had to shake my head and laugh.

And then as they departed some smiled and waved their farewells to me. That's 'our' reality in Dewsbury.

Having said that, we had an Asian witness of our own who claimed to have seen everything that went on that day in Savile Town, and when he'd finished on the stand I wanted to go throw myself in front of a London bus.

Barrister Crystal – a great bloke by the way – was in a state of shock. I think he wanted to throw his wig at Taylor-Heath and us for lumbering him with this character. Wankowski and Tamsin Allen could barely contain their glee. Our witness had either watched too much Perry Mason or Judge John Deed – or maybe even X-Files – because he really got caught up in the moment, embellishing the day's events as he went.

What a complete ball of wax.

I could write a book on its own about the two weeks of that trial, of my digs in what I termed the 'Hotel Sangatte' (after the refugee camp outside Calais) which was run by a group of Serbian émigrés. I swear there were bullet holes in the plaster. The net curtains hadn't been taken down since the Blitz. God, but was it an ordeal.

After two weeks of absolute agonies, the jury went out. Then they returned from their deliberations with a list of questions as long as your mum's weekly supermarket shop – there were clearly so many vital issues left unanswered by the evidence.

That's where Eady, in his attempts to narrow the entire case down to the specific meanings of expressions in Scott's letter and refusing to contemplate all the wider issues of our defence, failed in his job. He couldn't answer many of their questions. He sent them back to consider their verdict, then a majority verdict, but the poor sods weren't getting anywhere near any kind of verdict.

On that final Friday afternoon with the jury out deliberating, I took myself across The Strand from the court to the pub and banged down several pints in rapid succession as I stared hard into the likelihood of losing not just my business and livelihood, but the very real possibility of the roof over my wife and kids' heads. Mrs L would love that. What a bloody fool. A vain and proud fool.

Then my phone went and it was Scott. The jury were coming back. I know what it must feel like for a man to walk to the gallows, because that's how I felt. And I knew it was all my own fault. Bloody foolish pride.

When they filed back into the box I noticed one or two jury members look down at Malik who was sitting closest to them, almost under their noses, and smile at him. I couldn't find a friendly eye to catch. Shit, shit, shit.

And then the jury foreman revealed that they simply could not reach a verdict, and in answer to Eady's promptings regarding the possibility of reconvening after the weekend, that no, he didn't think they could even get close to a verdict. They were implacably, irrevocably split. And then I saw one or two smiles coming my way.

With a resigned sigh – he must have realised he'd ballsed the process up – Eady thanked and dismissed the jury. With a sense of deflation having fallen over the lawyers – Malik looked puzzled – and something akin to a rapture pervading Scott and I (in the realisation that at least we'd not lost) Eady said he'd like to take instruction from both sides.

There was a problem from our point of view. Stephen Taylor-Heath was already in a taxi on his way to Heathrow for a jolly in South Africa. The judge was about as far from chuffed at hearing that news as you can get.

He adjourned matters eventually, but the next step was then clear – we would need a re-trial, and this time we might need three weeks of court time.

It was with a sense of elation that Scott and I travelled back up to Yorkshire on the train that night. Crystal had offered to carry on giving his service on the CFA basis. Heath had intimated the same, although there was to be an unhappy ending there.

Later, after I phoned Malik and we sat down and talked some sense into each other, we agreed a statement respecting each other's position, the battle and the principle we had all stood by, and shook hands and walked away, bloodied, bruised, battered and hopefully wiser for the experience. I respected Shahid Malik that day. He had certainly matched my dogged idiocy/pride in seeing the fight through.

I don't know how he settled Bindmans' affairs, but that dropping of his suit triggered Fox Hayes – who had 'blanked' us since the end of the trial – to come after me and Scott for £120,000. They considered the outcome a 'win' for them and were claiming their doubled-up success fee from us, not Malik.

It isn't germane to this story, but there followed another year or more of sky-high stress as Scott and I went through as much of an ordeal fighting Taylor-Heath's employers as we had Malik. We represented ourselves and ultimately a judge in Leeds High Court threw their case out.

Bastard lawyers.

17 – MOVING ON

BY THE END of the Malik trial in November 2007 I had packed in as editor of The Press and gave up almost all my involvement except writing my weekly 'Ed Lines' column. I needed to concentrate on my own publication and the one that paid my wage, League Weekly.

The whole Malik affair – indeed the whole pressure of holding the 'front line' on The Press since 2002 – had pretty much worn me out. The pressure on my marriage and my family certainly wasn't decreasing.

My son had attended my old primary school, St Paulinus, where, a bit like me, he hadn't had the easiest of times. A reasonably bright lad, he decided he would like to sit the entrance exam for the state-funded Heckmondwike Grammar School – a very high achieving seat of education in a neighbouring town – rather than the Catholic high school, St John Fisher.

He did pretty poorly in the 'mock' exam, but decided he wanted to try some private tuition, just an hour a week for six weeks, and in the event he sailed through the entrance exam and won a place. It proved a mixed blessing.

Education has been a thorny issue in Dewsbury even pre-dating even the 1989 riot, when white parents in Thornhill Lees insisted on having a say in where their children were educated, taking Kirklees Council to the high court and winning a landmark case which was a slap in the face for the social scientists of the liberal left.

Because schools by their geographic nature will almost always reflect local demographics, there has been a consistent pattern of schools becoming predominantly white or Asian. That does not preclude ethnic minority families being every bit as ambitious for their offspring and often instilling far greater work ethic and disciplinary values in them. Just as Councillor Karam Hussain sent his boys to St Paulinus and then St John Fisher Roman Catholic schools, so Heckmondwike Grammar School has long been identified as an exceptional seat of learning for children regardless of colour or creed.

There's a growing trend within Muslim communities to clutch their young people closer to them and focus on faith-based education; to bond them with the glue of their religion, contracting philosophically even while expanding numerically, which flies in the face of anyone's idea of integration. Young students within the mainstream system typically go straight to madressah for religious tuition after school, while stand-alone religious schools like the Paradise Primary are springing up with increasing regularity.

Heckmondwike Grammar School is an interesting case in point, however, where there is a very high admission of young Muslim pupils coming from homes where educational attainment is at the centre of the family ethos. The mix brings its occasional challenges but the school generally manages to balance the disparate cultural issues calmly and professionally. It couldn't protect my son though.

He first travelled past Heckmondwike Grammar when he was about one week old and in his little car safety seat, on our way to the Samarkand restaurant, just 100 yards down the road from the school. Sammy's is the best Indian restaurant in the world – at least it is to diehard devotees like the Lockwoods.

The owner Shabir 'Sammy' Laher and his wife Julie have

been like an aunt and uncle to our kids. It was the first restaurant either of them ever went in, and given the choice today, still the first one they would opt to go to.

The food at Sammy's is distinctive mostly because Julie, although Indian, was brought up in South Africa and she brings some distinctive qualities to their cooking. Trust me – if ever you get the opportunity, go and try a Sammy's in Heckmondwike town centre.

Julie would supervise the kitchen with one of our babies on her hip, later they would crawl and toddle around customers' feet. When the option arose of sitting the Heckmondwike Grammar entrance exam my son used to say that he could always pop up to Sammy's house, just up the hill, after school. He would have been made welcome.

Sammy, Julie and the gang, Rahil, Tosif and the ever genial 'Smiler' have long felt like part of the family to our kids. Some years ago I managed to arrange a 12-month work placement in the IT department at the Yorkshire Post for one of Sammy's staff, Tabasum Aslam, which was a huge career step-up for the young man. He later went on to serve as a Liberal Democrat councillor in Heckmondwike.

My son meanwhile has always found it somewhat difficult to cut along easily with his peer group and being thrown into a new school environment where he barely knew anyone – I think only one other pupil from St Paulinus made the move to Heckmondwike Grammar that year – was always going to be a challenge, even if one he'd looked forward to. In that, we were prepared for a bit of a bumpy ride.

Unfortunately the ride wasn't just a bumpy one. It went completely off course.

I was probably naïve, thinking that I could insulate my family from the repercussions of dad being an outspoken – controversial even – editor, especially in a community as inward looking as ours with issues so raw and provocative.

Was it coincidence that it was Muslim children who managed to taunt my son into trouble? I thought so at first. I didn't later.

Were some Muslim youngsters, even at the age of 11, sophisticated enough to know that their parents might have a very low opinion of one of their schoolmates' fathers? I hoped not, but in hindsight I expect they did.

Ryan was born with a faint birth mark on the side of his face, that's pretty much faded now. He'd been teased over it in primary school – I think he'd been called 'gravy face' a few times – but it wasn't a big deal. On this occasion one of his fellow pupils went a bit further.

"Hey Lockwood, you've got shit on your face, did you know? Hey, shit-face. Yes you Lockwood, shit-face." Etc etc.

My son is nothing if not a chip off the old block.

"So what?" he replied. "You look like you've got shit all over your face."

Now when I heard all of this later that day, I thought that was a petty sharp retort. And when I spoke to him that evening I believed him completely when he said there hadn't been the first thought in his mind that it could be construed as a racist insult.

The other boy had started it, mocking the colour of his birthmark, he'd hit back mocking the colour of his skin. Kids' stuff, eh?

Except no, it wasn't. Whether the boy went and took advice at lunch, at break-time, phoned home or whatever, later that day he turned up at the headmaster's office to report my son for racist abuse. And the school took it seriously as, in these happy-clappy days of Political Correctness, they are forced to do.

The headmaster, Mark Tweedle, wasn't happy about it, I could tell. Indeed he did not just discipline my boy, but the other one as well. He also asked my lad to write a letter of apology, which he duly did. I've never been more proud, because what he wrote was a salutary lesson for people of any age.

My son said sorry for his remark if it caused offence on the basis his antagonist took it to mean, but that he truly hadn't intended anything of that sort. But he was equally sorry that the other boy felt it was acceptable to mock his appearance.

For an 11-year-old I thought it was a very mature piece of work. And you'd like to imagine that was a satisfactory conclusion, except of course it wasn't.

My son struggled with his temper and now the other boys knew how to get to him. The next time it all blew up he ended up with two detentions – one for the fight he got into inside the school, the other for finishing it off outside.

Again, the school struggled with the situation. The four boys who had taunted my son into the confrontation turned up to the head's office word perfect in their recollection of what my boy was supposed to have said that was 'racist' – and they stuck to their guns even though independent witnesses disagreed with their version.

My lad was in a fury at the injustice of it all. I was in a fix how to make his next five or six years of education survivable.

One sunny Sunday afternoon in 2008, our family drove out towards York and meandered through a few little villages. In one we stopped at the pub for a bite of lunch, watched the locals playing tennis on the grass courts by the village hall, we sat out on the green, and we delighted at this almost 'foreign' – to us – picture of England.

I returned to that same village four days later to cast an eye over a converted barn rental, we all came back and paid a visit to the local schools, and six weeks later we moved in. Fifteen months later we bought a house here.

It's only a 40 minute drive into Dewsbury on a decent run and, nearly three years on as I write this, I'm back at the helm of The Press, sticking two fingers up at the PC politburo and asking difficult questions again.

Earlier in this book I mentioned an incident where Shahid Malik's sidekicks organised a protest outside the police station in Dewsbury. As part of that process they also set up an anti-Press/Lockwood Facebook group which they invited their fellow foot-soldiers to sign up to. I even subscribed myself in order to engage some of the characters in debating their various objections.

It was interesting to note that the Heckmondwike Grammar School pupil who made the 'shit face' remark to my son was signed up to the group.

Coincidence?

Who knows. At least my wife and children are well out of it now. My son is vice-captain of his House at school and in a good place, in more ways than one.

That's all most of us want for our children.

18 – HER LADYSHIP

WHEN SAYEEDA HUSSAIN-WARSI breezed into the public consciousness in Dewsbury in 2003 it was a breath of fresh air in more ways than one. She wasn't – so far as any of us were aware – remotely party political, but she was a common sense-speaking young Muslim woman, extremely articulate, and a welcome recruit to the robust, barrier-breaking common sense of Councillor Khizar Iqbal and his fellow modernist Muslim Tory Imtiaz Ameen.

Well, I say modernist. Imtiaz, like Warsi a Dewsbury-based immigration lawyer in the main, stood unsuccessfully against Home Secretary Jack Straw for the Labour seat in 2005. He was also, I later understood, privately mightily aggrieved that Warsi had usurped his ambitions closer to home for the Dewsbury candidacy, which was perhaps understandable.

That resentment would surface during our 2007 Malik trial when Ameen, rather surprisingly, offered himself as a witness in the Labour MP's cause and in opposition to The Press and our erstwhile allies (and his fellow Tories) Scott, Iqbal and Warsi. It wouldn't prove critical to the case, but it would be instructive to those of us trying to make sense of Muslim political relationships.

Sayeeda was a fresh-faced 33 back then and had cut her teeth as a solicitor in the offices of former Conservative MP for Dewsbury (1983-87) John Whitfield, before setting up her own practice George Warsi along with another solicitor Michael George. Together with a few other local, enlightened young Muslims, Sayeeda had already set up the Savayra Foundation, a charity aimed at helping empower young women back in Pakistan.

Someone else will undoubtedly produce the definitive account of Britain's first female Muslim minister of state. For my purposes, and notwithstanding the strong personal relationship that I felt I'd had with her for a number of years, it is more instructive to touch on specific incidents which might in their own way give a clue to Sayeeda's nature, her ambition, and the way they impacted on Dewsbury.

If I considered myself a friend when she introduced me to Benazir Bhutto at a private luncheon, or later when she publicly applauded and thanked me in front of 400 fellow Muslims from the stage at Dewsbury town hall after receiving her peerage, then I can only say that there's no fool quite like an easily flattered one. That'll be me then.

Sayeeda Hussain-Warsi played me like an old piano.

Perhaps unwittingly to many British observers she was first seen by a national audience during a series of television documentaries by the esteemed business guru Sir Gerry Robinson, during which he stepped in to help turn around a variety of struggling companies.

One such was Shire Beds in Dewsbury, started by Sayeeda's migrant father, initially a mill worker who created a thriving little business and brought up five strikingly able and confident young women, all who went to a school in Dewsbury – Birkdale High – not renowned for its scholastic excellence, but which can be rightfully proud of the Hussain girls.

By the time of the Robinson programme Mr Hussain had pretty much turned over the running of the business to two of his daughter's husbands – one of them Sayeeda's spouse,

Naeem. She had been taken back to Pakistan when she was just 15 and invited to 'pick' a husband from mum and dad's approved list of candidates which, in its own way was reasonably emancipated. They were married when she was 19 and for long enough she feigned that it was wedded bliss.

Some years later and it was clear the Shire Beds business was going down the pan, perhaps not unexpectedly given the background of both young men, who apparently to business guru Gerry Robinson were out of their depth. But, in this still hugely male-dominated society, and despite the assertive qualities of the very attractive and articulate Hussain girls, change was not easy to bring about.

A series of at-home television documentary shots of the girls and their parents – and some highly uncomfortable interviews with the husbands – made for fascinating viewing, the upshot being that his recommendation, the only way he could visualise survival/progress of Shire Beds, was for one of the sisters to come in as Managing Director, with authority over the husbands.

I recall cringing at that – and with tv cameras blazing in their faces, the men had no choice but to concur.

It was culturally face-destroying in a manner that takes some beating in their closed society. And it was being watched by everyone at their mosque, in their social and family groups, and worse still, by the men they employed. The young Hussain girls were stars of the show, but I can still see the haunted, pained look in Naeem Warsi's eyes.

But Sayeeda already did, and still does, revel in the camera, the stage, and as best witnessed by her single-handed emasculation of BNP leader Nick Griffin during his infamous Question Time appearance in the run-up to the 2010 General Election, she can play the good-old, down-home Yorkshire lass role to a tee.

When the publicity opportunity knocks, Sayeeda Warsi isn't far from the door handle.

If she has a problem at the very top table of British politics it is that, like Shahid Malik, the rank personal ambition and opportunism – not a rare trait in politics I accept – isn't always backed up by joined-up political thinking.

During her 2005 election campaign she was accused of homophobia for comments made in her election leaflets. They were seized on by gay rights group Stonewall. But as uncomfortable as they may have been for her new public audience, they were clearly genuinely felt.

And to be fair Sayeeda was, after all, trying to find her feet in a very deep pool with some dangerous currents – and having to do it on the hoof. The odds were stacked pretty dauntingly against her, with all kinds of interest groups ready and waiting to pounce on the slightest slip.

As someone who puts his foot in his mouth as often as I do, I cannot be overly critical of a young woman so suddenly elevated to a position of state beyond the imagination of most people.

But still ... this was a woman wanting to empower Muslim women, but then saying the burkha does not limit them from engaging in everyday life. This was a woman shouting the virtues of arranged marriages to first cousins from Pakistan, yet who would be involved in what I consider a breath-taking deception which left me stunned.

And that takes some doing.

AS PREVIOUSLY explained, the 2005 general election battle between Malik and Sayeeda was filthy. And as she found out, if Muslim affiliation trumps Party affiliation in these matters, male also trumps female.

Vanquished by Malik, and briefly on the sidelines of public life until elevated rapidly to prominence by Michael Howard, she contained a bitter loathing for the new MP who rarely missed an opportunity to gloat.

What was rapidly clear to me at least was that for all the Muslim-Christian antagonism that might publicly prevail in our communities, there were and are bitter rivalries within the Muslim community itself rarely revealed to the wider public, but which often kicked our petty or imagined tussles into a cocked hat.

One day prior to our legal troubles with Shahid Malik I received a phone call from a very urbane and articulate young man, Iftikhar Azam. He was a local chap, married with four children, he worked as a food scientist for an Oxfordshire based company, and he invited me to his house to hear his story.

Ifty – as he became known to me, on friendly first-name terms – professed no political affiliation, but he had some juicy tales to tell about some of Malik's electoral tactics. It made for a decent story.

He also said that he, and a number of similarly perturbed modernist young Muslims, had tried to hire a community centre in Ravensthorpe to stage a public meeting, its aim being to put questions to Shahid Malik, but that they had had the booking suddenly cancelled. What's more, they had proof that Malik himself had intervened to have the (Muslim) community centre trustees cancel their meeting.

I put the allegations to Malik, who in turn ratcheted up the story another gear. He said he couldn't divulge 'security service confidentialities' – some real James Bond stuff – but directly accused Iftikhar Azam and his accomplices of being members of Hizb ut-Tahrir, the proscribed Islamic extremist organisation.

I don't mind admitting that I struggled to tiptoe around the writing of that story, and if anything it ended up marginally favouring the version of events that Malik was standing four-square behind; I was delicate enough with it not to alienate Ifty Azam as a source. Indeed he became an even closer confidante as the legal problems with Malik erupted.

With the legal battle in full swing Ifty and his 'apolitical' friends finally staged their anti-Malik public meeting after being forced to hire another community centre in Batley, at which they flogged the MP's reputation.

At the end of the meeting they even passed a hat round to raise cash for the Freedom of Speech campaign which had been started by supportive readers of The Press to help us fight our case against Malik.

It was comforting to realise we had independent supporters within the mainstream Muslim community, who saw that The Press wasn't here to rabble-rouse but to address serious issues which were not going to improve by being ignored, or silenced by the race industry.

Meanwhile on the trial-front Sayeeda was a willing witness for us and gave a statement, but the real value we would have felt, of having her appear on the stand as the vice-chairman of the Conservative Party (as she was by then) was completely deflated when Malik's legal team managed to persuade Judge Eady that her presence wasn't required.

With her new job increasingly requiring her presence in Westminster, and her stratospheric career by no means hindered by failing to beat Malik for the Dewsbury seat – possibly the best thing that could have happened to her in hindsight – my regular contact with Sayeeda became confined to occasional political briefings over the phone.

Every so often she would call me before going in to talk to Michael Howard or later David Cameron, on subjects where she felt I might have a 'grounded' view of how policies might play in towns like Dewsbury, or we would chat about how she looked/performed on an edition of Question Time etc etc. It remained very cosy-friendly.

But as ever, nothing was really quite as it seemed. I realised that when, out of the blue, Baroness Warsi of Dewsbury divorced her husband Naeem in the town's Sharia court and swiftly married Iftikhar Azam.

You could have knocked me over with a wet fish.

IF SAYEEDA was in the midst of her own happy-ever-after, and beyond the tentacles of Dewsbury's constricting Muslim society, there were still battles and issues remaining for those of us nominally left behind.

You'd think that after years of newspaper campaigns and voicing righteous indignation, at venting frustration about our British way of life and Dewsbury institutions being eroded before all our eyes; of being treated as second class citizens – and worse, as fools – in the town we and our forefathers built, that a man might be moved to try do something about it.

I'm not talking about editorials or launching petitions or taking a megaphone into Market Place, but actually doing something about it.

Wouldn't an editor, a publisher so passionate about a cause, consider adding a physical presence to his weekly voice of dissent? Wouldn't he care enough to give the unrepresented majority someone, something, to rally behind? If he thought enough people shared his care?

Anyone with a local voice as noisy as mine has been in the local press for so many years was always going to get the occasional 'you should stand for Parliament, Danny' pat on the back.

I'd thought about it often enough and at least by standing for election I would discover whether my ideas about the unrepresented majority were well founded, or not. I'd always considered it from an 'independent' standpoint.

But my absence from the green benches of the House of

Commons isn't for the lack, ultimately, of effort or intent.

The year 2008 was not an auspicious one in economic terms for anywhere in the UK and certainly not in Dewsbury. The spectacular nature of the global financial collapse of that year would roll across our hills and valleys like the Passover plague that visited the Egypt of Moses, with few houses left unbloodied by its passing, just like the rest of the country.

But local people in the Heavy Woollen district had other matters of grievous import on their minds, certainly in the early months of the year.

If a town is capable of suffering from communal hurt feelings and low morale, then three years of being the spiritual home to many of Britain's leading Islamic terrorists, and worse, the physical home of Karen Matthews, slatternly mother of 'kidnap' victim Shannon, had left Dewsbury residents with a definite sense of parochial embarrassment.

BBC and ITV journalists were on nodding terms with half the residents of Dewsbury Moor and Savile Town, respectively the public repositories of our more prominent and numerous members of the Benefits Class and Islamic Fundamentalism. I'm still not entirely sure which faction does the town the greater disservice.

But if in the summer of 2008 you went on holiday – pretty much worldwide, but certainly on the beaches of Europe – and were asked by new acquaintances where you were from, the temptation was to say 'near Leeds' or 'close to Wakefield'. Huddersfield and Bradford would have done equally well, Dewsbury sitting plonked pretty much slap bang in the middle of those four major conurbations.

We'd had several murders – a teenager attacked outside a nightclub in the rather more white, middle-class adjacent town of Mirfield, besides two young men killed on Dewsbury railway station and in the town's main park.

As one tv staffer from the north-east said to me on the occasion of that last story, "Dewsbury, I'm sick of the bloody sight of Dewsbury". The feeling was mutual, I reflected. "TV crews, we're sick of the bloody sight of tv crews."

In the regional newspaper game in 2008 we got a preview of what the rest of the economy was soon to experience when estate agents were being driven to their knees early in the year – months before the banks were collapsing like so many houses of cards.

Advertising revenues in newspapers are always first to suffer in such times, and they were with us.

Job losses weren't felt as badly in Dewsbury, one reason being that such a large proportion of the local populace was already what I unfondly describe as 'the benefits class'. And beyond but not exclusive to that, was the 'black economy' – no pun intended – of people falling solidly into the first category, but busily beavering away in cash trades.

So when the banks blew up in all our faces and the global markets went into meltdown, the people of Dewsbury could be forgiven for wondering what a few more boarded up shop fronts were between friends? Retail property occupancy in the town centre can't be much higher than 60-65% as I write this.

By October 2008 Dewsbury's residents were already resigned to what remained of the decent retail businesses following Marks and Spencer out of town – they'd jumped ship to a shopping mall near Leeds – while an unhealthy proportion of estate agents had found themselves well and truly crunched, their newly whitewashed windows bearing visible testimony to the grinding halt of the housing market.

That collapse claimed one other notable victim, which directly affected me at least. The Prospective Parliamentary candidate for the Conservative Party, Kevin Hollinrake, a self-made millionaire estate agent, found himself fighting for his business life back in his home town of York.

He had to put those obligations first and aspirations of a Westminster career on the back burner, at least for a while. On the very same day that Kevin stepped down my mobile phone rang. It was Diane Clarke, the Tories' no-nonsense Field Director in the north of England, asking me if I would be interested in standing as their general election candidate in Dewsbury and Mirfield.

Yes, you read that correctly.

To put this into some kind of likely perspective, the first libel writ I ever had thrown at me when I was the editor on the Dewsbury Reporter in 1993 emanated from the town's Conservatives – specifically Sayeeda Warsi's old boss and former MP of 1983-87, John Whitfield.

They'd decided they would make an early impression on this gobby, opinionated local oik, a working class hack from a family of window cleaners.

In time the Lib Dems, Labour and even the BNP would take their turns deploring my opinionated style, and public name-calling abounded with insults healthily hurled around our news, opinion and letters pages, first when I ran the Reporter and latterly The Press.

Good old fashioned journalism in other words, with the editor's job being to hold everyone in the political spectrum to robust account, but never anyone more than the holders of public office, which in our district's Kirklees Council was to include all three major parties from time to time – and of course the MPs who represent the two Parliamentary seats our newspaper covers.

Funny how yesterday's allies became today's enemies the minute they assumed the mantle of power. I'd like to think we never changed, but they certainly did.

Because I wasn't so hands-on at The Press by the time the Tory call came through in October 2008, I could actually consider it. No matter that I'd detested Margaret Thatcher with the venom of anyone whose best rugby and pub mates had been miners who lived on the frontline of 1984.

No matter that I'd voted for Neil Kinnock in 1992 and Tony Blair and the bright New Labour dawn in '97. By the time 2001 came around I'd seen through Blair and voted for an Independent Labour candidate. But I'd seen enough of politicians of all colours to consider them with equal disregard and disrespect, and, as I explained to the Tories as I considered their offer … "as much as I'll be making a compromise, you have to understand what you are taking on."

I'd never considered myself party political, but whatever else David Cameron was (at that point at least) he wasn't Tony Blair or Gordon Brown. And he certainly wasn't John Major, or mortally tarnished by the vainglorious arrogance of that corrupt regime. I didn't think so at that point at least.

Would I be interested in any other constituency than Dewsbury, I was asked? No. The issues I cared about, the people I cared most about, were here in Dewsbury, or maybe Batley at a push.

I could swallow the bitter-ish pill of partisan alignment by becoming a Conservative, if it empowered me to do something meaningful for my town. Action, not just words.

Very noble, eh? Very bloody naïve, as it turned out.

Apart from Diane Clarke's phone call, I was then bombarded by calls and messages of support from what seemed like the entire constituency party. I even received the 'blessing' of recently departed nominee Kevin Hollinrake, who put on a lunch at his magnificent Crayke Castle home outside York, where I met and discussed various topical issues with almost the entire Dewsbury constituency Tory executive.

What were they getting?

I was a Dewsbury bloke born and bred, schooled in the

town, brought up on some of the roughest of its council estates, a footballer and rugby player on the local sports fields, trainee journalist and finally editor and publisher of newspapers in the town, notwithstanding some highly entertaining interim years globetrotting with my rugby boots as far afield as California and Australia.

My dad, like several uncles and cousins, was a window cleaner before his untimely death from cancer at 52. The female side of the family worked in the mills, sorting and ripping rags. I think I can say with some safety that I was the first member of my family to get an 'O' level, and I was the first Catholic editor of the town's newspaper.

The records show my tenure at the Reporter was a successful one. Heck, having been acting MD in my final year our 'little' weekly newspaper group had delivered profits above £1 million for the first time ever. And then I threw my teddy out of the cot (a recurrent professional theme) and spent three years as a bit of a journalistic maverick, until I founded The Press in 2002.

Throughout all that time I had witnessed the continued social and economic decline in a once moderately prosperous place. I cared deeply about the issues beguiling 'my' home town and nothing was more frustrating than the continued weasel words spoken, but lack of action taken. Surely if anyone could make a difference, an MP could.

No one appeared to be listening outside our borough's boundaries, I'd so often thought.

Everyone who rolled into town in a position to make positive differences ended up spending more time feathering their own nests and furthering their own careers it seemed, with barely a benefit in kind for the people who put them there.

Now there was an opportunity to sweep Shahid Malik out of power and find out if I could do better. I had never been party political and even though I have a torn up

Conservative Party membership card on my desk, I am still not.

But if the Tories could put up with my occasionally outspoken ways as the price of winning Dewsbury, then I could at least occasionally toe the party line and bite my tongue. This was, after all, an opportunity to make real change in a town desperately needing it.

The family had actually moved home just a matter of weeks before the Tories offered me the opportunity of the Dewsbury nomination. I think if I'd still been living in town I couldn't have considered it – I doubt my marriage would have survived!

I confess to having been flattered when the local Conservative party executive came calling, courting and enthusing about us fighting the general election together and ridding the town of Malik.

I went to a dinner, a lunch, to fund-raising socials. The entire committee was behind my candidacy, or so it appeared, led not inconsequentially by chairwoman Amelia Bolton, who not unhelpfully (I thought) was the girlfriend of the man who had replaced me as editor of The Press, Martin Shaw.

A young and thrusting Muslim solicitor and committee member, Naeem Hasmi, sought my company at the annual dinner and confided that he thought it was great I was considering standing.

What a winning combination, eh? The outspoken but well known local publisher, backed up by a Conservative party machine which was already looking hot favourite to remove Malik because of boundary changes to the constituency!

He'd lost a chunk of his working class heartland vote to the Batley seat and had it replaced with some true-blue Tory villages out in the hills to the south of town. Then there was Malik's controversial nature plus the general malaise of Gordon Brown's Labour. We could run up a 10,000 majority!

I succumbed to the temptation. In quick order I was hurried through the Tories' Parliamentary Assessment process and approved at Millbank Tower in London by the Conservative high command. Even the constituency selection process for the new candidate was delayed until I was qualified to formally apply.

When applications for the seat were closed some 30-odd Conservative party hopefuls from all over the country had submitted their CVs for the Dewsbury and Mirfield seat. Only one of them – me – was from the town or even from the wider constituency.

And of course I already had the backing of the party executive who would essentially select the winning candidate. They'd wined and dined me and already started the local lobbying process with influential members.

What lay ahead after an initial sifting of the applications by a three-person sub-committee was interviews for the shortlisted candidates with the wider party membership, and then a public 'primary' style of selection.

During both of those elements – in front of the local party membership and then the open meeting – I'd get the opportunity to display the passion of my belief in this cause, and spell out my message of how we could deliver real change for real people's lives. Or so I thought.

On Friday the 6th of February 2009, while preparing to celebrate my wife's birthday that evening, I received a one line email from an anonymous Tory party bureaucrat.

Thanks but no thanks, we won't need to see you for an interview.

The three-person 'sifting team' of Amelia Bolton, Naeem Hasmi, and a chap I'd not met by the name of John Taylor, had for some inexplicable reason decided that the only local candidate did not even merit an interview, let alone the chance to contest the selection process, and beyond that try to unseat Shahid Malik.

I'd been stitched up, well and truly.

How? I can't say for certain that it was 'Paki Politics' whatever my suspicion. More likely it was just the common-or-garden variety of simple, backstabbing politics.

After all those years, I hadn't learned a damned thing.

I CONFESS to being stunned by the cursory nature of the dismissal, bloody furious at the time and money I'd wasted putting myself through the qualifying process and, finally, puzzled at what exactly had gone on. I still don't know what lay at the bottom of the stunt, whether it was a nudge from on high, or somewhat closer to home.

I rang Amelia Bolton the party chairman, quite a timid little thing and as I mentioned my business partner Martin Shaw's girlfriend. She lamely said that they simply thought there were far more better suited candidates.

"Not even an interview Amelia?"

Erm, no.

But what about Naeem Hasmi? He'd been all over me like a rash in the run up to the candidacy. Again, despite all the face-to-face bullshit, he'd simply changed his mind he said. And that was that.

Except of course it didn't escape me that Her Ladyship – Sayeeda Warsi – was the political patron of both Bolton and Hasmi and (at that time at least) generally dictated local Conservative affairs at arm's length through them. She had seen off Khizar's aspirations with little more than a helpless shrug. Did she really want Lockwood's questionable baggage hanging off the back of her sedate ride to power? Would any association with me ultimately taint her greater ambitions? Possibly.

Sayeeda in fairness had told me that she wouldn't be

supporting my candidacy – she'd already committed her support to some metropolitan London chap – so I was probably naïve not to have realised that she had the means, should she wish, to ensure I didn't get to put my case to members.

But Sayeeda was a friend, a like-minded soul wasn't she?

She was a Muslim moderniser who knew how passionate I was for everyone in our town, didn't she? She believed like me that in order to make meaningful progress on the ground we needed honesty and fair play?

I still believe that if I'd got that far – to the interview by Constituency members – with my knowledge of the town, its issues (and the not-inconsiderable benefit of owning a newspaper), that if I was being judged against hooray-Henrys from Tory Central, that I'd have won the nomination.

As it happened, the local Conservative Association went into meltdown as a result of the stunt pulled on me. At least they rejected Sayeeda's favoured candidate too, with the group plumping instead for a lawyer from Hull who managed to oust Malik narrowly.

Back on the Tory party ground in Dewsbury and Mirfield fundraisers and campaigners were disgusted by the charade and some resigned over what had happened. Even Amelia Bolton and Naeem Hasmi are now long gone – but then again so is Sayeeda Warsi. She doesn't need them any longer and long ago moved out of Dewsbury to set up home with her new husband and my old 'friend', the self-styled non-political Iftikhar Azam.

The woman of conviction, who stood up for arranged marriages to cousins on a national stage – thankfully their child isn't as mutilated and deformed as so many in Dewsbury – snuck off and got herself a Sharia divorce from Yakub Munshi and his fundamentalist pals very quietly, once her fame and fortune in London had been established.

I twitched my first clue of something changing at the public event in Dewsbury town hall celebrating her peerage, when I was surprised to spot Ifty there, though nothing clicked at the time. I didn't see her husband Naeem present.

Some time later I met her for a coffee in the House of Lords while I was attending a function there – just a couple of weeks before I got the heave-ho from the Tories – and she was being coy about what was happening in her personal life. It clicked.

"So you and Ifty are an item then."

Cue big blush ... "how did you know?"

And suddenly it dawned. All those anti-Malik stories being fed to me by my new pal Ifty, the non-political Ifty – like those letters in The Press from her sisters, I was being used as a proper Sayeeda stooge.

It turned out the pair of them had known each other from their schooldays. Funny how they neither of them mentioned it to me during all those turbulent political times when their respective names and pictures were in the paper. I never saw it coming.

On that occasion in the House of Lords tearoom Sayeeda skirted around the little matter of Ifty's wife and four kids – and with good reason as the Mail on Sunday would later reveal. Sayeeda married Ifty and his wife (another import who barely spoke more than a word or two of English after all her years here) didn't even know she'd been divorced!

The story had actually come to me first from a contact in the Muslim community – a friend of her ex-husband Naeem Warsi if I'm taking an educated guess – who filled me in on the predicament of Ifty's wife, suddenly, inexplicably, finding herself usurped.

The poor woman was nothing more than a semi-literate house-slave, an imported baby factory like so many hundreds and thousands in this valley, and when everything blew up she was even treated like dirt by her own children, as the national newspaper reporters who went to see her would bear witness.

When it came my way I had no hesitation in deciding I wasn't touching that news story with a bargepole, thanks. I'd had enough of being manipulated by one faction or another within the Muslim community. So I rang a contact at the Mail on Sunday and put them on the trail.

Sayeeda had befriended the woman, Ifty's wife, ostensibly posturing as a political acquaintance and old school friend of his; she had accepted his wife's hospitality, and yet all the time they were presumably planning their new life together.

It's nice when a 'happy ever after' story comes together, don't you think?

On a human level I have to say good for them; the cultural lie of their happily-arranged Islamic marriages was exposed but come on, shouldn't 'true love' prevail? (I know I can be a bit of a romantic at times.)

But still it didn't make any more palatable the fact that, not for the first time, and probably not the last time either, I felt like a bloody fool.

Would I have made a difference as an MP? I don't know. Probably not. Could I have survived the nasty machinations of Westminster? Again, unlikely. Dewsbury's Don Quixote was probably just tilting at another windmill, although I do like to think I would have chinned the odious little Speaker of the House John Bercow.

Locky in the Tower? Attaboy! Keep your blindfold, bring on the axeman!

Simon Reevell, who won the Tory nomination and ousted Shahid Malik, certainly won't be working his fingers to the bone in the town's cause. Figures released after his first year as a sitting MP showed the barrister billing for approximately 500 hours of work, earning over £60,000 in fees of which £48,000 was legal aid funded; he further made 79 court appearances and logged another 30-odd meetings of various sorts.

Even before The Press made those numbers public MP Reevell's allies had tired of me revealing his thriving commercial activities. They were the same chaps formerly 'courting' my Tory candidacy and they manufactured a meeting between us.

"Simon's a nice guy!" I was told over beers.

"He should have told the people of Dewsbury he was going to be a part-time MP," I replied.

"Ah, but he never said that he wouldn't be!" one of them limply tried. I wasn't having that. Simon Reevell achieved his nice little Westminster ambition and Dewsbury had to make do with an occasional surgery, photo-shoot, lots of well-meaning words, but still a part-time MP. At least Shahid Malik put plenty of hours in.

Baroness Hussain/Warsi/Azam? She's now right up there with the two Baroness Bettys and that other scheming self-server, ex-MP and Labour stooge in the Lords, Ann Taylor.

Sayeeda is still around town from time to time, unlike the others. I'd like to think that she probably wipes her shoes every time she leaves Dewsbury behind.

The rest of us just keep buying bigger pairs of wellies.

19 – FIGHTING THE GOOD FIGHT

I'VE BEEN BACK running The Press for a few months now. Martin Shaw and the previous directors couldn't lift the business out of the swamp of the trial debts and the economic crash of 2008/09 sufficiently for it to become a viable business. They hit the buffers at the end of February 2011 and with no other saviour in sight I bought the paper off the administrator.

I must be a bloody fool, but I breathed first life into this newspaper and I'm damned if anyone else will be the one to administer its last rites. I've had a bit of breathing space from the frontline of Dewsbury's shenanigans this last couple of years, I've been around for the kids as we settled into our home away from the trenches, and for my wife while she's fought steadfastedly against breast cancer and all the surgeries, chemotherapies, radiotherapies and drugs that that lousy disease brings with it.

It puts things into a bit of perspective. In hindsight maybe it was a good job that Sayeeda's sidekicks shafted me after all.

And now I'm back at it, full tilt, running my rugby paper with one hand, trying to help keep afloat a couple of golf magazines I'm involved in with another, trying to be a half decent dad and husband, and save a struggling weekly newspaper into the bargain.

Pass me that sweeping brush – I'll shove the handle up

my jacksy and clean the office floor while I'm at it!

Early into the office today, Monday June the 6th.

I suspended one of the sales staff yesterday and need to jump through all the legal hoops of formally terminating someone's employment. Luckily his three-month probation was just coming due and I'd already sounded more warnings than the Edison Lighthouse in a thick fog.

I have a quick chat with Dave Bentley, the acting editor – a good lad – and things seem to be going smoothly. He's going round the town centre tomorrow (market day) to conduct a bit of a vox pop with the traders regarding who intends opening their shop this coming Saturday.

The BNP may have died a death in Dewsbury, but a bunch of characters styling themselves the English Defence League have announced that they are staging a rally here on Saturday. Dave is too young to remember the BNP rally almost 22 years ago to the day which triggered the Scarborough pub riot, but the echoes are eerily similar.

I have already editorialised on the issue: If it's a police problem the EDL have then go rally outside the police HQ in Huddersfield. If it's political, then go on, bugger off to march outside Westminster. We don't have much left of a town in Dewsbury, but the last thing we need is a bunch of someone else's hooligans kicking over the traces.

Does this place look like Little Big Horn? No, so please stop using it like a battlefield.

Mid-morning, we're out of milk, so I decide to pop round to our town centre newsagent, Faz, pick some up and pay the newspaper bill as well. Faz once said he might have to stop stocking The Press because some of his 'brothers' were giving him grief after one particular ethnic strop, but it blew over as it always did and it was business as usual. Faz is a good guy.

On the way out of his shop I bump into an old friend. Mick's a top man. I've golfed with him a bit over the years. I also went to school with his kids. They are an ex-Irish Westtown family; have been for generations. We're looking around us at a town on its knees. Half the shops are empty and the rest are closed – this is Tuesday, which is traditionally half-day closing (full day in reality) for many of the shops.

An old boy stops and asks us where he can find a cobbler/key cutting shop that's open because the one that usually fashions a ferrule for the tip of his walking stick is shut. We guide him back up Bond Street to see if the other key-cutting shop in the town centre happens to be open. I doubt it, but he shuffles off to look.

We regard the characters passing us by. A souped-up Mitsubishi roars past with heavy rap music blasting its echo between the town centre buildings with decibels a Tornado pilot would envy. There aren't any police officers around to flag him down and enforce some peace, even though that was one of last Superintendent's bugbears. We both shake our head.

"I don't know what the answer is Mick."

"Me neither Danny lad."

Mick inquires how things are going with my family out in York, then surprises me with his own news – for the first time since childhood he and his wife have departed 'Daw Green' – the old original Irish migrant name for the Westtown settlement. They'd long ago bought their semi-detached council house. The quotes are not quite verbatim, but they are close enough.

"Well, it's been changing for years Danny. Our lot's moved out, they've moved in. But you know me. I made a lot of them welcome. Helped out with jobs and stuff with the neighbours when they needed it. When our new neighbours moved in next door I invited them round a few times. I wasn't happy with his wife having the face veil on all the time, but there you go.

"One day he's sitting in our front room and he's looking around like, admiringly. And he says to me, 'just you and the woman here yes?' I said 'me and my wife, yes'. He nods and says 'just you and the woman, no children, very big house for two people. If you sell you tell me yes?'

"And that was it Danny. Literally, from that moment on. Aggravation, day and night. A football being bounced against our bedroom wall at two and three in the morning. Constant bother. I tried talking to them, reasoning with them. Nothing. For fifteen months.

"I called the Council's anti-social unit and they gave me the run-around long enough. I kept calling them and getting shoved from one number to another, before they said it was a police matter. But could I get anyone to come and deal with it?

"Finally one Sunday afternoon I've had my Yorkshire puddings and roast and a glass of red and I'm settling down to watch some sport on the telly. The phone goes and it's the police saying 'can we come see you'? I said yes.

"They said '20 minutes' and sure enough, 20 minutes later there's a knock at the door. And its two Asian officers – actually, I tell a lie, one lad was probably half caste. But I hadn't a prayer. It was all my problem, basically my imagination! I might as well have been talking to the wall."

Mick, however, had the last laugh.

"Well I wasn't bloody selling it to this character next door who wanted it for his 18-year-old son and the wife they were planning on bringing in from Pakistan."

Mick also knew that he hadn't a chance of selling the house to a white family. He was already one of the last few remaining on the street that in my childhood had been a colony of Irish Catholics.

So he went across the road to some other Asian neighbours and said he would be selling, had a firm idea of the price he wanted, and they had 24 hours to make an offer before he put the house up with agents.

"It was funny. They were straight across in no time – except it wasn't the bloke across the road but three others. They said they wanted the house, had to have the house, and then of course started playing silly buggers over the price. I told them 'stop there, leave now, because you're wasting both our time. Either come back with a serious offer by the next day or that's that.'

"They left and were back again in no time. My wife couldn't handle the horse-trading though, she had to leave the house!"

With a twinkle in his eye – he obviously enjoyed getting his pound of flesh – Mick explains how they agreed on a price and then his purchasers started on the 'we both agree we pay this price and then we give you rest in cash' routine – but how he eventually got things sorted.

"I managed to keep the news from the bloke next door until a week or two before we were done and dusted," says Mick. "I was in the back garden and his son was looking over the wall. They'd built a four-and-a-half-foot breeze block wall round it for some reason. I was about 15 feet away, doing a bit of gardening, and this lad looks at me and says 'you fucking bastard'."

Mick chuckles.

"We bought a lovely little bungalow up near the golf course," he adds. "We can sit out of an evening, nice and peaceful. It's lovely."

"A bit of peace of mind," I say. "That's worth its weight. But you were still forced out of Daw Green, Mick. We're still on the retreat."

Mick thinks, smiles ruefully and shakes his head.

"No, not on the retreat. This battle's lost, lad."

POSTSCRIPT I.

IT'S THE same day. We have an advert in the paper for a new takeaway in the town centre. Adam's Cafe. Little Adele, our office manager, who's worked with me on and off for more than 30 years, and walked out on The Reporter to join me at The Press, tells me about an encounter she's had with a customer who came in to pay cash – up front – for an advert.

"It was that Shaf fellow," she says. "He was calling you all sorts of names Danny, but he wanted to pay cash for an advert. Anyway he kept going on about you, and I know it's not like me but I said 'well it's good to see that you're not in prison Shaf' and that shut him up."

I didn't need to ask which 'Shaf' it was. Shaf Siddique, our old friend from Trade Price Beds, half of whose friends and family were still presumably rotting in a Brazilian prison cell, and whose other acquaintances had previously been dragged off the streets by the Dubai authorities.

Shaf who told anyone who would listen that Lockwood's a racist pig, and don't do business with The Press – but who for some reason kept turning up like a bad penny and booking adverts. And paying – eventually – even though in the past I've had to go into their former bed shop and threaten to physically drag someone to the bank. Now he pays up front.

Apparently Shaf is taking a career break from flogging beds and bunks and is now professing to cook 'Yorkshire's best chicken' – plus kebabs, curries and various other exotic sundries including a full English breakfast. I presume that must include bacon and sausage.

And it must be a good trade, because the shop Shaf has opened is the fourth takeaway in a row of just five shops – and at possibly the most decrepit end of town with the fewest likely customers. I have to see this.

I pop my head into his new establishment, 'Adams Café' and the lights are dim – it's 1.15pm, still lunchtime presumably – and a small pile of cold-looking chicken wings are sitting forlornly in a turned-off food warmer.

The window at the side of the door has been kicked in. There's no sign of staff, let alone customers, and nary a cooking appliance that looks like it's been used. At least not today.

Shaf hears footsteps but he's in the dark footwell at the back of the takeaway. "Can I get you something mate? Best chicken in Yorkshire here!"

"No, you're all right pal," I shout back, edging my way out the front door. "I just wanted a look."

Too late. Here he comes.

"Danny! How are you? Can I get you something? Best chicken in Yorkshire mate! I've been in this game for years you know, not just beds. My family have restaurants over in Beverley you know. Do you know Beverley?"

I do.

"Down from the races, past the pub at the crossroads, across the other side, there's a Thai restaurant and a curry house round the back. That's us. Best chicken in Yorkshire!"

He's bang on with his geography, whatever the veracity of his culinary boasts.

"No thanks Shaf. I just couldn't believe what I was hearing about you being back in business in town. I had to have a look for myself. I'll try something later in the week maybe."

"You give us a write-up Danny, I'm telling you mate, best chicken in Yorkshire."

I try to make my excuses and leave, but I should know better. The next 20 minutes are spent out on the pavement in front of Adam's Café in Northgate, opposite the mosque that used to be the old Parish Youth Club.

A friend of mine, pub landlord John Foulstone, drives by and notices this seemingly fraught exchange, so he circles the town unbeknown to me, to make sure I'm ok. I am. This is just Shaf.

The town is going to shit, says Shaf. You need to do something about it, he tells me. Parking wardens are killing the town's trade.

"All those years up at my bed shop, parking on the double yellows, I only ever got one or two tickets Danny. I've been here hardly any time at all and I've had 14 parking tickets already.

"You stop to unload a bunch of leaflets and they hide round the corner and stick you with a ticket before you can do anything. Why can't we have parking passes like they do in Hornsea and Bridlington and towns where they know how to keep business and get people shopping? You need to do summat about it Danny.

"Know what they do? Blokes just dropping off, they get your number and send a ticket to your house! Bastards. Just driving people out of the town they are. You ought to do summat about it Danny.

"Them and the taxi drivers, private hire you know Danny, killing this town. They're not insured you know if they don't get a phone call first booking 'em. You can't move through the town on a Friday and Saturday night for them parked all over. It's wrong you know.

"That Black Bull pub Danny, it's a fucking nightmare. They have bouncers on there who kick shit out of local white lads, and there's Pakis hanging around just waiting to finish them off. The coppers don't want to know Danny. Just fucking take their time wandering round and hoping there isn't a body to pick up.

"But you know these (white) Dewsbury lads from up Chickenley and Dewsbury Moor estates, they aren't going to the cops are they? Take their hidings and come back for a bit more. You wouldn't believe it down here at 4 o'clock on a Saturday and Sunday morning. I've had 'em crawling into my café and I've looked after 'em and made sure they're safe."

Apparently Shaf stays open until 5am in the wild west landscape he describes as Dewsbury town centre on a Friday and Saturday night, dispensing his 'best chicken in Yorkshire'. There are only four or five pubs left in the town centre (it varies as one opens and another closes). 'Rough and ready' would be a fairly kind description. You wouldn't impress a girlfriend on a first date if you took her out there, let's put it like that.

"You should come down with your camera Danny," Shaf raved. "Get across by the town hall with a long lens and take photos of the shit that goes on."

"I'm usually in bed at that time Shaf. Not my gig any more."

"You get up to buy a paper early don't you sometimes…?"

I can still see the dent on Shaf's head where one of his countrymen hit him over the skull with a lump hammer a few years back. He came to the paper saying it was a mugging. Course it was. And I take it he's still not had the £35,000 that the police confiscated under proceeds of crime legislation returned to him. He's obviously still earning money though – he says he's investing £100,000 in his new café venture.

"I don't get up to go for a paper at four in the morning Shaf."

"Well you ought to. You wouldn't believe it. You know these Paki private hire drivers aren't insured unless they're called and pre-booked, don't you Danny? It's illegal you know, but the company doing it, the bloke runs the private hire stuff round here.

"They're all taking backhanders Danny. The Hackney

cabs, they're the only ones supposed to be doing this job, but they're mostly Indian lads and they get shit from the Pakis. They get bullied out of it. It's wrong."

"You're a Paki Shaf. If I said that you'd be calling me a racist all over town, like you usually do."

Shaf shakes his head, spitting accidentally through his top gold tooth as he regularly does.

"No Danny, I'm a Dewsbury lad. I live on Crackenedge Lane. A Dewsbury lad like you Danny. But this town isn't what it used to be. It's gone to shit mate.

"You and the paper need to do something about it. Parking wardens and Pakis Danny, they're fucking ruining this town. Parking wardens and Pakis mate. You ought to do something about it!"

Well I've tried Shaf mate. You're a Dewsbury lad, your turn to do something about it now...

POSTSCRIPT II:

BREAKING NEWS ... Police are investigating a race attack on an Asian Dewsbury businessman. Shaf Siddique, 41, of Crackenedge Lane, Dewsbury, claims he was assaulted in the back of a taxi near the Black Bull pub in Dewsbury town centre.

Shaf, who used to run Trade Price Beds in Dewsbury, said his attacker shouted: "We don't like Pakis," before jumping on him and that the same man confronted him near the market gates and threatened to "rape his kids".

Shaf, who is investing £100,000 in a new food takeaway business in Northgate, Dewsbury, fought back. "I had to defend myself," he said. "I had to hit him back. My nickname is Mad Shaf and I didn't get that by selling lollipops."

He is looking for witnesses to the attack, which

happened at about 3.45am on Sunday, to come forward.

Police confirmed they were treating the attack as racially-motivated.

A spokesman said the victim was believed to have been refused entry to the Black Bull, and an argument broke out with a doorman. Police inquiries are ongoing...